QUEST FOR SPIRI

QUEST FOR SPIRITUAL COMMUNITY

RECLAIMING SPIRITUAL GUIDANCE FOR CONTEMPORARY CONGREGATIONS

Angela H. Reed

t&t clark

Published by T&T Clark International
A Continuum Imprint
The Tower Building, 11 York Road, London SE1 7NX
80 Maiden Lane, Suite 704, New York, NY 10038

www.continuumbooks.com

Scripture quotations, unless otherwise noted, are from the New Revised
Standard Version Bible, copyright 1989, Division of Christian Education
of the National Council of the Churches of Christ in the United States of
America. Used by permission. All rights reserved.

British Library Cataloguing-in-Publication Data
A catalogue record for this book is available from the British Library

ISBN13: 978–0–567–19019–2 (Hardback)
978–0–567–03883–8 (Paperback)

Typeset by Fakenham Photosetting Ltd, Fakenham, Norfolk
Printed and bound in the United States of America

Table of Contents

Acknowledgements

It has been a holy gift to sit with all of those who graciously shared with me their stories of spiritual guidance in the course of my research for this book. I hold these stories gently and treasure each one in the same way that I have learned to treasure the story of every directee. I was astonished at the large numbers of pastors, spiritual directors, professors, and congregational members that agreed to meet with me to share their joys and concerns about spiritual direction in the congregation. There is a great deal of energy surrounding this work in many pockets of the church. Their testimonies are beautiful offerings before the Mysterious One who is in all things and holds all things together.

This book began as a dissertation project while I was a PhD candidate at Princeton Theological Seminary under the direction of Dr Richard Osmer. I offer my deepest thanks to him for challenging and encouraging me in my development as a practical theologian, educator, and spiritual guide. He is a remarkable teacher and mentor that I am blessed to know. I also offer my thanks to Dr Kenda Dean whose wisdom and insight was tremendously helpful to me as I began the process of developing a research design and visiting congregations. I had much to learn, and she provided exceptional support in her winsome way. Thanks also to Dr Bo Karen Lee and Dr Gordon Mikoski who provided valuable feedback that strengthened my writing. I am especially appreciative of the Lilly Endowment and Princeton Seminary for sponsoring the Faithful Practices Project. My research for the project became the heart of this book. It was an added blessing to have a publishing contract in place when I finished writing the dissertation. I am so thankful to the editorial staff at T&T Clark, including Thomas Kraft and Burke Gerstenschlager, who gave me the opportunity to publish this work and patiently answered my questions along the way.

Professor emeritus Dr Marcus Smucker, has been a true spiritual guide to me, and I will always be thankful for his input in my development as a spiritual director and writer. Many thanks to Ruth Workman and Gayle Kerr who served faithfully as my spiritual directors during my years in Princeton Seminary's PhD. program. Their passion for spiritual direction nurtured me when I needed a sounding board for new ideas. I thank my dear friend and introverted colleague, Carmen Maier, whose gift for listening allowed me to work out my thoughts verbally like the extravert that I am.

Finally, I must offer thanks to my family who has been with me through the journey of study, writing, and teaching. Thank you to my husband, David, and our children, Joshua and Ashley, who joyfully accompanied me to New Jersey and Texas, making many sacrifices so I could pursue this work. The relationships we share are filled with a holy grace that could only come from God. Each one of you is a part of my spiritual journey in profound ways that God alone can measure. Many thanks to our parents, siblings and other family members who offered extra special care during these years. Your phone calls, visits and prayers kept me going. I could not have completed this project without all of you.

Foreword

"I'm spiritual but not religious." In thousands of variations, many emerging adults in the United States today affirm this truth. "My congregation means everything to me. It brought me to God. It awakened my spiritual life." In thousands of variations, many members of religious communities in the United States affirm this truth. Angela Reed provides us with help in understanding and responding to these two truths.

Research by Jeffrey Arnett, Chris Smith, and Robert Wuthnow documents changes in the spiritual quest of emerging adults in America today. They have discovered that many young people between the ages of eighteen and thirty are engaged in an intense process of exploration. They are searching to find themselves and to determine what they will do with their lives. Their lives are frequently unstable and filled with short-term relationships and commitments. Though they often experience loneliness and disap-pointment, they remain hopeful that they will ultimately find what they are seeking. By some estimates, around 75% of emerging adults do not find organized religion helpful in their journey of self-discovery. Yet many view themselves as spiritual, if not religious. They are asking questions about the meaning of life and about the kinds of relationships and work that will bring purpose to their days.

At the same time, it is also is true that many American adults *do* find meaning through their participation in religious communities. A large percentage of social scientists today no longer hold to the secularization thesis in the form that dominated mainstream sociology for much of the twentieth century. This thesis portrayed religion as gradually withering away while modernization spread around the world. At most, religion would play a role in the private lives of individuals, with little impact on public life. This thesis has not been born out by events around the world. It is impossible to imagine the Civil Rights movement in the United States or the Solidarity movement in Poland without the important role of religion. Nor is it true that religion has withered away. For many people, their congregations are vital sources of meaning. They influence family life and voting preferences. They impact involvement in voluntary organizations and charitable giving. Many would say that their congregations are the primary source of awareness of God's presence in their lives and in their world.

How are we to make sense of these social trends? In a very real sense, emerging adults are the future of the church. Is their departure from the church a temporary glitch in the overall trend toward strong participation in religious communities? Perhaps, the answer is found in a central thesis of Angela Reed's book: at the beginning of the twenty-first century, the human longing for spiritual meaning is as strong as ever and the future of the church largely rests on its ability to respond to this longing.

Reed's book is part of a broader literature on contemporary Christianity that is retrieving ancient practices of spiritual guidance and formation that may help the church recover its ability to respond to the human longing for spiritual meaning. Her book makes a unique contribution to this literature along two important lines. First, it emphasizes *congregation-based* spiritual guidance and formation. Much of the contemporary literature in this field focuses on the individual, exploring the practices of one-on-one spiritual direction. While there are notable exceptions to this trend, the literature of contemporary spirituality and its training programs and guilds reveal many parallels to the Clinical Pastoral Education movement that flourished during the middle decades of the twentieth century. That movement championed an individual-therapeutic approach to pastoral care. It also moved toward the professionalization of pastoral care, establishing training and counseling centers with few ties to the church. If the contemporary discussion of Christian spirituality were to continue moving in this direction, its potential contribution to the church would greatly diminish.

The importance of Reed's book is to point the discussion of spirituality in a different direction. She argues that spirituality is best nurtured in religious communities, focusing especially on local congregations. She develops models and guidelines of congregation-based spiritual formation. The individual is important; spiritual guidance is important. But these are best understood in a community of spiritual practices and friendships that seeks to deepen the ties of individuals to a larger community and, through this community, to the world.

A second reason this book is important is its exploration of contemporary spirituality through empirical research. This is part of Reed's commitment to an understanding of practical theology in which the empirical investigation of what is going on in a particular context shapes her understanding of the ways Christian spirituality might be nurtured in living communities in the present. Her research does not rely primarily on social survey methods, but rather looks closely at congregations in two different Christian traditions. This gives depth and plausibility to her proposals. They are grounded in an assessment of the strengths and limitations of spiritual formation in actual congregations. She does not claim that what she has discovered is applicable in exactly the same way in other congregations situated in very different circumstances. But she *does* offer examples of living practices of spiritual formation and guidance that may be adapted by other congregations to fit their own needs and possibilities.

I share Reed's commitment to the importance of the contemporary discussion of Christian spirituality. I also share her commitment to pointing this discussion in the direction of congregation-based models of spiritual formation that are grounded in research into the ways formation is actually occurring in living communities today. Perhaps, here, the church will begin the journey toward a spiritual awakening that can speak to the needs of emerging adults and to the deepest longings of those who already members of Christian congregations.

Richard Osmer
Princeton Theological Seminary

For my parents, Nick and Dorothy Heide,
who nurtured the early stirrings
of my own spiritual quest.

Introduction

Kathryn hadn't given much thought to ministry as a profession until she entered Bible College. During those critical years, she began to realize that people tended to confide in her, especially about matters of faith and spirituality. She relished these holy moments and developed a yearning to give her life fully to walking with people on their spiritual journeys. This yearning led to seminary and finally a call to pastoral ministry in a Christian denomination. Kathryn began her work by giving attention to the things the church expected of her, including biblical and theological preaching and teaching, planning educational programs, supporting committees and providing pastoral care.

With all of the organizational responsibilities, Kathryn began to feel the passion for her work draining away. She reached out to a retired pastor who practices spiritual guidance, and she got in touch again with the initial yearnings that led her into ministry. Kathryn began to pray for the courage to connect with people at the level of soul. As she experienced a relationship of spiritual guidance, she realized that providing spiritual guidance was what she thought ministry was supposed to be about, so she trained in spiritual guidance for herself. In her preaching, teaching, committee meetings and even unexpected conversations at the supermarket, she is finding new opportunities to help others pay attention to the presence and activity of God in everyday life. Kathryn wonders now if she can learn and grow from spiritual traditions outside her own without being associated with 'New Age' spiritualities. Can she help people in her congregation to transform habitual rituals into genuine experiences of God, and develop a language to describe them?

Before middle adulthood, Sam would not have thought of himself as a 'spiritual' person. Though he had always believed in God and occasionally prayed, he did not pay much attention to anything he might have described as 'spirituality.' The occasional attendance at public worship on major holidays did not leave him with a positive impression of the church. Sam struggled with alcohol in young adulthood. When he came to realize that he had become powerless over alcohol, he joined Alcoholics Anonymous. As he worked through the twelve steps, he paused to acknowledge that his very essence is spiritual, and he needs a higher power to stay sober. At times the higher power appears to be core relationships in the AA group; at other times, he tries to focus more intently on a God he cannot understand. Regardless, Sam views spirituality as a key element in his recovery and is hungry to develop this dimension of himself further. Recently he has considered seeking support through the church that hosts his AA group, but he is still unsure if a church can really offer him what he is looking for.

Jordan first attended church as a child during his parents' spiritual awakening. He became heavily involved in the youth group where he found a sense of welcome and belonging. Jordan has begun to think about serving God further in a mission project outside of North America. Just after graduation from high school, he sought the help of his youth pastor in a more intentional way through one-with-one spiritual guidance. In these sessions, he asked questions about God's unique purposes for his life, and he discerned a sense of call to venture beyond his comfort zone to participate in a program serving poor children in other parts of the world. Jordan suggests that spiritual guidance enabled him to hold out his options and discern God's invitation more clearly. He hopes he can continue to grow his spiritual life through some of the practices he has learned in spiritual guidance. Yet he fears he might struggle to stay connected with God when he is without the support and accountability he has come to rely on in relationships in his local church.

The Spiritual Search

Kathryn, Sam and Jordan reflect dimensions of the hunger for spiritual depth pervading contemporary North American culture.[1]

---

[1] Most individuals mentioned in this book shared their stories as part of a qualitative research project in congregations with active ministries of spiritual guidance. Names and some details have been changed in order to protect anonymity. Occasionally, several individuals from the research are drawn upon to create composite figures representative of the research findings. More details about the research project itself will be addressed in a later chapter.

Not so long ago, the term 'spirituality' would have been most closely associated with religious movements or practices on the periphery. Today this term is commonplace from corporate head offices to the curricula of public universities. Interest in spirituality has become a popular dimension of contemporary life. While the content of spirituality is certainly wide-ranging and the term itself is nebulous, Americans overwhelmingly convey to pollsters that their spiritual lives incorporate both belief in God and communication with God.[2]

A recent nationwide survey reported that over 75% of Americans believe in God and another 12% believe in some form of higher power. Over 85% of respondents say they pray outside of religious services, and most pray at least a few times a week. Studies show that Americans are reaching out to communicate with a being or presence beyond themselves whom they believe is loving, ever-present, and concerned with their personal well-being.[3] Personal expressions of spirituality remain strong in contemporary American life. These statistics may seem surprising given the role that science has played in the last several centuries in our understanding of the world. The Western world tends to explain human life in terms of materialistic forces which we can study in scientific laboratories and describe using carefully reasoned thought. Yet this materialistic world view so prevalent in the West has failed to persuade the majority of

[2] While our culture has progressed along a path toward secularization, some concept of a divine being is still very much a part of western culture and psyche. Psychological studies from the time of Sigmund Freud have given extensive attention to representations of God and the accompanying development of belief in God in the West. Psychoanalyst Ana-Maria Rizzuto makes a strong case that 'no child in the Western world brought up in ordinary circumstances completes the Oedipal cycle without forming at least a rudimentary God representation' even if the individual chooses not to believe. See Ana-Maria Rizzuto *The Birth of the Living God: A Psychoanalytic Study*, Chicago: University of Chicago Press, 1979, 200.

[3] The data were downloaded from the Association for Religion Data Archives, www.TheARDA.com, and were collected as a part of *The Baylor Religion Survey, 2005*, and *The Baylor Religion Survey, Wave 2, 2007,* Waco, TX: Baylor Institute for Studies of Religion. These are representative surveys of the US population. Surveys in Canada report results that are fairly consistent with US data, though there are some differences. According to a major survey in 1995, about 80% of Canadians believe in God and about 42% believe they have experienced God; 60% report that they pray at least once a month. The Canadian data were downloaded from the Association for Religion Data Archives, www.TheARDA.com, and were collected as part of *Project Canada 1995*.

Americans that they are not intrinsically spiritual beings who relate to the divine.

A Widening Gulf Between Spirituality and Religion

This widespread recognition of the spiritual dimensions of human beings appears most striking in the face of waning participation in religious institutions. At the start of the twentieth century, a large percentage of Americans practiced their faith within a Christian or Jewish framework. They were members of particular traditions and attended services their whole lives. Experiencing church as a foundation for the spiritual life in the way that Jordan does would have been typical at this time. However, many more today understand their spiritual identities apart from religious institutions, not unlike Sam. Long-standing denominations have experienced steady declines in both church membership and attendance over the last half century.

While Americans are interested in spirituality and are reaching out in prayer, less than half participate in a religious service even once a month. The number of people indicating no religious preference has more than doubled in the last two decades. Of those who do affiliate themselves with a particular religious group, only about a third would consider their affiliation strong.[4] These statistics tell a story of religious change in America. Religious institutions no longer serve as the sole source for spiritual wisdom they once did. The search for God is strong, but many Americans are not looking to traditional religious institutions to light the way.

A few years ago, the New York Times featured the personal story of one woman whose spiritual yearnings the church, in all its forms and functions, has somehow been unable to address:

> I don't remember exactly when or how I lost my belief in God. As a child I attended Sunday school and church, was confirmed

[4] The data were downloaded from the Association of Religion Data Archives, www.TheARDA.com, and were collected as part of *The General Social Survey, 2006* by The National Opinion Research Center. The 1995 Canadian survey revealed that more than half of Canadians believe they have spiritual needs, but only about one third reported attending a religious service at least once a month. The Canadian data were downloaded from the Association for Religion Data Archives, www.TheARDA.com, and were collected as part of *Project Canada 1995.*

and took my first communion at the age of 12, volunteered in the church nursery and was a member of [a Christian mainline congregation's] youth group. But in my teens I felt pained and angry about going to church, and I began to experience my own tentative faith as a sort of betrayal. During services from my favorite perch in the balcony, I had a marvelous view of the two symmetrical rows of stained-glass windows, the vaulted ceiling and the wood pews, the beautiful pendant glass lamps, the minister's white cassock and the enormous bronze pipes of the organ swelling with music. The entire glorious pageant felt like a siren song calling me to accept what was impossible, urging me to confess an essential desire that would forever be unfulfilled. I sensed even then a fundamental human longing within me, and I felt that longing was being toyed with and manipulated. Observing the glorious pageant week after week, I began to feel like a starving person being given a picture of a plate of food ...[5]

We cannot begin to know the multitude of factors involved in this writer's rejection of the church, but what is clear is her inability to accept the invitation to participate in the life of Christ and the church as it is offered. In times past, she might have had no choice but to stay and hunger for more. In the contemporary context, she feels free to leave the church and join a support group to address her spiritual needs while remaining openly agnostic. One can only suspect that many *within* the church have also been touched by the contemporary spiritual quest and wonder about the place of the church in their spiritual identities. The church faces a great challenge as it seeks to understand and address the spiritual yearnings of those in the pews and those who have already turned towards the door.

John Drane discusses the dilemma of the Christian Church's relationship to blossoming expressions of spirituality in the West by raising the critical question after which his book is named, *Do Christians Know How to be Spiritual?* He suggests that the Western world has experienced a move from religion to spirituality. 'Religion' now tends to be understood by many in the average populace as an ...

---

[5] Julie Schumacher, 'A Support Group Is My Higher Power', *New York Times*, July 6 2008.

'externally imposed world view and set of practices, requiring conformity on the part of those who engage in it, backed up by narrow-minded attitudes based on dogmatic understandings of the meaning of everything – all of this is enforced by hierarchical structures that are riddled with hypocrisy and self-serving in a way that exploits others and prevents them reaching their full potential as human beings ...'[6]

Nothing about this definition sounds remotely appealing. Why would anyone want to participate in something so oppressive and heavy-handed? On the other hand, Drane notes that 'spirituality' tends to be seen in a more positive light; as a journey towards wholeness and healing which encompasses our full potential as human beings. Spirituality attends to the fullness of life and freedom without the pressure to conform to external expectations.[7] Essentially, spirituality in the eyes of many people might be described as an individual's search for the sacred which involves personal identity and purpose. What is clearly evident in this description is the emphasis upon 'me.' Drane puts his finger on a critical point: many people are looking outside traditional forms of church to pursue their spiritual longings.

The loss of influence of traditional religious institutions has created a variety of options for Americans. As conventional forms of authority, including religious authority, are viewed with suspicion or indifference, we are seeing a burgeoning marketplace of spiritual goods and services arising to fill the void. Like Sam, many are nurtured in the spiritual life by the raw honesty and accountability of a self-help group.[8] The marketplace also offers various opportunities to explore spirituality beyond the Judaeo-Christian tradition from zen meditation practices to shamanic healing to spiritual hiking adventures. Other religious traditions also welcome seekers who want to explore their options. The hunger for greater spiritual depth continues to be satisfied by incorporating spiritual practices

---

[6] Drane, *Do Christians Know How to Be Spiritual? The Rise of New Spirituality and the Mission of the Church*, London: Darton Longman & Todd, 2005, 10.

[7] Ibid.

[8] Self-help groups have become increasingly varied and popular. Sociologist Robert Wuthnow estimates that between eight and ten million adults in America participate in this kind of support group. See Robert Wuthnow *Sharing the Journey: Support Groups and America's New Quest for Community*, New York: Free Press, 1994, 70–73.

and intentional relationships as in traditional religious life, but these practices and relationships are increasingly formed in a myriad of ways which may not show clear evidence of traditional religious convictions.

Many congregations feel the pressure to meet the demands of religious consumers. At the same time, they want to be faithful to fundamental convictions based in Scripture, theology, and church history. This challenge reminds me of the classic childhood race featuring an egg and a spoon. The goal of the race is to balance the egg on the spoon and avoid dropping it while hurrying to the finish line. Racers must concentrate on doing two things well: keeping the egg on the spoon and moving quickly. In a similar way, congregations struggle to hang on to cherished convictions while keeping pace with an ever-changing religious marketplace.

The Rising Interest in Spiritual Guidance

While the task is not without its challenges, various segments of the church are attempting to bridge the gulf between traditional religious institutions and the contemporary spiritual quest by looking to old avenues with new vision. In fact, ancient Christian practices with long and storied histories are being revitalized and retooled for expression in the contemporary context. The ministry of spiritual guidance is an example of a practice that has recently caught the attention of leaders and lay people across many sections of the Christian Church. This renewal of interest is evident in seminaries, retreat centres and local churches that provide spiritual guidance and offer training programs or degrees in spiritual formation and spiritual guidance practices.[9] The ministry of spiritual guidance is particularly effective in bridging the gulf between spirituality and religion because it gives credence to the genuine spiritual yearnings of our time. It provides a sacred space for Kathryn to explore the possibilities of her own spiritual formation with a wise guide outside her congregation, for Sam to

---

[9] It is important to note that some denominations, particularly the Roman Catholic Church, have never stopped practicing some form of spiritual guidance and direction in intentional ways, yet even these denominations appear to be giving spiritual guidance increased attention. What is especially striking about the current emphasis in the religious life of North America is the wide-ranging ecumenical interest in spiritual guidance practices among Protestant, Catholic, and sectarian Christian groups, including both lay people and clergy.

unpack his culturally-formed understandings of God without fear of judgment, and for Jordan to engage in vocational discernment with a fellow-Christian who can join in listening for God's call. Spiritual guidance practices clearly have a contemporary relevance. At the same time, spiritual guidance has strong roots in the history of the church that have weathered changing cultural trends and withstood the test of time. The historical significance of spiritual guidance will be explored further in the third chapter. For now it is necessary to provide some defining characteristics for spiritual guidance.

The term 'spiritual guidance' can be understood in various ways. *By spiritual guidance, I mean a ministry of companionship in which Christians support one another in their Christian formation by helping each other to notice God's presence and activity in their lives.* Spiritual direction is a key practice within the ministry of spiritual guidance, classically defined by William Barry and William Connolly as 'help given by one Christian to another which enables that person to pay attention to God's personal communication to him or her, to respond to this personally communicating God, to grow in intimacy with this God, and to live out the consequences of the relationship.'[10]

The term 'spiritual direction' is something of a misnomer because it implies a kind of heavy-handed practice in which a person in authority tells another person exactly what to do in the spiritual life. This kind of approach would be particularly grating to a culture suspicious of externally imposed structures and practices. In order to avoid any misunderstanding and to broaden the possible practices and relationships that might be included, I use the language of 'guidance' more often than 'direction.' At the same time, it is critical to connect spiritual guidance with the practice that has historically been known as spiritual direction, dating back to relationships between the early mothers and fathers of the desert and those who sought their council. As I understand it, spiritual direction is not spiritual in the sense that it is only concerned with some kinds of esoteric practices foreign to everyday life, nor is it direction in the sense that one person tells another exactly how to live a spiritual life and to please God. Instead, spiritual direction is spiritual in that it looks for the presence and activity of the Holy Spirit in all of life, and it is direction in that it is a relationship

---

[10] William A. Barry and William J. Connolly, *The Practice of Spiritual Direction*, New York: Seabury Press, 1982, 8.

of coming alongside another who seeks *God's* direction for living. In this book, spiritual guidance is rooted in the kind of helping relationship defined above, but may take many forms, including one-with-one spiritual friendships, small group spiritual direction, and traditional one-with-one spiritual direction between a director and a directee.

Can Spiritual Guidance be a Faithful Practice?

The booming interest in the ministry of spiritual guidance raises some critical questions for today's congregation. What tangible difference does spiritual guidance make in Kathryn's pastoral work? Would spiritual guidance simply encourage people in Kathryn's church to pursue further the individualized spirituality in the culture around them, or would it help to build a spiritual community that challenges cultural norms? Have pastors who offer spiritual direction reflected sufficiently upon how their practice relates to their theological convictions?

These are earnest questions among those who seek to be faithful to the church's community and mission. In response to contemporary interest in spiritual guidance, some voice concerns that incorporating spiritual guidance practices in congregations and seminaries mirrors the overwhelming tide toward individualism.[11] In other words, we are interested in spiritual guidance these days because it feeds the need we are trained in from birth to give greatest attention to what helps *me* live a fulfilling life – the essence of contemporary spirituality. According to this argument, increasing attention to interiority actually harms the church. Spiritual guidance practices may inadvertently reinforce Christian faith and practice that focuses on self rather than communal formation, interiority rather than an outward missional focus, and a de-traditionalized eclecticism rather

---

[11] Because of my inclusion of Mennonite congregations in the empirical research, I point to the concerns raised by Arnold Snyder, 'Modern Mennonite Reality and Anabaptist Spirituality: Balthasar Hubmaier's Catechism of 1526,' *Conrad Grebel Review* 9 (1991). Snyder is critical of the training in spiritual guidance and formation offered to students at one Anabaptist-Mennonite seminary because he believes it may undercut Anabaptist theological convictions regarding participation in corporate worship and the integration of the Christian spiritual life with 'life in the world.' Snyder's comments are part of a passionate dialogue among Anabaptist-Mennonites regarding spirituality, ethics, and community.

than a firm theological grounding. This raises a key question: Do spiritual guidance practices contribute to the formation of *person, community,* and *mission* or do they emphasize one of these three at the expense of the others? Throughout this book, we will be using the formational concerns of person, community, and mission to direct our exploration of Christian thought and practice.[12]

Criticisms about contemporary spiritual guidance practices are worthy of careful consideration if the church is to be faithful to the biblical call to live as God's witness in the world. But do these concerns find any traction in real congregations that incorporate active ministries of spiritual guidance? Literally thousands of congregational leaders have trained in spiritual guidance practices in a multitude of seminaries and spiritual formation programs across North America, yet we have surprisingly little sustained research into what this kind of training actually does for pastors and for the churches they serve. One need only look at the *Spiritual Directors International* website to see how many of its members are ordained church leaders in communities small and large across the continent. How do these leaders employ what they have learned? This book is based upon case studies of actual congregations with pastors or lay leaders who have trained in spiritual guidance and have active ministries of spiritual guidance in congregations. I place this empirical research and analysis in conversation with a theology of spiritual guidance addressing the work of the Holy Spirit in the life of the church.

Instead of simply accommodating a self-serving appetite, we explore the conviction that spiritual guidance practices may actually nurture Christian community and Christian witness in the world while at the same time giving critical attention to personal spiritual growth. Despite the strong cultural pull toward practices that end in

---

[12] Anabaptist theologian Thomas Finger makes the argument that person, community, and mission are often separated in contemporary Christianity. However, they are inseparably intertwined in God's vision for the new creation. Although the Anabaptist tradition is often recognized today primarily for contributions to Christian ethics, Finger notes that Anabaptists historically attended carefully to person, community, and mission as one unit. This included an emphasis on inner transformation. He calls for a retrieval of person, community, and mission as a framework for contemporary Christian thought and practice. See Thomas N. Finger, *A Contemporary Anabaptist Theology: Biblical, Historical, Constructive,* Downers Grove, IL: InterVarsity Press, 2004, 105–9.

the self, spiritual guidance ministries may have a deep social relevance when intentionally rooted in theology, grounded in communal Christian formation, and interconnected with the church's mission. The resulting vision is a congregation-based ministry of spiritual guidance which nurtures the spiritual quest within the context of the theology and practices of the church.[13]

A Writer's Perspective

Just as practices of spiritual guidance, indeed even the nature of spirituality itself does not develop in a vacuum, so my perspective mirrors my own training and religious history. I come to this work formed by my Anabaptist-Mennonite background with experience in pastoral ministry in that context. As a recipient and provider of spiritual direction, my development in Christian life and faith has been indelibly influenced by the intentional spiritually formative relationships God has blessed me with. In the sphere of academia, I have come to approach any activity of the church with the lens of a practical theologian who gives attention to present practice, analysis of practice incorporating biblical theology and the human sciences, and an imagination for the possibilities of future practice.[14]

Organizing the Work

In order to explore the issues, we approach several key tasks in five chapters. The first chapter provides a description of the contemporary spiritual quest for congregations and their leaders who are

[13] Most contemporary texts in spiritual guidance serve as handbooks for practitioners and offer little in the way of theological frameworks. There are a few notable exceptions, including William A. Barry, *Spiritual Direction and the Encounter with God: A Theological Inquiry*, rev. ed., New York: Paulist Press, 2004, W. Paul Jones, *The Art of Spiritual Direction: Giving and Receiving Spiritual Guidance*, Nashville: Upper Room Books, 2002, Gary W. Moon and David G. Benner, *Spiritual Direction and the care of Souls: A Guide to Christian Approaches and Practices*, Downers Grove, IL: InterVarsity Press, 2004, and William E. Reiser, *Seeking God in All Things: Theology and Spiritual Direction*, Collegeville, MN: Liturgical Press, 2004.

[14] Richard Osmer has outlined the practical theological method I use in Richard Robert Osmer, *Practical Theology: An Introduction,* Grand Rapids, MI: Eerdmans, 2008. The method carries out descriptive-empirical, interpretative, normative and pragmatic tasks in an integrated project of practical theological reflection.

frequently ill-equipped to understand the spiritual environment in society around them. The sociological frameworks of Wade Clark Roof, Robert Wuthnow, and Christian Smith offer insights into the contemporary cultural milieu, and provide direction for recovering ancient practices of spiritual guidance in the current context.

The second chapter explores the experiences of some who participate in congregation-based spiritual guidance. This empirical research involves qualitative case studies of three Mennonite and three Presbyterian congregations in which a pastor or lay leader has been educated in spiritual guidance and engages in an active spiritual guidance ministry in the congregation. Ultimately, the chapter considers how spiritual guidance practices impact the congregation's ability to create meaningful responses to a questing culture.[15] The third chapter uncovers biblical and historical models of spiritual guidance, including the apostle Paul and the Thessalonians, Julian of Norwich, Susanna Wesley, and Dietrich Bonhoeffer. These four moments in the life of the church are examples of excellence that provide practical insights for contemporary spiritual guides. In each case, we pay attention to the manner in which person, community, and mission are interconnected.

The theological discussion in the fourth chapter lays the foundation for a Protestant theology of spiritual guidance. We draw upon Jürgen Moltmann's understanding of the Holy Spirit and the church to talk about encountering God in all creation. The fifth chapter provides a pragmatic vision for a congregation-based model of spiritual guidance. We bring together the resources of previous chapters to generate key insights about spiritual guidance and the journey of spiritual formation. We also articulate initiatives for the pastor as spiritual guide and outline potential models for congregation-based spiritual guidance practices.

Why Theatrical Improvisation?

Throughout the book, we draw on the art of theatrical improvisation as a metaphor to analyse and creatively adapt practices of

---

[15] The research project I am referring to was conducted as a part of the Faithful Practices Project which was funded by the Lilly Endowment with the support of Princeton Theological Seminary. The Lilly grant allowed me to carry out case study research on six North American congregations.

spiritual guidance for congregations. Theatrical improvisation and spiritual guidance utilize many of the same concepts and tools. Like spiritual guidance, improvisation is based in a tradition that requires on-going practice. With this foundation in place, the actor gets on stage and tells a story by attending to the action of the present moment and the contributions of the audience and other actors. Masters of theatrical improvisation emphasize presence and draw on the human capacity for sensation, memory, and imagination.[16] Spiritual guidance incorporates these abilities in order to make sense of God's presence in the world and in everyday life. When congregations draw on the traditions and practices of the faith to create meaningful responses to contemporary culture, they are improvising. We will consider these and other insights from the art of theatrical improvisation in order to enrich our formation of spiritual guidance practices. This will be especially useful for developing a theology of spiritual guidance.

A Call to One Anothering

It is possible to complicate any ministry of the church while hunting for definitions, observable practice in the historical record of the church, theological principles that support our understanding of practice and contemporary social constructions. Exploring spiritual guidance in each of these arenas assists in creating a three-dimensional picture of meaning and method. Yet there is also a certain beauty in simplicity. Spiritual guidance in one form or another has always been a part of the life of the church in the way one follower of God would simply be present with another, providing an opportunity for conversation about spiritual things.

An adviser and mentor once pointed out to me that spiritual guidance is fundamentally a matter of living out the biblical mandate to 'one anothering.' The New Testament gospels and letters include the invitation to encourage *one another* (I Thes. 5:11; Heb. 3:13), instruct *one another* (Rom. 15:14), speak to *one another* in psalms and hymns (Eph. 5:19), admonish *one another* (Col. 3:16), confess sins to *one another* (James 5:16) and spur *one another* on toward love and good

---

[16] Ruth Zaporah, *Action Theater: The Improvisation of Presence*, Berkeley, CA: North Atlantic Books, 1995, 17.

deeds (Heb. 10:24).[17] These and other forms of 'spiritual conver-sation' are indicative of active relationships of spiritual guidance. Spiritual guidance provides a kind of on-going discernment, care and accountability in order that each one might fulfil more completely God's best for their lives, including participation in Christian fellowship and service as a part of God's arm that reaches out to draw in the world.

[17] I am indebted to Dr. Marcus Smucker for many insights and ideas on the topic of contemporary and historical practices of spiritual guidance. He has pointed to the concept of 'spiritual conversation' in the Christian community and 'one anothering' in the New Testament letters as examples of the ministry of spiritual guidance. Included in his works on the topic is an unpublished document entitled *A Rationale for Spiritual Guidance in the Mennonite Church*.

Chapter 1

Spiritual Communities in a Culture of Individuals: Understanding the Contemporary Spiritual Quest

Of all the stories of spiritual guidance in the congregation included in this study, Anna's was perhaps the most unexpected. As a pastor's wife in a large Protestant congregation in the late 1990s, Anna was active in many lay leadership roles which brought fulfilment and a sense of purpose. Anna had a deep faith in God and believed in God's call to worship and serve together in the communal life of the church. At the same time, Anna was hungry for more. Beyond the local church, she sought out classes and retreats on various streams of spirituality across denominational lines to meet her own spiritual needs. Anna found that this widening exploration nurtured her spiritual life and inspired her to minister to others in new ways, supporting her sense of call. Anna was excited about the new ways she was communing with God and bringing her gifts into her church home.

Unexpectedly, the relationships Anna most relied upon began to crumble around her. The life of ministry she relished slipped away from her and none of her efforts to get her life back under control seemed to make any difference. A painful break occurred between her husband and the congregation. After failed attempts to mend the break and work out difficult issues, Anna and her husband ultimately left the church. The spiral of pain continued as the severed relationship with the church took its toll on Anna's family life. Her marriage disintegrated and her husband left. She was alone with primary custody of two young boys.

In all of her plans for the future, Anna never imagined things could go so wrong, and the pain was nearly unbearable at times. This was not what she had expected out of life – not what she believed she signed up for as the wife of a pastor seeking to serve God, love her family, and share her gifts with the church. Anna felt keenly the desire to protect her sons from torn relationships in the midst of her own heartbreak. She could not look to the church to provide support, not in the congregation she had once loved nor in any other. There was too much pain associated with participation in church life and too many relationships left unrepaired. Deep inside, Anna still believed in God's purposes for the church, but she could not bear to participate in its life. Anna let go of the church just as she had let go of her husband. She carried away aching wounds leaving a chasm between the church and herself that would not easily be crossed.

For some time, Anna struggled to reconcile her convictions about God's call to Christian community with the reality of broken relationships. In addition to therapeutic support, Anna found some comfort in the occasional Catholic mass, but she experienced any church relationship as 'iffy.' Anna found herself getting 'cold feet' whenever someone came too close – she learned to keep her distance. In hindsight, Anna recognizes that she needed space to recover from the shock of life changes she had not expected. She needed to grieve and feel the losses; to be angry and to be empty. Yet Anna would not finally sink into bitterness. Instead, she chose to respond to love.

God's gentle call to a new phase of life began around the time Anna met Sandra, a pastor at a local Protestant congregation who was just beginning training in spiritual direction. Anna was taking a break from a period of counselling and accepted the invitation to enter a spiritual direction relationship with Sandra, a kind of relationship she had experienced during her spiritual explorations of the past. Anna was not ready to attend public worship in the congregation, but believed it was time to embark upon a significant healing process with Sandra's support. While it was hard at times to separate Sandra from her role, Anna found that Sandra was available to her as a spiritual companion who met her exactly where she was at, emotionally and spiritually. This meant space to be as close or as far away as needed; space to allow a mysterious God to guide the healing work; space to risk honest reflection on her inner world in a contemplative manner. One of the most profound gifts Sandra offered Anna was companionship in the spiritual journey with no strings attached, whether or not Anna ever chose to settle into a congregation again.

Eventually Anna hesitantly attended worship in Sandra's congregation a few times, a decision spurred on by her eldest son who participated in the children's ministry. With halting steps she allowed herself to be drawn in again to the life of a congregation. This was not a smooth transition, and there were times when she felt compelled to pull back from Sandra and from the church, but slowly she was able to open herself up to the possibilities of new relationships. Today Anna is an active church member and participates in leading worship. She points to her relationship with Sandra as a key factor in her ability to return to the church and even to gain a sense of belonging there, allowing others into her life along the way. In her own words, spiritual direction with Sandra 'has given me the courage to step back into an arena where I have been severely hurt. I believe we're meant to be in community with people of faith. [Spiritual direction] has given me the courage to take those steps.'

Today Sandra and Anna continue to meet, as Anna discerns future vocational decisions and pays particular attention to the loves and losses of ministry in the past. Recently Sandra invited Anna to develop a list of her life experiences and aptitudes and ask, 'What does this picture form?' Anna reports that spiritual direction is helping her stay on course to dream new dreams even when they seem insurmountable for someone in her middle years. With a deep sense of gratitude, Anna recognizes that Sandra has encouraged her to be open to the Spirit and to hear what God is saying in her individual spiritual journey, while at the same time welcoming her into Christian fellowship. Through this process, Sandra provided a kind of transitional relationship to Anna as she navigated the difficult journey from alienation to trust, a tenuous thread slowly woven into a web of church relationships that Anna is able to embrace. In this transitional space, Anna appreciates Sandra's openness to various streams of spirituality that she explores in spiritual guidance while once again finding her footing in a local congregation.

Spirituality in Church and Society

Several aspects of Anna's story reflect the life experiences of many people in our time: (1) the depth of her spiritual hunger and her longing to explore her spirituality; (2) her desire to be formed and grow spiritually; (3) her embrace of various spiritual streams and ecumenical perspectives to nurture growth; and (4) her desire for a spiritual community to provide healing, support and guidance along the way. These dimensions of Anna's spiritual journey are not uncommon in the contemporary spiritual search both inside and outside traditional religious institutions. While some may not identify with Anna's particularly painful relationship with the church, her spiritual search is common to many. Anna's experience of spiritual direction with Sandra raises an important question: How might churches and their leaders best minister amid the intense, eclectic spiritual hunger of our time?

Effective ministry to church and society must begin with some awareness of the contemporary cultural context. Unfortunately, congregations and their leaders are often ill-equipped to understand the spiritual environment in society around them. Many seminaries train their students to excel in the study of Scripture, theology and church history, but give less attention to the study of the cultures congregations are steeped in. Pastors may be skilled at reading commentaries, but are they also skilled at reading contemporary challenges faced by the long distance driver, the stay-at-home mother and the college student in a multi-faith environment? Addressing these challenges with any kind of adequacy requires a deep reading of culture. The field of sociology of religion is especially helpful as we grapple with issues of contemporary spirituality.[1] In this chapter, we explore these issues by: (1) considering briefly a recent history of Christian spirituality and spiritual guidance; (2) addressing concerns about self-focused spirituality; (3) mining the sociological insights of Wade Clark Roof, Robert Wuthnow, and Christian Smith to understand changing patterns of spiritual life and practice; and (4) discussing practices of spiritual guidance that engage contemporary culture.

---

[1] Practical theological methods that incorporate interdisciplinary research in the human sciences bring important insights to the study of spirituality. As we pay attention to research in fields such as sociology or psychology, we may increase our understanding about how historical practices such as spiritual guidance bring meaning to persons and communities. While we typically think and talk about the contemporary church through the lenses of Scripture and theology, the social sciences give us useful perspectives that help us to view our congregational contexts in new ways. This is not to say that social sciences are placed on the same plane as Scripture or our theological convictions, just that they enrich and enlighten our use of Scripture and theology.

Linking Contemporary Spirituality with the Past

In my perspective, improvisational theater is a courageous art. I say *courageous* because actors get up on stage without having a clue about how the drama will unfold. Many of us get nervous when we have to stand in front of an audience. Sweaty hands cling to carefully worded scripts with the hope that we might get through it unscathed. If we dare to face the crowd without written words, we anxiously rehearse what we have planned to say again and again in our minds. Even the most confident preachers who know their congregations would hesitate to go forward without key points in mind. Few of us would consider approaching a stage in front of strangers without knowing what we will say or do. Yet this is exactly what improvising actors seem to do, at least from the observer's perspective. The audience does not see the skills and tools the actors practice endlessly before they ever face a public audience. They engage in an art with a lengthy tradition and a host of techniques that guide their words and movements. While there are fresh twists and turns in every developing plot, the fundamental elements of improvisation are not new at all.

In a similar way, the spiritual climate the church faces may seem like a strange new world. Congregations are up on stage facing a fast-changing, hard-to-understand culture with sweaty palms – a culture that no longer respects the church's authority as it once did. Yet the church has a long history of spiritual traditions to draw upon. The skills and tools of practices like spiritual guidance are really nothing new. While it may appear that Sandra's training in spiritual direction has little relationship to the historic traditions of her faith community, dimensions of the healing relationship she shares with Anna have always been a part of the church's life.

Long before the term 'spirituality' drew 30 million hits on the internet and 'spiritual guidance' over one million, interest in spiritual things has been a vital part of the church. Christians in the past and present have been concerned with our nature as spiritual beings and the human relationship to God who continues to be present in the world as Spirit. Practices of spiritual guidance and direction which support formation of Christian spirituality have been an integral part of church life. In the West, the Roman Catholic Church has employed these practices since the time of the fourth century holy men and women of the desert whose followers came seeking guidance and wisdom.[2]

While the Protestant Church has not placed an emphasis on classical spiritual direction in the same manner as the Roman Catholic Church, Protestant spirituality has given considerable attention to the 'cure of souls.' A generation before contemporary Protestants looked upon spiritual guidance and direction with renewed interest, John McNeill penned an historical account of the 'cure' or care of souls in both Roman Catholic and Protestant contexts.[3] According to McNeill, care for the soul was essential to the ministry of several Protestant leaders and lay people. This included various forms of spiritual guidance involving wisdom and discernment for spiritual well-being.

William A. Clebsch and Charles Jaekle have also studied the history of Christian soul care. They suggest that the Christian ministry of the cure of souls can be identified with the modern language of 'pastoral care.'[4] Certainly pastoral care incorporates many concerns, such as crisis intervention, which go beyond the scope of contemporary spiritual guidance and direction; however, Clebsch and Jaekle clearly identify the importance of *healing, sustaining, and guiding* as core functions of pastoral care. The type of care-giving Sandra offered to Anna included each of these functions. The authors make the point that these functions ought to go beyond directing thought and action to the spiritual significance and implications of any situation in pastoral care. Pastoral care involves specific attention

---

[2] Janet Ruffing offers a brief exploration of six historical models for spiritual direction relationships. She outlines the manner in which the spiritual direction relationship developed from the time of the desert abbas and ammas who became parental figures to those seeking a 'word' from the Lord, to communal monastic institutions, to various mystical leaders who became spiritual directors in the medieval period. Ruffing also highlights the Ignatian Interventionist Model of spiritual direction which emphasized self-observation in order to find the will of God and the post-Tridentine Director of Conscience who expected obedience of directees and placed a heavy emphasis on sin. In Ruffing's view, the contemporary model is rooted in a relationship of shared Christian faith in which God as the Holy Spirit is acknowledged as Guide, and the director assumes a listening/ reflective position in relation to the directee. See Janet Ruffing, *Uncovering Stories of Faith: Spiritual Direction and Narrative*. New York: Paulist Press, 1989, 3–17.

[3] John Thomas McNeill, *A History of the Cure of Souls*. New York: Harper, 1951.

[4] William A. Clebsch and Charles R. Jaekle, *Pastoral Care in Historical Perspective*. New York: Jason Aronson, 1983, 1.

to the spiritual insights and growth of the one receiving care. An even more explicit tie between spiritual guidance and pastoral care is made by William Clinebell in the classic work, *Basic Types of Pastoral Care & Counseling,* that calls for the ancient tradition of spiritual direction to be recovered and integrated with pastoral care and counselling.[5]

Surging interest in spiritual formation and spiritual guidance has caught the attention of numerous theological educators in recent years. They are engaging the interests of pastors like Sandra who are well-trained in the traditional Protestant functions of ministry, but feel a call to go beyond their seminary education into the study and practice of spiritual guidance. Numerous theological schools have developed Master of Arts degrees in spirituality and spiritual formation, or Master of Divinity degrees with concentrations in spirituality. Programs like these were rare only a few decades ago. Even institutions without specific programs in spirituality frequently encourage students to participate in individual or group spiritual direction often available on or off campus.[6] While long-established institutions explore spirituality with renewed vigour, new groups are springing up such as the Society for the Study of Christian Spirituality, an academic guild, and Spiritual Directors International, a world-wide membership of spiritual directors.

Self-focused Spiritual Direction

It seems evident that a strong trend emphasizing spirituality and spiritual formation has begun to take hold in theological education in both the church and classroom. While many, like Sandra and Anna, are enthusiastic about the renewed interest in spiritual practices such as spiritual

---

[5] Howard J. Clinebell, *Basic Types of Pastoral Care & Counseling: Resources for the Ministry of Healing and Growth,* revised ed. Nashville: Abingdon Press, 1984, 113–14. Clinebell notes the Protestant rejection of the term 'spiritual direction' because of the suspicion that it may undermine the place of Christ as mediator between people and God. Yet a kind of personal direction was practiced by Martin Luther, John Calvin, John Wesley and others Protestant leaders. Clinebell's interest in the recovery and incorporation of spiritual direction into pastoral counselling comes as a result of the heavy emphasis on psychological insights and psychotherapeutic techniques which he considers to be valuable but often lopsided in the contemporary context.

[6] These changes have been undergirded by surveys in which some students suggest that their time in seminary did little to nurture their own spiritual formation. See Robert J. Banks, *Reenvisioning Theological Education: Exploring a Missional Alternative to Current Models.* Grand Rapids, MI: Eerdmans, 1999, 200.

guidance, others are cautious or even suspicious. As we noted in the introduction, there is concern that the current emphasis on spirituality and spiritual guidance simply turns the tide towards a Christian faith that ends in the self. If this happens, it will certainly undermine the church's God-given call to community and mission. No doubt Sandra would have reason for concern if many members of her congregation became so enamoured with an inward spiritual journey that they disconnected themselves from healthy congregational relationships and lost interest in the congregation's missional activities. Her church would be a group of 'spiritual' people rather than a community of faith.

This caution about the implications of an inward journey is not without foundation, especially when we consider the recent history of the 'cure of souls' in the Protestant context. Spiritual guidance practices face some of the same dangers today that have dogged the field of pastoral care over the last hundred years. The strong interest in the self and the goal of self-actualization that developed through the mid-twentieth century tended to focus on the individual apart from the community.[7] In this view, healing requires an inward journey towards personal growth that gives little attention to the individual's relationships or interaction with the world. The client-centred therapy developed by Carl Rogers, for example, has merit as an alternative to giving advice, but even his optimistic view that the self is capable of making change does not necessarily become a 'nudge' toward growth and healthier interaction with the world.[8] The field of pastoral care has made many changes in the last several decades to account for social context and issues such as social justice.[9]

Contemporary spiritual guidance has given some attention to psychological approaches, including client-centred therapy, and it faces the same potential criticisms. The impending problems are epitomized in one story recounted to me by a seminary professor. He spoke of a man he knew who sought a spiritual director outside the church to assuage his guilt about an extra-marital affair. The spiritual director did nothing to discourage the man from continuing this

---

[7] For an in-depth discussion of the history of therapy and the self in pastoral care, see E. Brooks Holifield, *A History of Pastoral Care in America: From Salvation to Self-Realization*. Nashville: Abingdon Press, 1983.

[8] Robert C Leslie, 'A History of Pastoral Care in America,' *Journal of Pastoral Care* 37, no. 4 (1983), 308.

[9] Ibid., 313.

secretive relationship, giving him full freedom to pursue his personal spiritual quest without concern for the way his actions might affect others. If this is the result of spiritual guidance practices, we ought to run far away, and fast!

As the recovery of spiritual practices progresses in the church, we must learn from the lessons of pastoral care. We must be self-critical, and we cannot rely on a model of spiritual guidance that is based on the highly individualistic trends in our culture. Fortunately, some spiritual direction theorists are beginning to ask questions about contemporary patterns of spirituality, preoccupation with the self and the work of spiritual guidance. William Reiser makes the point that spiritual direction attends closely to the individual's relationship with God, and so care must be exercised that direction 'does not unwittingly play into the age's preoccupation with the private, individualized self making its mark upon the world.'[10] We are fundamentally social beings, who deeply form and are formed by our relationships with others for good or ill from the time of our birth to our death. The contemporary focus on the individual tends to obscure the social nature of the human self. As a result, the cultural pull toward seeking personal meaning and fulfilment as the key purpose of spirituality could be seriously detrimental to God's call to lovingly support the formation of each other.

In order to develop spiritual guidance practices in a self-critical manner, we must be aware of the cultural influences all around us. We turn next to a sociological reading of spirituality in culture.

The Contemporary Spiritual Quest: Searching for the Sacred in Ourselves

Wade Clark Roof is a sociologist who explores the nature of American spiritual patterns in *Spiritual Marketplace: Baby Boomers and the Remaking of American Religion*. Roof suggests that boundaries for religious life in America are being redrawn through the influence of post-World War II generations. This demographic group is concerned with spiritual searching supported by the rise of a spiritual market-place.[11] What makes Roof's work especially useful for congregations

---

[10] Reiser, *Seeking God in All Things: Theology and Spiritual Direction*, 6.
[11] Wade Clark Roof, *Spiritual Marketplace: Baby Boomers and the Remaking of American Religion*. Princeton, NJ: Princeton University Press, 1999, 10.

that want to understand contemporary spirituality is his discussion of *the spiritual quest*. Essential questions asked in the quest include*: Does religion relate to my life?; How can I find spiritual meaning and depth?;* and *How can I feel good about myself?*[12]

Many social scientists argue that religion has to do with two major concerns: personal meaning and social belong. Roof suggests that religious energies flow more toward the former these days. Popular terms such as 'inwardness,' 'subjectivity,' 'experiential,' and 'soul' reflect the predominant questing mood in which people are seeking greater self-understanding and a sense of connection with the sacred they may discover within themselves. Many individuals have lost their traditional religious grounding and are looking to enrich their lives by embarking on a spiritual quest that nurtures the autonomous self.

Both cultural and social trends have contributed to a questing culture. Roof notes that the boundaries once structuring society so rigidly, including race, gender and socio-economic class, have become more permeable. As the boundaries flex, ideas, beliefs, practices and even people cross easily. A case in point is the current emphases in elementary schools in some parts of the country that provide acknowledgement and even some education on holiday traditions rooted in various religious groups. Young children might be invited to bring religious artifacts to school to symbolize Kwanzaa, Hanukkah or Christmas, or colour pictures that teach the meanings of symbols from various religious traditions they are unfamiliar with. Public school curriculum writers would not have considered including such a wide variety of religious perspectives mere decades ago. Religious boundaries themselves are being redefined, and personal and group identities are being reconfigured. Roof argues that spiritual searching should come as no surprise in a pluralistic culture that has become increasingly free in its willingness to peer over the sides of existing religious boundaries.[13]

With greater proliferation of varying religious symbols, beliefs and practices, the individual tends to be responsible to judge between the various options available, even to embrace multiple practices and beliefs from various sources. Yet alongside a greater variety of beliefs has come a general decline in a depth of knowledge and

[12] Ibid., 67.
[13] Ibid., 44.

understanding of religious 'scripts' such as biblical stories which have long been cherished for the universal truths they carry. Children and even adults may see Santa at the mall near a nativity scene and have no sense of which symbol the Christmas holiday is truly rooted in. Universal truths have lost their authority amid greater scepticism and relativism.

As they grow increasingly disconnected from the meaning and purpose communicated through religious traditions, Americans have begun to look within themselves with the desire to find God. Interest in personal mystical or spiritual experiences grows, while knowledge of traditional religious stories and ideas decline. Roof suggests that individuals turn inward, grasping for the hope that *their own* life stories might somehow provide personal insights into the sacred. As people seek to appropriate beliefs and commitments at a deeply personal level, they are essentially becoming theologians in their own right.[14] In this environment, a flexible spirituality is born which requires seekers to attend to their own spiritual formation, creating a textured cloth of brightly woven threads drawn from various religious symbols, stories and practices for their own individual benefit.[15]

Finding Something *Good* in the Spiritual Quest

The language of the 'autonomous self' can certainly be a grating sound to our ears. This may be especially true for congregational leaders with theological convictions about creating community and participating in God's work for the sake of the world. The church cannot fulfill its God-given role as the body of Christ if it simply is a gathering of autonomous selves, each seeking their own benefit. We may be tempted to reject outright the kind of popular spirituality described by Roof.[16] However, Roof would probably caution against this drastic action. In fact he argues that the kind of self-fulfillment which was a cultural theme in the 1960s and 1970s had a somewhat different flavour from the prevailing mood we find today. Roof suggests that the quest has matured beyond the self-centred, therapeutic cultural characteristics of the earlier period. Popular spirituality may *appear* shallow but something more substantial lies

[14] Ibid., 48–57.
[15] Ibid., 67–75.
[16] Ibid., 9.

beneath. At its heart, the yearning of the spiritual quest is born out of our deepest energies and our most genuine inner desires.

Theologians and church leaders who reject or deny the value of the spiritual quest risk missing an opportunity to nurture the open, searching mood of our time towards the kinds of things the Christian faith proclaims will truly satisfy. If congregations are to accomplish this, they must provide a space for the spiritual quest. Some churches have so accommodated the rational tendencies of the scientific mindset by emphasizing doctrinal beliefs that they have lost the experiential dimension and the depth of faith that comes alive in Jesus' invitation to 'love the Lord your God with all your heart, and with all your soul, and with all your mind' (Matt. 22:37). When we lose touch with emotions, indeed our very souls, we risk losing touch with the heartbeat of this generation.

Roof suggests that there are great possibilities for congregations in reclaiming spiritual roots. Religious communities may recover the spiritual diversity strongly evident within their own histories when they welcome the rich spirituality of the past. This involves assessing and embracing the spirituality in our own traditions along with the wisdom of other traditions. We will be better able to bridge the gulf between spirituality and religion when we consider *reclaiming* spirituality for the purposes of *redefining* the religious.[17] In a nutshell, this is what Sandra has done for herself first, then also for Anna and her entire congregation. Sandra was willing to become vulnerable with a spiritual guide in order to deepen her connection with God. This prepared her to provide the same kind of relationship to Anna in her spiritual quest, which led to a healing relationship between Anna and the church. Every time Sandra preaches, leads worship, teaches a Sunday School class or chats in the church foyer, she has an opportunity to listen for the spiritual quest in the life of another. Her experiential knowledge of spiritual practices, especially spiritual guidance, has enabled her to embrace a ministry of participation in the spiritual lives of others.

There is no doubt that providing a hospitable space for spiritual questing may be a bit messy for congregations and will quite likely

---

[17] Wade Clark Roof, *Americans and Religions in the Twenty-First Century*, Annals of the American Academy of Political and Social Science, V. 558. Thousand Oaks, CA: Sage Publications, 1998, 222–23.

lead to some insecurity on the part of leaders.[18] How will we be certain that the spiritual quest will engender the answers – the theological perspectives – that we hold to be true? What happens if there is greater spiritual diversity in the congregation, both in practices and perspectives? Who will hold everything together? The truth is that we cannot fully know the outcome of redefining the religious through openness to spiritual quests. What may inadvertently be of the greatest benefit in the process is the necessity for congregational leaders to give up some control of where their churches are headed. This does not mean that leaders give up interpreting contemporary spirituality in the light of Scripture and theological convictions. In fact they may actually reflect more deeply on sacred texts and practices as a part of embracing the quest. Yet leaders may also have to let loose the rope that reins in the congregation in order to point to God.

Shifts in Contemporary Spirituality: From Dwelling to Seeking

Sociologist Robert Wuthnow provides a compelling reading of consumer-oriented religious life in *After Heaven: Spirituality in America since the 1950's*. His description of current trends flows along a similar vein as the theories offered by Roof, but he includes some alternative sociological insights that illuminate particular factors driving spirituality in America. Wuthnow argues that profound change has occurred in the way Americans have practiced their spirituality since the mid-twentieth century. A traditional spirituality of dwelling has gradually given way to a spirituality of seeking. A spirituality of dwelling or habitation rests upon a theological conviction that God can occupy a particular place in the universe. In essence, God creates a sacred space in which human beings are welcome to reside with the divine. Wuthnow likens dwelling spirituality to the biblical tradition of kings and priests who led the people to worship at the temple. A sacred place provides shelter and boundaries for those who desire to encounter God in a predefined space. Wuthnow points out that any trend in spirituality is reinforced by the social conditions of the times in which we live. Periods of relative stability, when individuals

---

[18] Robert Wuthnow, *After Heaven: Spirituality in America since the 1950s*. Berkeley: University of California Press, 1998, 198.

tend to remain in one community throughout their lives, reinforce dwelling spirituality.[19]

A spirituality of dwelling can also be identified with strong trends toward denominationalism. Throughout the period up to and including the 1950s, congregations did not generally view themselves as individual entities. American religious life was structured by denominational affiliation.[20] Congregations and individuals themselves tended to identify themselves according to a denomination. People experienced a strong sense of community within a denomination, and a boundary separated insiders from outsiders. In some cases, individuals were discouraged from marrying or even building friendships across denominations.

The bulwarks of denominational structures can be seen in towns and neighbourhoods which are dotted with churches of various affiliations built in the last few hundred years and located within a few blocks of each other. In the past, the congregation frequently became the home of both religious practice and social life, a space to participate in spiritual practices and a place to enjoy pot luck suppers and picnics as the primary social interaction of the week. In the words of one respondent in Wuthnow's research, 'The church was the centre of our lives.'[21]

Since the 1960s there has been a trend in America toward a spirituality of seeking. Freedom lies at the heart of the spiritual quest, freedom to choose from multiple forms of social support and an abundance of communities in which to worship God. Wuthnow compares this form of spirituality with the biblical paradigm of the tabernacle religion led by prophets and judges. This was a journeying period without one definitive sacred place or designated ruler. In

---

[19] Ibid., 3.

[20] See Robert Wuthnow, *The Restructuring of American Religion: Society and Faith since World War II* Princeton, NJ: Princeton University Press, 1988. In this text, Wuthnow articulates the historical importance of denominationalism in the American religious life. In 1800, there were about three dozen major denominations in America, a number which rose to over 200 by 1900 as a result of various forces including massive numbers of immigrants arriving on American soil and the ongoing tendencies toward schism within denominations. Denominations continued to grow in strength internally through the 1950s, increasing their numbers. However, significant social forces have undercut denominations since the 1960s.

[21] Wuthnow, *After Heaven: Spirituality in America since the 1950s*, 25.

a similar way, contemporary seekers may incorporate ideas and practices from a variety of traditions rather than remaining loyal to any one congregation or denomination.

Anna and Sandra are examples of the spiritual seeker. Anna was interested in growing her spiritual life by participating in classes and retreats outside her local congregation or denomination. While Anna returned ultimately to the Protestant Church, she chose the congregation because of relationships with church members rather than loyalty to a denomination. Sandra, too, has drawn from various spiritual streams to nurture her search. She enjoys participating in religious practices that are not rooted in her own religious tradition. Yet Sandra is also respectful of the denomination she serves, and she recognizes that some members of her congregation are more comfortable with dwelling spirituality. She tries to attend to elements of both dwelling and seeker spirituality in her ministry.

Spiritual seekers often explore various religious options before deciding upon a congregation, formative relationship or set of practices their spiritual needs. Anna and Sandra's congregation is a prime example of a community of faith that has grown considerably in the last decade with many individuals coming from a wide-ranging background of religious traditions. The fact that this church is related to one Protestant denomination and not another makes little difference to those who were not raised in the Protestant Church. We no longer assume that the religious tradition of parents will match the choices of their children. Many Americans think through their options and select a congregation and a faith tradition that seems to nurture their spiritual journeys and supports what they believe to be true.[22] Denominationalism has declined as congregations in any given denomination may have less in common with each other than with other congregations across the street or across the country. Individuals already suspicious of institutionalized structures

---

[22] Jeffrey Arnett suggests that a period of emerging adulthood following the teen years is characterized by an insistence on personal spiritual choices. Emerging adults predominantly want to decide for themselves what to believe and what to value based upon their own process of searching and questioning, a journey that may lead them far afield from the religious beliefs and practices they were exposed to in childhood and adolescence. See Jeffrey Jensen Arnett, *Emerging Adulthood: The Winding Road from the Late Teens through the Twenties*. Oxford: Oxford University Press, 2004, 165–87.

embark on a spiritual search to 'rediscover that God dwells not only in homes but also in the byways trod by pilgrims and sojourners.'[23]

Another major social force drawing Americans toward a spirituality of seeking is the consumer mentality. Wuthnow theorizes that our experiences of God and the spiritual life are heavily influenced by our socio-cultural context. This explains the lines blurring between the religious industry and other industries in America. A religious marketplace has arisen offering a wide variety of goods and services. In the 1960s people learned to shop as advertising budgets soared to convince consumers of their need for the seller's goods and services. Over time, religious entrepreneurs began to model the techniques of advertisers and retailers, launching an era of television evangelists, religious publishers, spiritual guides and others who provide opportunities for encounter with God outside the institutional church. The religious industry has contributed to making spirituality both popular and relevant to 'buyers' in ever-changing times. Religion is marketed and participants are taught to be faithful consumers.

As church membership declines in many settings and Americans grow more open to meeting their spiritual needs beyond traditional religion, congregations feel the pressure to enter the spiritual marketplace by providing spiritual services that will appeal to consumers. These might include programs for children and families, and ministries to special interest groups of every kind, particularly those that emphasize support or recovery for the problems of everyday life including addictions, bereavement and divorce. Larger congregations become multi-service communities attempting to meet every need from schools and daycare to contemporary worship music to coffee bars and mission trips. Smaller congregations strive to find a niche ministry that appeals to certain groups in the community, such as food pantries or youth ministries. The congregation with a highly cherished history and tradition that does not strive to meet the needs of the contemporary individualized seeker may find itself wondering where God is as it struggles to address a powerfully pervasive consumer culture.

The Pitfalls of Seeking and Dwelling

While there are good reasons to support the climate of genuine spiritual seeking which shows no signs of waning, there are also

---

[23] Wuthnow, *After Heaven: Spirituality in America since the 1950s*, 57.

reasons for concern. Congregations are in danger of participating in the buying and selling of religious goods and services without reflecting on why they do what they do. They may not give much attention to the ways they mirror the consumer-oriented habits of our culture. I suspect that some congregations give little emphasis to confronting the cultural milieu with the Gospel – to grappling with the values that give life meaning, and the sources of these values. Do Americans ask questions about the kind of spirituality that is important to them or the manner in which they will choose a church to attend? Do we take on consumer-driven priorities like marketability and customer satisfaction in our congregations and denominations? Addressing questions like these begins with recognition of who we are as consumers and how this ought to relate to our lives of faith. These issues can be rich fodder for sermons, educational classes or leadership meetings.

Neither the spirituality of dwelling nor the spirituality of seeking may be the most faithful path for individuals and religious communities. A spirituality of seeking alone is too fluid to provide individuals with the social ties they need, and it lacks the stability to support sustained spiritual growth toward maturity in Christian character in the image of Jesus Christ. This maturity is a key goal of spiritual formation! While seekers may be nurtured in the spiritual life by the freedom of exploration, they may also falter, as the wide variety of spiritual paths seems confusing, and opportunities for significant illumination are few and far between. Many more individuals and congregations will tend towards seeker spirituality in the future since it is more reflective of the consumer culture we live in; however it is likely that a certain appeal toward dwelling-orientated spirituality will always remain. Americans who are disquieted by continual societal change will desire the safe haven of secure spaces and the opportunity to meet with God in familiar ways.

The downside of dwelling spirituality is the tendency to encourage dependence upon communities of faith that are innately undependable.[24] Anna's story is a case in point. While she relished her spiritual search, she was also firmly and comfortably planted in a church home. Unfortunately her experience of the congregation as a safe haven of shared worship and loving community was shattered. In

[24] Ibid., 15–16.

31

her time of brokenness, it was a spirituality of seeking that sustained her more than a spirituality of dwelling. Her commitment to seeker spirituality became a strength in her journey of return to the church. If she had relied solely on dwelling spirituality, she may never have found a way back.

A Third Alternative: Practice-Oriented Spirituality

Robert Wuthnow suggests a third possibility other than seeking or dwelling spirituality: a practice-orientated spirituality. Spiritual practices address the seeker's desire for participation that is freely chosen. The responsibility to engage in practices lies squarely on the shoulders of the individual. At the same time, they are embedded in historic religious traditions and institutions that pass on the practices from one to another. Many practices, such as spiritual guidance or direction, have a long historical development rooted in the spiritual formation of the church. Spiritual practices invite individuals to engage reflectively in conversation with the past, to examine themselves and how they are shaped, and to instruct people in how they should behave – a moral dimension.

In essence, practice-orientated spirituality provides the freedom for individual initiative and sacred exploration so treasured by the spiritual seeker, while at the same time offering a stable spiritual home in which to communicate with God.[25] Individuals longing for home will find the support of spiritual guides who are also on the journey and can point to God as the faithful one. Contemporary writings on relationships of spiritual guidance consistently emphasize the importance of taking the attention off the self as the one who guides the way, and instead pointing to God for direction in life.[26]

While the relationship with the spiritual guide who represents organized religion is critical, as in the case of Anna, it is God who does the work of formation and transformation. Sandra provided a transitional relationship for Anna while pointing to God. In the

---

[25] Ibid., 14–18.

[26] For example, see Margaret Guenther, *Holy Listening: The Art of Spiritual Direction.* Cambridge: Cowley Publications, 1992, 32–9. Primary attention is given to the Holy Spirit who is the true Guide. The spiritual director is neither guru nor authority. In fact sometimes the role of the spiritual director is to stay out of the way as directees give voice to their stories.

process, Anna was able to recognize that *God* has been the Healer, not any individual or congregation. The shared practice enjoyed by Sandra and Anna draws upon the strengths of both the spirituality of dwelling and spirituality of seeking. A focused and disciplined relationship rooted in the background support of a spiritual home met the needs of one woman's personal spiritual search. Taking on responsibility for her own spiritual formation puts the weight of responsibility on the individual rather than some marketplace to accomplish the task on the individual's behalf. Growth in faithful character cannot be 'purchased' by consumers.

Spiritual practices may provide an important alternative for congregations in a 'me' orientated culture; however a troubling problem remains. In Wuthnow's research, those whose spirituality is deeply formed by spiritual practices vary on a spectrum from significant involvement in local churches to none at all. Of the two individual cases Wuthnow describes, one has little connection to a congregation and the other is heavily involved in a congregation, yet finds primary spiritual nurture for formation through practices outside this setting. Wuthnow acknowledges that many in his research would support the hypothesis presented in the introduction – that a distinction can be drawn between spirituality and religion.

In Wuthnow's research, Coleman McGregor is a representative example of those who continue to participate in congregational life while pursuing a practice-orientated spirituality. Yet Coleman is more drawn to retreat centres and less towards a local church to nurture his spiritual life. He acknowledges openly his need to withdraw from the circle of people in the congregation who focus too much attention on its members and not enough on their relationship to God. In this case, the congregation has not been able to nurture Coleman's spirituality adequately through communal practices. In turn, Coleman's spiritual awakening brings little benefit to the life of his congregation.[27]

While we cannot know all the stories of individuals who participated in the research, the key figures symbolic of contemporary spirituality *go outside* the local congregation to enter into a personally formative journey. What they gain outside the congregation tends to stay outside the congregation. Wuthnow makes it clear that this is likely to occur in religious institutions that do not support the

---

[27] Wuthnow, *After Heaven: Spirituality in America since the 1950s*, 178–92.

exploration of spiritual practices. If seekers cannot find resources and encouragement for the spiritual journey in a congregation, they will find a social network somewhere else that helps them meet the need. From a theological perspective, this is deeply troubling. If the congregation is to be a primary *source for spiritual formation* it must also be a *source for spiritual practices* that nurture the spiritual journey.

The challenge to the church is quite clear: How are we communicating to the Colemans of our congregations that we want to know about their spiritual searching, and support them in it? What would this kind of support look like? Wuthnow's reading of culture is very insightful, but he does not provide descriptions of congregations who are successfully incorporating spiritual practices that support the seeker. These questions will need to be addressed in future chapters.

Accommodation or Creative Adaptation?

Roof and Wuthnow provide an excellent foundation for understanding spirituality in contemporary culture, but our own quest into this issue is not quite complete. Christian Smith offers one more perspective that we will look at briefly to fill out our understanding. In *American Evangelicalism: Embattled and Thriving*, Smith discusses the evangelical church's interaction with contemporary culture. A dimension of his *subcultural identity theory* helps congregations pinpoint their potential for introducing spiritual practices within the contemporary spiritual climate. Smith states that *'religion survives and can thrive in a pluralistic, modern society by embedding itself in subcultures that offer satisfying morally orienting collective identities which provide adherents meaning and belonging.'*

Essentially, Smith is arguing that American evangelicalism has blossomed despite the challenges facing churches today because the evangelical community has created a place for people to belong and find their identity. This is especially important in a complex, rapidly-changing world without many firm moorings. Religious groups can thrive as they discover ways to be distinct from other groups, even while they may find themselves in tension with these groups.[28]

The key dimension of this theory for spiritual practices is proposition 3: *'Religious traditions have* always *strategically renegotiated their*

---

[28] Christian Smith, *American Evangelicalism: Embattled and Thriving*. Chicago: University of Chicago Press, 1998, 118–19.

collective identities by continually reformulating the ways their constructed orthodoxies engage the changing socio-cultural environments they confront.'[29] Smith proposes that religious groups who modify themselves in response to culture or incorporate new elements from the surrounding culture are often labelled as 'accommodating' culture. As a result, congregations that struggle against the tides of secular life are giving away more and more of what they hold to be true, including practices and moral convictions, in order to appease.

Rather than being 'in' but not 'of' the world (in theological terms), congregations have become both 'in' *and* 'of' the world. Many a faithful Christian might shudder at the thought, yet it seems extraordinarily difficult to find a balance between accommodating dimensions of culture while resisting what is deemed incompatible with the Christian witness. This is a hard-won balance sought in the lives of individuals, families, congregations and denominations. Some believe that religious groups have a specific number of orthodox 'goods' they must protect from modernity at all costs. Smith argues that this is not the case. Instead, congregational responses to religious change have *always* required strategic adaptation of the life of faith in order to address more adequately the contemporary context. This may include 'reclaiming and reinvigorating lost and dormant sacred themes, traditions and practices; [or] generating new religious goods while relinquishing others.'[30]

The invaluable tool that Smith offers is a sociologist's insight into the manner in which the church has always negotiated with culture. We may fear, as some have suggested, that welcoming the spiritual will lead to accommodating ourselves to culture. We will be in danger of losing our theological moorings and risk irreparably damaging our witness to the ways of God in Jesus Christ. We may address the person, but lose community and mission because we opened ourselves to the contemporary spiritual quest. Once we cross the bridge from traditional religion to contemporary spirituality we may never return. However Smith provides a vision that looks upon the possibilities positively – as creative adaptation rather than accommodation.

The crucial challenge for churches will be to hold fast to the tradition's essential orthodoxy while at the same time reformulating it in

[29] Ibid., 97.
[30] Ibid., 97–102.

a way that is appropriate for the context we live in, a challenge that must always be re-evaluated. Smith notes that this is a critical skill of religious masters (and discerning spiritual guides, I might add). In the process we will do what the church has always done: we will reclaim and retool the historical spiritual practices of the church which will enable us to attend better to the spiritual cries of the contemporary world. *Smith provides a theoretical analysis for what thousands of congregational leaders are already doing: introducing practices of spiritual guidance to bridge the gap between the contemporary spiritual quest and traditional religion.*

Practices of Spiritual Guidance Engage Contemporary Spirituality

After discussing contemporary spiritual trends, the stage is set to return to the rise of spiritual guidance practices in contemporary congregations and theological institutions. It is clear that Robert Wuthnow, Wade Clark Roof, and Christian Smith are not the only ones who see a benefit in drawing upon spiritual practices from historical traditions to reframe contemporary spirituality for the church. More and more people are engaging in spiritual guidance practices in our time. Yet how can spiritual guidance relationships be rooted in theological commitments to person, community and mission while still supporting the church's work of creative adaptation for our context?

We have already discussed concerns that spiritual guidance practices may inadvertently reinforce cultural trends by attending to self rather than communal formation, interiority rather than an outward missional focus, and a de-traditionalized eclecticism rather than a firm theological foundation. Without a doubt, current forms of spiritual guidance relationships do reflect key features of contemporary spirituality, but they need not stop there. Instead of watering down the gospel in order to accommodate the whims of culture, religious tradition can be creatively adapted through spiritual practices in order to provide a taste of genuine Christian spirituality in a palatable form to those inside and outside the church. This will be possible if we balance out what is personal, interior and eclectic with attention to community, mission and theological foundations. Finding this balance is critical for spiritual guidance relationships that honour Christ.

Personal *and* Communal Formation

The research we have considered so far is clear: contemporary spirituality is more heavily absorbed with the self than with community. Wuthnow reports that small groups have grown exponentially in recent years, but even in a group, the goal is often individual. One of the main reasons people join a group is the personal need for social interaction. When this need is no longer met in one group, individuals often leave with the intent of finding a new group that will better support their own spiritual growth.[31] We see the same pattern happening in churches. Rather than resolve conflicts or work for change in a congregation, many church members leave to find a church that is a better fit for one reason or another. In the western world, we tend to be interested in spirituality for the purposes of self-fulfillment. We are concerned with charting a spiritual path that will bring inner contentment and peace in a fast-paced, ever-changing context.

Contemporary spiritual guidance practices directly address the personal journey and the desire for individual spiritual growth. A longing for peace and inner contentment are common threads in spiritual guidance conversations. Spiritual guidance watches for the presence and activity of God in an individual's personal life. It brings together everyday life experiences and convictions about God for the purposes of growing the relationship with God which will certainly include a greater sense of fulfillment and purpose in life.

Spiritual guidance practices are also communal by their very nature. The manner in which the spiritual guide or director provides a hospitable space of time for the other to reflect upon the spiritual quest is truly a communal act. Douglas Steere once said that 'to listen another's soul into a condition of disclosure and discovery may be almost the greatest service that any human being ever performs for

---

[31] While American culture is often characterized as individualistic, massive numbers of people across the country participate in groups for various reasons, including spiritual growth. According to Wuthnow, small groups tend to support a safe, domesticated version of the sacred. This form of community may not lead to transformation into the image of Christ through genuine 'one anothering,' nor do they necessarily point to congregations as a locus for spiritual formation. See Wuthnow, *Sharing the Journey: Support Groups and America's New Quest for Community*, 6.

another.'[32] In the very act of serving as a spiritual guide, the director models genuine care-giving that is offered for the benefit of another rather than the self. Those on the receiving end comment frequently on how they have truly learned to listen to and care for others because of the experience of having received the gift of attentive listening from someone else.

Interiority *and* an Outward Missional Focus

Working intentionally at personal spiritual growth often means an inward turn in contemporary spirituality. Instead of looking to outward authority for meaning and purpose, there is a tendency to view one's own subjective experiences as authoritative. In this way, the inner world takes precedence over social organizations such as the community of faith.[33] When people speak about becoming centred or connected within themselves, they may be describing an interiority that brings a greater sense of wholeness in a culture suffering from fragmentation and compartmentalization. As growing numbers are estranged from traditional forms of religion, a sense of the sacred tends to be separated out of their lives. The inward journey is often an attempt to reconnect with the sacred. However, when the search for the sacred is limited to an inward search for the self, it becomes more difficult to pay attention to God who is also an external presence.

Spiritual guidance practices are intently concerned with the inward journey. As greater self-understanding develops, spiritual growth may occur as well. Spiritual guidance pays attention to mystical experiences and personal encounters with God which includes reflection on the inward self. Unpacking images of God that have developed over time certainly requires a process of interior reflection. Spiritual guidance supports the interior work of accepting the loving presence of God in the life of the individual. However, this presence also guides participants beyond the interior journey to a journey outward – to seeing God's presence and activity in the world and to an invitation to participate in God's activity. Spiritual guidance practices have the potential to be truly missional. As we delve more deeply

---

[32] Douglas Steere, *Gleanings: A Random Harvest.* Nashville: Upper Room Books, 1986.

[33] Roof, *Spiritual Marketplace: Baby Boomers and the Remaking of American Religion,* 39.

into the heart of God and grow to know more fully our purpose for life on this planet, we hear the true Spiritual Guide call us into participation in God's plan for the world. Relationships of spiritual guidance serve as sounding boards for discerning this call. Spiritual guidance best serves the church when it attends to both a journey inward and a journey outward.

De-traditionalized Eclecticism *and* a Firm Theological Grounding

Wuthnow's description of seeker spirituality can be characterized as eclectic and de-traditionalized. The seeker is open to a variety of sources for spiritual guidance and is not necessarily concerned that one traditional religious institution is the only provider. As Roof points out, the boundaries become permeable and opportunities abound to make choices that appeal to the spiritual life of the individual. Scepticism towards traditional religion has altered the landscape of religious life drastically, creating a culture less guided by tradition yet more intrigued by all things spiritual. At the same time, people face new challenges because there are fewer foundations to stand on. Seeker spirituality does not easily suffice in periods of personal and public crisis. Overflowing church buildings in the weeks after 9/11 are a stark reminder of the genuine need for stability in spite of the American love for exploration and freedom.

Spiritual guidance ministries today tend to promote eclectic exploration. Certainly Sandra and Anna can attest to this. Spiritual guidance practices in the Protestant Church are inherently eclectic because they draw on traditions largely untouched by Protestant denominations since the time of the Reformation. Contemporary writings in spiritual guidance support the notion that drinking from a variety of spiritual streams actually enhances the fullness of our relationship to God. At the same time, spiritual guidance practices draw explicitly on historical forms of relationship which have been tested in a variety of times and contexts. They are usually taught with the help of biblical, historical and theological writings of the church.

Today, Protestant students of spiritual direction read Teresa of Avila and Ignatius Loyola with a willingness to be enriched and formed. Writings like these are rooted in Scripture and theology. Contemporary resources in spiritual guidance are also exploring the intersection of theology and practice. Spiritual guidance relationships have the flexibility to be formed uniquely in each situation, yet they draw on the wisdom of a Christian practice dating back thousands of years. It is possible to embrace a variety of spiritual practices and still hold on to a firm theological foundation.

Learning to Improvise

Improvisational theatre is a vibrant metaphor for understanding the life of the church in our time. Congregations are like the actors who get on stage. They have choices to make. Will they look at the unfamiliar audience and realize they have nothing to say – nothing to offer? Or will they pause, take a deep breath, and trust their training and the skills they have learned. Will they remember how they have been taught to engage observers, providing opportunities for the audience to present an idea or question and then incorporating it into the existing dramatic sequence? Will they remember that the most creative thing they can do sometimes includes turning an idea around and running with it in a new direction? Are the actors willing to risk failure in their practice?

Congregations face the same decision to stay on stage and address the ever-changing spiritual climate or run with fear. For some it will mean meeting the genuine questions of those who have serious doubts about the Christian faith. For others it will mean learning about ancient spiritual practices and trying them out in worship or small groups. Still others will open themselves to listening for God in new ways in church business meetings or grocery stores. All of these possibilities will be explored further in the chapters to come. The key piece we take from this sociological reading of contemporary spirituality is the need to draw on the resources of our spiritual traditions and improvise in order to address the spiritual longings of our time.

Conclusion: The Heart of Spiritual Guidance in the Life of John the Baptist

Spiritual guidance practices can and do lead to *both* a personalized faith *and* a socially relevant Christianity. Creative adaptation has the potential to transform traditional religion in a manner that relates to the contemporary spiritual quest, a quest that resounds with the hungry cry for meaning and purpose in this world. Practices that are rooted in both self and community, interiority and outward mission, and eclectic openness alongside the theological and practical traditions of the church can reinvigorate the congregation.

While I have suggested that social relevance is an integral part of contemporary spiritual guidance, few of us would celebrate the opportunity to live a life solely to draw attention to someone else. Yet the witness of Christian Scripture points to exactly this purpose for God's people. In fact, there may be no more counter-cultural biblical figure for his own time and ours than John the Baptist. John was clear about his mission and goal. He had been born with a purpose: not to fulfil a spiritually in-tune calling for his own sake, but to come before another, a cousin, who was also the Son of God. People travelled many miles to hear John speak and be baptized by him. They held him in awe, questioning if he might be Elijah, another great prophet, or even the Christ. John had every opportunity to draw attention to himself, to let the ministry be about *him* so that he could nurture his own personal needs and wants. So many people choose this path. Yet John knew with great clarity that his work was to point to another. He was a messenger and a harbinger of something greater which could only be outside himself. When John's own followers recognized that Jesus was encroaching on their territory, John clearly stated his purpose, 'he must increase but I must decrease' (John 3:30). Choosing to decrease is not human nature, certainly not in a self-orientated culture.

John's life poses a challenge to those who serve as spiritual guides. While he had opportunity take up the role of groom, he chose the path of friend of the groom (John 3:29). Likewise the work of spiritual guidance is a calling of pointing to another, to God who is the true spiritual guide. While individuals may look to a spiritual guide for wisdom, the guide knows that they are truly looking for what only God can give.

★★★★★★★★★★★★★★★★★★★★★

Spiritual Exercise: Naming your Quest

Spiritual guidance practices involve reflecting on our stories of faith. Over the course of this book, you are invited to ponder your own spiritual autobiography as you consider the material of each chapter. Understanding how you have been formed spiritually up to this point is critical for developing a vision for on-going formation. One helpful way to approach the spiritual autobiography is to begin with a symbolic image. Each exercise will draw upon the metaphor of theatre in keeping with the theme of improvisation. Along the way, you will consider the people and events that have had an impact on your spiritual life. If you choose, you may jot down some 'actor's notes' to keep a record of your journey.

Find a comfortable and quiet space and take a few slow, deep breaths. Ask God to be present with you and guide you through this practice. Begin to reflect on your whole life as a play comprised of several acts. Be attentive to the natural transitions of your life which signal the beginning of a new act, such as early childhood, teen years, college, employment, major moves or family transitions. If you find it helpful, create a timeline of your life that identifies each act and jot down key features of those periods. As you look at the dramatic movement of your life, pay attention to God's presence and activity. How would you describe your awareness of God in each act? Are there particular spiritual traditions or practices that have been meaningful for your relationship with God at different times? Take note of points on the journey when you experienced a genuine spiritual quest. How would you describe the quest?

Read Revelation 3:20 to yourself a few times. Consider how you would like to commune with God. Respond to God in prayer in whatever way you choose.

★★★★★★★★★★★★★★★★★★★★★★★

Discussion Questions

- How would you describe the contemporary spiritual search in your community?
- In your perspective, how does an emphasis on the inner self impact an individual's commitment to community and mission in our time?
- How has the consumer-driven culture affected the life of any congregations you have been involved with over the last few years?
- Consider the role of popular culture (e.g. movies, books, sports, celebrity) on contemporary spirituality. What impact do these influences have on the way people understand and relate to God? How can the church address this impact?
- Are you more drawn to seeker or dwelling spirituality? Why?

Chapter 2

Hearing their Stories: Congregations that Practice Spiritual Guidance

Reggie paused in his preparations for Sunday's sermon to consider the church visioning weekend concluded just a few days ago. In keeping with tradition, the deacons and elders held an annual retreat early in September to reflect on the life of their Presbyterian congregation. The theme for this year's retreat was based upon Isaiah 43:19, 'I am about to do a new thing ...'. As a pastor, Reggie felt deeply grateful for the fellowship shared at the retreat again this year, but he wondered if anyone in the group had even considered the possibility that God might want to actually *do a new thing* in their community. These days, people Reggie speaks with are mostly concerned with maintaining the status quo. Any changes are borne out of a desire to keep their children or grandchildren in the congregation. It seems that every month or so Reggie hears about a member who is visiting another church 'just to try something new.' While choosing a church based on denominational affiliation was paramount in his youth, it isn't that way anymore. Now people talk more about music styles, children's programs and coffee bars. Reggie expects that some who have left, like one of his young nephews, still believe in *God* but not in the *church*. They have dropped out altogether since they feel the church does not offer anything truly necessary for being a 'spiritual' person.

As a pastor, Reggie recognizes the importance of evangelism, but he isn't certain how to go about it, and he doesn't see a lot of people in his congregation open to the change that would be necessary. After twelve years serving in this church, Reggie finds that most people who attend faithfully want things to remain the way they have always been, a congregation teaching about Jesus Christ and creating a safe haven in a mixed-up world; a place where fellowship is comfortable and church is predictable. Reggie admits that those who raise significant doubts about faith or the way it is lived out in this congregation usually move on. As he reflects again on Isaiah 43, Reggie prays that God might open the doors for a new thing among them, something he and his congregation would be able to see clearly and embrace. Reggie is beginning to crave this for his congregation ... and for himself as well.

A few hundred miles away in another Presbyterian congregation, Joelle prepares to serve tea to Sonja who runs the prayer shawl ministry. Joelle has been an associate pastor in the church for three years and she always looks forward to time with Sonja who has become a dear friend and a source of wisdom. It is Joelle's job to make the tea and compile a list of names of people who would benefit from prayer and a reminder of the love of the church through the gift of a handmade shawl. Joelle's congregation has many such unique ministries that seem to arise from the most unexpected individuals. While the congregation meets in an old historic building, the ideas are new and fresh.

The overall focus of Joelle's congregation is on-going spiritual formation toward maturity in Christ. She credits the senior pastor with creating a space for all to listen for God's invitations. He believes his training in Christian spirituality and direction has sharpened his attention to God's nudgings. He and Joelle talk often about the need for leaders to make space for God to speak, encouraging people to bring forward their sense of God's nudgings for communal discernment. Instead of voting 'yes' or 'no' in church meetings, leaders follow discussions with silent prayer to seek God's guidance. After the silence, everyone raises a hand according to what they believe is *God's* will for the congregation. They seek a consensus.

While this decision-making helps everyone to focus more on God and less on themselves, there are still disagreements. A few lay leaders have raised concerns that the congregation might lose its Presbyterian heritage with new songs, programs, and practices drawn from other traditions. Others wonder if it is really possible to discern God's call clearly. These are valid concerns, voices Joelle feels are needed if they will truly listen to God and grow as a spiritual community. As Joelle finishes making tea, she thinks of the single mother on her prayer shawl list today who lost her job recently, and she prays that God would continue to do new things.

Jason is rather surprised to find himself in church this Sunday. It is not something he ever expected to be doing, yet here he was again. Jason is openly agnostic and does not mind saying so, yet something draws him back to this place. It started when his friend Karina invited him to hear her band play on a Sunday morning. Jason was surprised to be invited but wanted to support his friend and was frankly a little curious about this place that she raved about. His parents had only taken him to church occasionally on holidays when he was a child, and he had found it utterly boring. He had come to think it was quite a pompous thing to believe that you knew the way to God – a God that probably doesn't even exist. Karina never said much about what her church believed and so Jason was curious about what she found so appealing. The first time he went, he was surprised to hear the pastor talking during the service about some of his own religious doubts.

Karina introduced Jason to pastor Thomas after the service, and they had an interesting conversation. Thomas did not seem to mind hearing Jason's challenging questions. In fact, he invited him to come again next week. Their relationship grew and now they meet together every month for coffee. Thomas accepts the fact that Jason is not easily swayed towards faith in God. He welcomes Jason's questions about God in a world of suffering and injustice. He even admits that he would rather talk with someone who has questions than someone who seems to have all the answers.

Clearly Thomas has a strong faith in God, but he doesn't push his perspective on others. Jason feels accepted right where he is at, as if Thomas genuinely cares about what Jason is thinking and feeling. Jason finds this completely surprising – in a good way. The more he thinks about it, the more he recognizes that many in the congregation seem to be this way, including Karina. While he does not feel ready to make any radical changes on his outlook, Jason appreciates what he has found in Karina's church and he expects to stay a while and see if anything new might come out of this for him.

Improvisation: Spiritual Practices for Changing Times

Most pastors are not unaware that participation in religious life is changing drastically in our time. They grapple with the possibility of doing something new in their own small corner of the wider church.

Like Reggie, some struggle even to consider the kind of change which would throw the majority of church members into chaos. Because of distinct theological perspectives or years of unchanging church experiences, it does not even occur to congregational members that God may be interested in doing a new thing among them. Reggie's church is most comfortable with dwelling spirituality, described in the previous chapter. There are many congregations that continue in this form. They would rather attempt to shut out the ever-changing developments of the culture around them than to engage those changes head on. While they can never truly escape the culture in which they live and work, they make every effort to sustain and live in the culture created within the congregation which results in clearly distinguishing 'insiders' from 'outsiders.'

Joelle finds herself in a congregation that has been careful trained over time to welcome the new thing and to consider the possibility that God's will can be discerned by congregations and very likely includes significant calls for change. While a few may express concern that denominational affiliations mean protecting certain established dimensions of corporate life, such as particular hymns or worship traditions, most are unconcerned about denominational loyalty. This is not surprising given the larger breakdown of loyalty to institutions in North American life.

In yet another context, Jason finds that Thomas has a strong faith in God, but he is open to hearing other perspectives. He is not afraid to listen to an agnostic and enter into a genuine relationship with him, even to the extent that he might grow and change as a result of a friendship with Jason. What Jason does not know is that Thomas learned to give up control of the convincing process years ago, in part through exploring spiritual direction training. He came to trust that the Holy Spirit is already at work in every human being to fulfil God's purposes. Thomas believes his primary responsibility in both evangelism and on-going congregational care is prayerfully to walk alongside another in the spiritual journey, even when the one he walks with is agnostic. Both Joelle and Thomas serve congregations that nourish seeker spirituality.

In the art of theatrical improvisation, the actor is never certain how the story will unfold. In order for creativity to flourish, actors must trust the process, acknowledging the role of the audience to present story ideas, images or words which will be drawn into the action of the drama and enrich what is already happening on stage. The process takes unexpected twists and turns. The actors hold the contributions of the audience carefully, drawing on the skill of *reincorporation* so that threads of the story are not lost as the drama plays on. These threads are rewoven into the story to bring together a completed whole.

Congregations that welcome seeker spirituality have a great deal in common with the art of improvisation. Like the actor who invites audience participation, these congregations and their leaders strive to engage the surrounding culture and bring faith into conversation with everyday life. It would not be unexpected to hear Thomas preach on a topic that grew out of time with Jason, or for Joelle's congregation to extend its prayer shawl ministry to providing food and shelter for a needy immigrant family as they discerned this response in prayer. Part of their improvisation also includes *reincorporation* of their own traditions and convictions as they attend to contemporary culture. When Thomas allows his preaching to be informed by conversations with Jason, he explores how the gospel interacts with Jason's questions. Other congregational leaders, like Reggie, long for genuine interaction with the culture but are unsure how to go about it or how to bring their congregations on board.

As we have already discussed in the previous chapter, congregations and their leaders respond to changing patterns of spirituality and religious participation in various ways. In some places, ancient practices of spiritual guidance are being reintroduced, or in the language of improvisation, *reincorporated*, in order to help feed the genuine spiritual hunger from within the scope of Christian tradition. It may be beneficial at this point to describe what we mean by 'Christian practices.' The term 'practice' can refer to all kinds of activities, from walking the dog to participating on a sports team to learning a piece of music on the piano. Practice is a basic dimension of human living. In this case, we are describing a kind of activity with the specific purpose of on-going formation in Christian faith.

An entire body of literature published in the last several years explores the formation of Christian faith through practice. In *Practicing our Faith: A Way of Life for a Searching People,* Craig Dykstra and Dorothy Bass describe Christian practices as 'things Christian people do together over time in response to and in light of God's active presence in the world.'[1] Two dimensions of this definition

---

[1] Dorothy C. Bass, *Practicing Our Faith: A Way of Life for a Searching People.* San Francisco: Jossey-Bass, 1997, 5. In a later book, they wisely suggest the words 'in

are particularly significant for spiritual guidance. First, Christian practices are activities we do together. One of the basic premises of this book is that the inward journey so popular in the contemporary spiritual search does not adequately reflect our God-given sociality. Even when we participate in solitary practices such as private prayer or Bible study, we do these things because we have been taught something about them at various points in our lives.

Second, we participate in practices as a part of our relationship to a God who is living and active in this world. We engage in Christian practices in response to God's invitation for the purpose of our ongoing Christian formation, our development toward personal and communal maturity in Jesus Christ. These practices take on special meaning as they nurture our relationship with God and with others, and we are empowered to do them again and again by the Holy Spirit. Participating in active practices involves recognizing that God is still engaging dynamically in the life of the church in a manner that supports God's ultimate purposes for the church and for the world. When we engage in Christian practices without giving much thought to their significance in our relationship to God, the practices tend to lose their power and purpose. When we think of spiritual guidance as a practice, we are speaking of a communal activity with a divine purpose that is rooted in relationship. In this chapter, we hear the stories of congregations and individuals who participate in a relational practice that attends to God's active presence in the world.

Listening to Congregations and their Leaders

Spiritual direction is one type of ancient Christian practice that contemporary leaders and congregations are drawing on in our time. This renewal appears to span the traditional denominational

Jesus Christ' could be added at the end to indicate the content and character of the divine presence. See Miroslav Volf and Dorothy C. Bass, *Practicing Theology: Beliefs and Practices in Christian Life*. Grand Rapids, MI: Eerdmans, 2001, 18. This description is further defined by four characteristics: (1) 'practices address fundamental human needs and conditions through concrete human acts;' (2) 'practices are done together and over time;' (3) 'practices possess standards of excellence;' and (4) practices are ordinary activities which reveal how 'our daily lives are all tangled up with the things God is doing in the world.' See Bass, *Practicing Our Faith: A Way of Life for a Searching People*, 6–8.

divide. While thousands of pastors and congregational leaders have received intentional training in spiritual direction, there is little, if any, research that explores the results of this kind of training for pastors and their congregations. When thinking about Thomas' approach to congregational formation, we might ask how he believes his spiritual direction training informs his role as a pastor. Does it affect the way he preaches, leads committee meetings or chats with people after worship? Does he ever offer the kind of one-with-one spiritual direction in his congregation that he was trained to give? To whom does he offer it and how is it received? If Reggie chooses to do something about his own spiritual hunger and he comes to Thomas for advice about training in spiritual direction as an entry into spiritual formation, what will Thomas tell him? In order for spiritual direction training and practice to be most effective, we must explore answers to some of these questions.

Empirical research in actual congregations among pastors and lay people with a passion for spiritual guidance offers one approach to understanding current trends. I engaged in empirical research in six congregations across North America, three Mennonite and three Presbyterian, to shed a bit of light on current spiritual direction practice. These denominations were selected because they do not have a history of explicit participation in traditional forms of spiritual direction since the time of the Reformation. Yet in the last few decades, many among their numbers evidence a renewed interest in spiritual direction which extends to training programs and ongoing practice in their seminaries and in local churches.[2]

Individual congregations were chosen based upon a 'best practices' approach in the tradition of researchers such as Diana Butler Bass who study congregations that engage in traditional Christian practices in meaningful ways that support characteristics of fervent life and ongoing growth.[3] Congregations were picked in which at least one pastor or lay person has trained in spiritual direction and has developed an active ministry of spiritual guidance

---

[2] I would consider this to be typical for many Protestant denominations. These denominations were also selected in part because of my own familiarity with their theological and practical traditions and my knowledge of individual congregations practicing forms of spiritual direction.

[3] See, for example, Diana Butler Bass, *The Practicing Congregation: Imagining a New Old Church.* Herndon, VA: Alban Institute, 2004.

in the congregation in some form.[4] They represent a mix of spiritual guidance models in order to describe the inner workings of each, and consider possible strengths and weaknesses of various approaches.

Individual and group interviews, along with participant observation in worship and other communal settings, make up the nuts and bolts of the study. In my exploration of six congregations, I do not make claims that can be broadly generalized to other contexts. At the same time, I will note the places of resonance between my findings and long-standing insights about spiritual direction and guidance. Theories about spiritual guidance arising from compelling descriptions of practice are what we turn to next.[5]

Shaping the Pastoral Role

I met Ryan in a tiny, hole-in-the-wall sandwich place in a quiet suburb of a mid-western city. It did not take long for me to figure out that Ryan was a deep thinker and a watchful participant in spiritual guidance practices. One of the most unexpected dimensions

---

[4] The trained spiritual directors/congregational leaders must have offered classical spiritual direction or some form of spiritual guidance practices in the local congregation for a minimum of two years to at least four individuals or groups. In reality, the congregations chosen generally had a much longer history of active spiritual guidance ministries and a greater number of congregants have participated. One congregation included in the study fits within the parameters, but has moved beyond them in recent years to create a congregational culture based upon spiritual direction principles without necessarily using this language. The analysis of this congregation provides numerous insights valuable to the questions of this study. Beyond the local congregation, I filled out my research by hosting meetings with other pastors/spiritual directors and visiting seminaries where spiritual direction is incorporated in various forms.

[5] This project employs a qualitative method of social scientific research. Through much of the twentieth century, the social sciences have tended to follow in the footsteps of other sciences by using quantitative research methods that are deductive: researchers begin with ideas taken from theoretical models and test them against broad generalizations. Where quantitative research makes broad sweeps, qualitative research explores more deeply meaning and practice in smaller samples. Qualitative research focuses on context-specific study which attends to diverse individual experiences. Using a qualitative research method allows me to explore the meaning of spiritual guidance practices in specific contexts in a deeper way. See Uwe Flick, *An Introduction to Qualitative Research*, 2nd ed. Thousand Oaks, CA: Sage Publications, 2002, 11–17.

of my conversation with Ryan was his keen observation of the way his pastor has incorporated principles of spiritual direction into his ministry. Ryan told a compelling story which describes his pastor's understanding of spiritual guidance ...

> 'My first meeting with Thomas was at a potluck dinner. Anyone could come to meet the guy that we were proposing for pastor. At the end there was a time for questions. And I think I was the one that asked, "What's your vision for this congregation?" And he said, "I hope you won't be disappointed, but I don't have a vision for this congregation ... I approach this more from a spiritual direction perspective. I'm trying to understand what *God* is doing for this community and move *that* forward."'

Three years later, Ryan still remembers Thomas' unexpected response to a very common question. He reflected on the significance of leading by intentionally looking for God in everyday life, by watching for God's presence and activity in every business meeting and in casual conversations in the church yard. He went on to describe a recent meeting to discuss Thomas' first three years of leadership, where it became clear that others had seen the same things in their pastor as Ryan himself had ...

> 'People were talking about how Thomas has led this congregation and is trying to understand where God's will is and move us forward together – as it relates to the administration of the church and being on committees; and I told that story. And [someone] said, "What I'm hearing is that he's actually doing it." And we all [responded], "Yeah, that's exactly what he's doing."'

Again and again, pastors like Thomas speak passionately about the importance of becoming spiritual guides of their congregations, and the people they serve are taking notice. The typical leader in North American culture is expected to be in charge: to clarify a vision others will follow, to monitor the goals of the company or organization, to report to a board of directors, and to take responsibility for successes ... and failures. In other words, leaders today are expected to be CEOs.[6] It is hardly surprising that this cultural model seeps into

---

[6] Andrew Seidel argues that most people are chosen to positions of leadership because of the competency they demonstrate in the external world, not because

pastoral leadership. With it comes the pressure to be a visionary who succeeds in making the church grow and mature. It is the pressure Reggie feels to set the tone and cause the church to be open to change.

Ironically, Thomas completed a business degree in college and when he first became a pastor, he naturally began to work using a CEO model by focusing on clarifying the vision, monitoring goals, reporting to a board of directors (aka: a church council or session) and striving to make the church a 'success.' His experience at seminary drew him to ponder this approach and incorporate a shepherding model of ministry, what he describes as 'sharing and caressing and overseeing and leading.' But it was not long before a desire for more personal spiritual formation grew within him. He sought to receive and later train in spiritual direction. That is when things started to change for Thomas in the way he understood his primary work as a pastor. Now he believes that he does the work of a shepherd or CEO at times, but this involves specific tasks rather than an overarching role. Instead, Thomas looks at all he says and does in ministry through a lens of spiritual direction.

Thomas is not alone is this re-imaging of ministry through spiritual direction training. One of the most overwhelmingly consistent findings of the research has to do with pastors discovering their role as spiritual guides of a congregation. In my conversations with pastors, five important findings emerge that speak to what becoming a spiritual guide means for pastors and the congregations they serve. This varies somewhat from one pastor to another, but there are clear patterns including: (1) *concern for self-care and ongoing personal spiritual formation*; (2) *a prayerful presence in all tasks of ministry*; (3) *an ear for God's presence and activity in people and projects*; (4) *a language for experiences of God*; and (5) *reconstructed standards of success*.

---

of a well-ordered internal world. See Paul Pettit, ed. *Foundations of Spiritual Formation: A Community Approach to Becoming Like Christ*. Grand Rapids: Kregel, 2008, 192. Congregations may be tempted to follow the cultural trend to separate the internal from the external. As a result, pastors are chosen and praised for outward signs of success, such as administrative excellence and effective public speaking skills. These abilities certainly have value, but they cannot be separated from evidence of attention to the inward self: on-going relationships with God and others, commitment to personal formation and well-being and the development of Christian character. Bringing together the internal and external dimensions of life and leadership will be discussed further in chapter five.

Self-care and On-going Personal Spiritual Formation

To begin, one of the most striking results of the study has to do with the impact of spiritual direction upon the pastors themselves. Many with training in spiritual direction first whet their appetites for the practice through their own experiences of receiving spiritual direction. Some note that in a profession of ministry to others, participation in spiritual direction allows them to slow down and step out of the role of minister. They have an opportunity to explore their own relationship with God in the care of someone who does not know them as pastor. The listening ear of a gifted spiritual director becomes a conduit for self-care. Pastors have the chance to set aside their concerns for others and give attention to their own issues in their faith journey. In the words of one pastor/director,

> 'It's so important for me to recognize myself as a child of God apart from the call that I have received in this season to be actively serving as a pastor. Spiritual direction does that. It provides me with a sense of having a pastor ... and I think everybody needs that in life; somebody that they can go to that will pray with them, tend to them, and seek God with them; someone [they] can trust who has insight and wisdom and can be that listening person with [them] for God's voice on the journey.'

I learned two things from this pastor's experience. First, she has a hunger to see herself as loved and cherished for *who she is* as God's child apart from *what she does* for God. The importance of this distinction cannot be underestimated. This pastor knows she needs to find her identity in the unchanging nature of God's love and commitment to her, rather than in her work, which may or may not bear fruit at any given time. Her identity is not tied up primarily in how she and others gauge the success of her ministry.[7]

---

[7] Pastors are not the only ones who struggle to separate their personal identity from the work they do. Our culture commonly connects identity with employment or work. When we are introduced to someone new, one of the first things we communicate is what we do with our days, whether we work as a carpenter, teacher, electrician, homemaker or student. In truth, human identity is developed in relationship with others from infancy rather than in vocational choices. Object relations theories explore this more fully. See, for example, the work of D. W. Winnicott, *Playing and Reality*. New York: Routledge, 2005.

Second, she knows her need for nurturing spiritual relationships apart from the congregation. In this case, she has found a spiritual director who has become a pastoral presence for her. Many pastors report that they experience spiritual direction as a kind of retreat to a space where their own relationship with God is deeply treasured. Without this retreat, they find it more difficult to stay nourished and strengthened in a lifestyle that tends to drain away energy. As pastors make the intentional effort to nourish themselves spiritually, they believe they have a greater capacity to stay in ministry for the 'long haul.'

One pastor noted that there are seasons of formation and de-formation in the life of the pastor. The ongoing need for inspiring sermons and teachings, wisdom in working with committees and boards, compassion in the personal crises of others and many other myriad expectations may certainly contribute to the pastor's seasoning and sense of purpose, but tends to cause de-formation. Danger arises when pastors become so drawn into the needs of others that their own relationship with God is pushed down the list of priorities. For many pastors in this study, spiritual direction provides a regular source of formation, accountability and a watchful eye that is concerned for the one who cares for others. Spiritual direction has become a 'life-line' for nurturing these pastors' own relationships with God, a necessary spring out of which flows the inspiration, wisdom and compassion pastors need.

Some congregational leaders report that attending to their own self-care in spiritual direction incorporates on-going education in the spiritual life. One pastor in particular expressed the belief that receiving and training in spiritual direction paved the way for an introduction to spiritual disciplines such as lectio divina and journalling that have deepened his relationship with God. The training opened him up to an entire category of Christian literature including a variety of readings from the mystics to historical spiritual practices rooted in his own tradition.

Another significant dimension of education is the explicit and implicit training in discernment, in other words, exploring the mysterious process of perceiving the quiet whispers and nudges of God. The director may offer explicit suggestions for reading or timely insights for paying attention to God's voice. The more implicit personal experience of learning to discern God's voice in one's own life is frequently mentioned by many congregational leaders. These are vital supports for one pastor who says she brings her own personal and vocational issues to spiritual direction, such as the decision to be a pastor full-time while raising young children. All kinds of personal and congregational issues are fodder for the practice of discernment.

One vital topic often addressed in spiritual direction is accountability. Relationships of accountability provide encouragement for personal change and on-going faithfulness to Christ. Leaders of congregations sometimes have difficulty finding friends or mentors with whom they can be completely honest about their shortcomings. The perceived expectations of congregations can leave pastors with the sense that their personal failings or limitations cannot be revealed before others. One pastor who has a growing ministry of spiritual direction to other pastors raises serious concerns about the lack of self-care among his colleagues:

> 'I see a lot of pastors burning out. I see a lot of pastors just succumbing to and yielding to the pressures ... pastors who feel like they're the lone dog, the lone ranger; that they can't reveal their cracks or their warts, their shortcomings. I just can't handle that. I get ready for work the same way everyone else does and I'm subject to the same temptations they are. I like to shake pastors sometimes – allow them to tell me where they're at and how they're feeling, and in some way I can salvage or help shake their souls to allow them to say, 'No, God really is at work here, and I just haven't taken the time to see it.' Some of them need a reality check that they are not God. It's good for the church if the pastors are cared for.'

This is a gut-wrenching response from one spiritual director who has seen colleagues slowly take upon themselves a persona of perfection, something that was described by one young pastor as the responsibility of being 'the God guy.'[8] In the process, pastors

---

[8] The pastor described the responsibility of being 'the God guy' as the recognition that we represent Christ before others. He felt this responsibility especially keenly as the pastor of youth who looked up to him. The problem, as he described it, is the tendency to take on too much ownership of representing Christ, so that it becomes difficult to accept one's own weaknesses and fallibility. In spiritual direction, he becomes aware of this tendency and is reminded that he is not God. Instead, he can point to Christ as the giver of salvation and the true model for right living.

lose track of themselves and, not surprisingly, lose touch with God who knows and accepts them as they truly are. According ᴛᴏ ᴏne spiritual direction educator, a privileged place with an objective care-giver helps the leader to guard against self-deception. In these cases, spiritual direction serves as a kind of preventative care. In the language of the health care field, it is the regular check-up that assesses blood pressure, weight, and cholesterol levels while making suggestions for healthy eating and exercise. Spiritual direction is a check-up for the spiritual life which attends to right-sized views of the self. Other forms of therapy attend to serious illnesses and crisis management. Spiritual direction for pastors supports on-going health in life and faith for those who lead God's people.[9]

Spiritual direction has provided an important type of formational relationship for participants in this study. Yet this kind of relationship is not always easy to find. More than one pastor tells of unhelpful relationships with a first spiritual director, but all have eventually found a good fit. Most would agree that spiritual direction is not for the faint of heart. One pastor pointed out that it is a very intense experience which takes a great deal of energy and a willingness to be vulnerable. In spite of the intense, at times 'horrible', process, it also comes with an incredible feeling of freedom. He notes, 'it's almost like I feel clogged going in, and I'm not aware of it ... [In spiritual direction,] I have been able to name certain things I've been wrestling with, and I feel a burden released afterwards.' One parishioner who works with him regularly comments that after spiritual direction he almost 'glows.' For pastors in this study, the desire for God is a profound reason for making a commitment to spiritual direction in spite of the time and energy required. The light of Christ shines more brightly in them as they pay attention to their own self-care and spiritual formation.

---

[9] Marlene Kropf, a professor and teacher of spiritual direction, argues that the pastoral care and counselling movement has limitations because it deals primarily with crisis response. As a result, many congregations have become therapeutic centers both in terms of pastoral care and in support group models that focus on treating sickness and crisis. This does not attend adequately to those who are not in crisis but simply want to grow. Spiritual direction is primarily about personal and spiritual health and growth, not sickness.

A Prayerful Presence in all Tasks of Ministry

Many pastors who participate in spiritual direction are not content to keep the nourishment they have received to themselves. What begins in self-care and personal spiritual formation extends beyond. One minister described her love for spiritual direction training and reflected that she 'had a deep desire to bring that back to [her] congregation' so she could share the blessing of what she has received with others. These kinds of yearnings lead pastors to engage in one-with-one and/or small group spiritual direction in their congregations, deeply significant forms of ministry that have had an impact on many interested individuals.

Perhaps even more transformational, and certainly more influential to the larger congregation, is the impact of spiritual direction training on how pastors conceive of their work. The practice has resulted in a fundamental change in their understandings of ministry. Spiritual direction has essentially become a lens through which pastors view all that they do. They are intentionally seeking to become spiritual guides for congregations. Many members of their churches, as in the case of pastor Thomas, have taken notice. When asked to describe the pastoral role as they see it, several were quick to note that they believe their pastors are first and foremost spiritual guides. This is evident both in congregational relationships and tasks of ministry. After listening to pastors talk about spiritual direction in ministry, I believe that the lens they employ might be described very simply as *a prayerful presence*. They seek to provide a prayerful presence in all that they do, and they invite others to do this same.

Prayer is certainly nothing new for the Christian Church. It represents a critical aspect of every renewal movement in church history. When pastors offer a prayerful presence, they place a priority on being attentive to God and other people simultaneously. One pastor, Karen, admits that in her early years of ministry, she would have been hesitant to stop and pray for people:

'As much as I loved God, I really don't think I just stopped to pray, and be with people, and now I do that all the time ... Last week someone stopped me at the bank from our congregation and I said, 'Okay, let's just pray,' so we went off to the side and did that. I would have thought I was really weird 10 or 15 years ago, even as a pastor, taking someone off to the side of the bank to pray.'

It appears that this changing approach towards prayer is rooted in a core belief about God, herself as a minister and her relationship with others. Karen expresses a confidence that God desires to be found by us in every place and every circumstance. In her perspective, the spiritual guide seeks to be 'attuned to what God is doing' and ready to encounter God alongside others when opportunities present themselves. Second, a major part of her role as spiritual guide is to help others become aware of God's presence and join them as they seek God for themselves. A third dimension of the change has to do with what she believes about humanity. At one time she might have worried that others would think, 'you're a holy roller, you're praying at the bank.' Now she is genuinely convinced that people are longing for God.

Spiritual caregivers begin to address this God longing when they are able to say, 'I am here, I am listening to you, and our interactions are holy because I am paying attention to you with the eyes of God at this moment. I can see your pain and acknowledge it and pray with you about it.' Pastors in congregations are making the same discovery as sociologists of religion who study the larger North American landscape: people long for the sacred. Karen takes on her role as prayerful presence to address this longing. Many congregants report that they have deeply appreciated the spiritual guidance of their pastors.

It is clear from Karen's perspective on her work as a spiritual guide that becoming a prayerful presence to others is more about *listening* than *talking*. She notes that 'as we honour what we hear in that prayerful way, it helps [people] to know that God is listening as well.' Spiritual direction literature points to the triangle of relationship that occurs in the setting including God, the director and the directee. The director is paying attention to God and the directee, not an easy task. It requires patience, a comfort with silence, and a commitment to listen without needing to plan the next verbal response. But when the director readily acknowledges God's presence and gives time for silence so both have opportunity to listen for God, directees may experience God's presence with them in a tangible way. Spiritual direction explicitly acknowledges God-with-us in an immediate manner that many contemporary ministry tasks do not. Pastors who have claimed the role of spiritual guide have taken the kind of listening they do in one-with-one spiritual direction outside the spiritual director's office.

One pastor noted that many of the conversations she has with members of her congregation have the *feel* of spiritual direction to them. She describes this as an approach to listening that occurs in committee meetings, when standing in line and shaking hands after Sunday morning worship and even with the youth group. She tells the story of one youth whose behaviour was distracting to others in the group. Her first response was irritation and an urgency to deal with the behaviour. Her next response was to pay attention to this young person and to watch for what was really going on. As she listened, she began to observe some things in his life that she had not seen before, and she was able to pray and respond. She believes that she might have arrived at the same course of action without spiritual direction, but understanding her role as a spiritual guide helped her go there more quickly than she would have before. In essence, spiritual direction has sharpened the gifts and skills she brings to pastoral work.

When pastors in this study speak of listening, it is clear that they have a growing comfort with silence that is not common in a society overflowing with iPods, internet and endless conversation. They have learned to sit in the quiet and recognize that it is not empty. In fact, the silence is rich and full of purpose. They cherish the opportunity to quiet themselves and wait for a prompting to speak at the right time. All of us have probably known a few individuals who have had a sense of the right time to offer an important comment in conversation. These pastors are learning to wait for the word to come and be content to listen until it does. They are teaching their congregations to wait in silence so that God might be heard more clearly. Listening is at the heart of spiritual guidance.[10]

These findings extend beyond the stories from congregations to the reports of professors who regularly teach spiritual direction. Students are quick to conceive of their ministry roles differently and often begin processing these changes toward the end of spiritual

---

[10] When pastors allow spiritual direction to become a lens for ministry, it impacts on the way they accomplish individual tasks such as preaching, pastoral care and administration. Pastors report that they approach these responsibilities differently because of their role as spiritual guides. We will explore spiritual guidance in specific tasks further in chapter five.

direction training. Pastors find that there is a 'sharpening of the core' in life and ministry.[11] This implies that the relationship with God and personal gifts and skills for pastoral work have already been in place, but pastors experience a deepening of connection with God and greater clarity about the purpose and direction of their gifts. I asked one pastor to describe the significance of spiritual direction in the life of his colleague. He recalled that she had always been a discerning individual with gifts in pastoral care and a yearning for God's presence in her life and ministry. The practice had not created these things in her, but her gifts in ministry were sharpened so that she uses them more skillfully with a clearer focus.

God's Presence and Activity in People and Projects

Pastors who are spiritual guides are giving priority to looking for evidence of God's presence and activity in people and projects. This is one way to explain what it means to view one's ministry through a 'lens' of spiritual guidance. It was certainly true for the pastor who looked underneath the behaviour of a disruptive youth in a new way. Instead of reacting quickly, she took the time to pray and discern an effective response. While she had always cared deeply for people, she now watches for God's movements intentionally. She began to perceive that whatever the problem might be, it was not hers to fix. She might be able to do or say certain things to provide support, but it is not her responsibility to change this young person.

As pastors contemplate the significance of spiritual direction, they often report that it impacts their responses to others, especially in difficult situations. One pastor was quite direct when describing his own personal change. While in spiritual direction, he was encouraged to watch himself more closely: his personality, his strengths and the things he finds irritating. A significant part of the practice is growth in understanding of the self. In the care of an effective spiritual director, this knowledge can develop into self-acceptance which, in turn, influences the way the pastor treats others. He puts it this way, 'My training has allowed me to appreciate that each and every person who crosses my path (the good, the bad, and the ugly) is loved by God with an infinite love. That

---

[11] Some individuals have used the language of 'sharpening the core' or 'sharpening gifts for ministry.'

may sound very basic, but it's a reality. It's a truth that has changed how I receive people.'

Because of his role as a spiritual guide, he has a deepened appreciation of the 'value of the individual soul.' Pastors in this study notice that they care for the soul best when they look for God's fingerprint in the lives of all people, both inside and outside the congregation. Before spiritual direction training, these pastors would probably have agreed with this theological position, but what has changed for some is the practical manner in which they are working out their beliefs.

This approach to watching for God extends to projects the church may embark upon. Pastors recognize that one of the responsibilities of the spiritual guide is to help in the process of congregational discernment. One pastor spoke about his role as a spiritual guide who releases people in his congregation to use their gifts and explore their interests. Parishioners know they are welcome to come to him with suggestions for church life and service, and he will be receptive. He acknowledges that he must sometimes say, 'I don't think it's going to work. Let's keep the idea but let's figure out a different way of doing it.' He wants to support holy nudges but seeks out a way of doing it on a 'concrete level.'

Rather than only going to the pastor/spiritual director to discern gifts and calling, he also encourages a communal approach by teaching people to help each other discern God's voice.[12] This approach to leadership development has resulted in many different ministries within and outside the church from prayer shawls to mission trips. When final decisions are made, people are asked to discern how God is calling, both individually and as a congregation. Spiritual guides do not necessarily assume that God gives the vision for the projects of a congregation to its leader. In fact, the leader watches for the longings

---

[12] The pastor notes that one-with-one spiritual direction developed in the monastic tradition actually functions in a communal context. Monastic groups such as the Benedictines have relationships of individual spiritual direction, but always within the setting of a spiritually formative community. Brothers or sisters in a religious order are participating in spiritual direction individually but also in all kinds of relationships and in everything they do in the community. He suggests that Protestant spiritual direction tends to rip this out of context and creates spiritual direction with individuals seeking their own unique paths. He posits that the church must create spiritual communities in which spiritual direction comes both through individual relationships and through patterns of the community, including liturgical life.

and giftings interspersed throughout the body of Christ and nurtures the God-given desires for service already present.

One pastor suggests that it is easy for churches to get bogged down in the regular functions of the church, including everything from music to children's programs to building maintenance. 'One of the things I'm constantly doing is reminding people not just to move in the functions. It's easy to care [only] about the function, but we're called to listen to what *God* is calling us to do.' Instead of simply following a curriculum or expending all their energy on the nuts and bolts of a task, he encourages them to attend to how God is calling. This involves listening carefully to God within the task at hand, perhaps making some changes or even doing something entirely different.

Pastors who meet with parishioners for one-with-one or group spiritual direction often find that they gain moments of clarity about some of the ways God may be leading the congregation. As they ask others what they believe God is calling them to do, they help participants to clarify their sense of call and sometimes this call emerges into a larger ministry of the church. One directee gifted in writing dramatic pieces reflected with her pastor/director on her sense of call to this work. As the pastor gave leadership to worship planning, she asked her directee if she would like to bring a dramatic element to a few services throughout the year. The directee accepted the invitation and helped to create several memorable experiences that parishioners continue to speak about months later. In this case, the pastor had a special window into the life of one member. This is not typically possible with the entire congregation, but pastors who view themselves as spiritual guides watch for evidence of God's presence and activity amid the stirrings of God's people whenever they have opportunity.

A Language for Experiences of God

Pastors report that spiritual direction training has helped them develop a language to speak about experiences of God. One spiritual director recalls that her first training class included an exercise in which she was required to share a personal experience of God with another trainee. Her partner listened without trying to relate the experience to her own spiritual life or offer any kind of perspective or opinion. Her only role was to listen. It was a memorable exercise for this director who reflected on how rarely people are free to share memories of sacred moments and how infrequently these moments are accepted and cherished by others.

What emerges from the stories of pastors and spiritual direction educators is the need to give words to experiences of God. Pastors with training in spiritual direction are helping their congregations to establish a *culture of spiritual conversation*. Many people are at a loss to talk about deeper experiences of God because they have not been taught to do so. Inviting personal dialogue about the relationship with God does not come naturally in our culture. Rarely does one friend confide in another about memorable moments in the personal relationship with God, such as a struggle to find God in one's life or an experience when God seemed especially near. Yet with some education and modelling in their congregations, these pastors have found that many people are open to having these kinds of conversations. A few pastors suggest that the well-developed theological language honed in seminary did not fully prepare them for conversation about experiences with God. They needed a way to explore everyday mysteries of relating to the sacred, both in a quiet corner of the bank on Tuesday morning and in the church sanctuary after Sunday worship. Spiritual direction has provided tools and opportunities to practice spiritual conversation.

Some pastors who talk about the language for spirituality refer specifically to what they call 'God questions.' They note that posing helpful questions is critical to the prayerful presence. The 'God questions' named by several pastors are widely varied but share a common goal of driving directly into the heart of the relationship with God. When meeting with individuals or groups formally or informally, pastors in this study have been known to ask, 'Where is God in this situation?;' 'Have you prayed about this? How?;' 'What did you notice about God in this experience?;' or 'Is there an invitation from God here?' These questions may be paired with time for silence and reflection. Follow-up questions allow time to unpack responses and reflect at a deeper level. Frequently individuals will come upon new insights not previously considered.

Spiritual direction teaches spiritual conversation for one-with-one relationships. The ability to adapt a historical practice to the contemporary congregational context is seen again in the spiritual guidance offered to a larger body. When they preach, meet with small groups or participate in business meetings, they may ask, 'How have we noticed God's presence with us this year;' 'What is God saying to us in this moment?;' or 'What is God calling us to do?' The questions they have learned to ask of individuals are adapted for the larger body of Christ. The typical North American leader is more likely to give opinions or set the direction with overt instruction. Instead, these pastors tend to raise questions which lead to prayerful reflection and discussion. The words vary but the intent is the same. The pastor is inviting exploration of God's presence in the life of this particular congregation and helping to tease out the congregation's response.

Specific words or phrases may become particularly important in churches that emphasize spiritual guidance. One pastor stated very clearly that his work in the congregation is not to point to what we *want* to do or even what we *should* do, but what we feel *called* to do. The language of 'call' has become central. Worship services may incorporate reflection on God's call in sermons, prayers, and songs. When I visited the congregation, the worship was full of 'call' language, even in the words of the young man leading music who felt 'called' to choose a certain song. Interviews with church members reveal that reflection on God's call for individuals and the congregation as a whole is seeping into the ethos of who they understand themselves to be.

In this congregation, the pastor has worked intentionally at teaching about discernment of call in every setting, something that is now at play in multiple levels of the church. He has influenced this process in his preaching and teaching, but the impact goes much further. One of his primary tasks is to train leaders to pay attention to what God is calling the church to do. These leaders are then asked to train others. The pastor believes that paying attention to the call enables each one to grow spiritually and move towards transformed living. As a result, it is common for congregational initiatives to come from all corners of the church body as parishioners are asked to pay attention to 'what God is calling [them] to do.' In every congregation in this study, pastors who view themselves as spiritual guides appear to have a significant role to play in developing a language for experiences of God and a language for living out the call of God towards spiritual maturity. This language influences understandings about who God is, how God functions in the world, and the role of human beings within God's purposes. Ultimately, spiritual guidance is rooted in theological convictions, something we discuss in chapter four.

Reconstructing Standards of Success

All church leaders probably wonder at times if their work is bearing fruit. One of the noticeable distinctions about these spiritual guides' approaches to ministry is their understanding of success. I will attempt to illustrate what I mean. I have a pair of sunglasses that never fail to surprise me. When I put them on, the colours of the outside world take on a richer hue – somehow the greens are greener and the blues more blue. I'm still looking at the same things, but my perspective has sharpened slightly and I notice the differences. Pastors who take on a lens of spiritual direction talk about viewing their roles differently in light of what they have learned about being a spiritual guide. Like the sunglasses, this lens brings a bit of sharpness and clarity to the pastoral role, and pastors are able to look at all kinds of tasks and relationships differently because of the altered perspective. We have explored some of these features already.

Yet the term 'lens' breaks down when we hear pastors in this study report inner change. Any kind of tinted or corrective lens can never fundamentally and permanently affect your sight. When you take the glasses off, they no longer make a difference. According to self-reports, pastors have experienced personal transformation that includes self-care and spiritual growth as well as a changed sense of purpose and fulfilment in life and work. This is much more than an external lens. One pastor suggested that for him it was a messy process of surrendering control and management of ministry to God. Earlier in the chapter we considered the meaning of successful leadership in our time for the CEO who is responsible for making the business or ministry grow and flourish. Most writing and teaching on successful leadership in our world does not include the language of surrender.

A mid-western congregation included in the research project has two pastors with training in spiritual direction who have given considerable thought to the goals of their ministries in light of spiritual direction. One pastor reflects on changing views of success:

'When I first started in ministry, I thought, "How can I make this church successful?" Now [at First Church], that's not my prime objective. This church is going to do what this church is going to do. How do I walk with it? It is the same way when I'm with directees – I release them in a sense … I would hope there would be some transformation and change and enlightenment, but I'm not expecting any particular outcome ... My task is to see where God is active and where God is moving and stirring in their lives. I take the same attitude [at First Church]. Of course ... I hope things continue to go well [here], but that's not my prime objective.'

This pastor extends what he has learned about working with individuals to the larger body. In his view, the congregation becomes the directee. The pastor/director senses the call to surrender his own will for the church and pay attention to what God is already doing among the people. In this way, he is not responsible for particular outcomes in the way a CEO might be. Instead he sees God as the true guide for the church, and he works to support what God appears to be doing among them.

The co-pastor in this congregation goes on to describe what a vision of spiritual guidance means for the long view of ministry, especially in light of the overwhelming pain and chaos that exists in our world:

'There is a way in which we are completely and utterly useless in the face of peoples' lives ... in the sense that you cannot right wrongs or make bad stories not be bad anymore ... We are powerless to change some of those kinds of things ... The goal of ministry is to be able to free people to encounter God, no matter what their journey is ... What I think spiritual direction did was give me some distance to say, *it's not mine to fix*. This is about what *God* is doing here.'

She acknowledges that spiritual direction radically changed her approach to ministry. For years she was the go-to person when someone had a personal crisis or an issue that needed resolution. Her desire to care for others made her a good fit for ministry, but she recognizes in herself the risk of despair at her inability to fix what is wrong. When she looks at the larger picture of her denomination she sees this same desire to meet needs and fix problems by taking action. 'Just as pastors can be in a fix-it mode, I think congregations can, too ... "Give us something to do and we'll do it. You want a pie, I'll bake you three!" We like action.' For this pastor, spiritual direction does not detract from the importance of action, but it helps the church remember that *God* is ultimately the one who changes lives. Success, then, might be characterized as trusting that the Spirit is already at work in every circumstance, and then living out what God is calling each one to do and to be in those contexts. Success means dependence and trust rather than specific results in terms of converts, church membership or even changed lives.

Pastors in this study cherish what they have learned about becoming spiritual guides, but they are clear that spiritual direction training may not be the right fit for every pastor. Most say that pastors should have a spiritual director or some other kind of intentional relationship that focuses on personal spiritual growth and accountability in the relationship with God. However, becoming a spiritual director may not suit the personality and gifts of all individuals. Spiritual direction is one kind of practice that has helped these individuals to grow in the ways we have discussed, but it is certainly not the only possibility.

Several pastors have also noted that spiritual direction has informed their ministry, but it does not replace the need for other skills such as public speaking, academic capacity, organizational gifts and political savvy.[13] What they are learning is to remove themselves from the middle of the congregation, allowing God to take up the space. When I showed surprise at how many people had been positively influenced by the practice in one congregation, the pastors were quick to respond, 'but it's nothing *we've* done.' They are finding a right-sized role for themselves which will, they hope, support long-term health in ministry.

Forming Congregations

When leaders begin to offer spiritual direction in their congregations, those who respond are often already on a spiritual quest. They fit into the cultural trend described in chapter one – the searching desire to encounter the divine in a genuinely personal way. Frank is one individual whose spiritual quest is fostered in his

---

[13] One pastor noted that spiritual guides must have other skills, including the ability to be politically astute. Working with people and accomplishing projects requires more than good listening skills or attentiveness to God. In her words, 'you have to be smart, or you get roasted in this job.'

own congregation. A self-described introvert who likes to 'think things through,' Frank speaks easily and candidly about the internal struggle he faced some years ago when he began honestly to try to make some sense of the world and of his place in it. He had been a faithful participant in his congregation for over 20 years, not one to make waves, but now something deep inside him boiled over in frustrated questioning about his own spirituality and his purpose in the church. In the middle of a worship service he found himself thinking, 'If the pastors knew what I really thought, I would be out of here.'

During this period of inner ferment, one of Frank's pastors began a training program in spiritual direction in a nearby seminary. Frank took a risk and responded to the invitation to become her first directee. He found that his questions and doubts were met with warm acceptance. What's more, he describes his pastor/director as someone who 'pushed me out of my head and helped me open up to the Mystery.' At times, this meant encouraging him *not* to think so much but instead to *experience* the movements of God.

Spiritual direction was a turning-point for Frank. He began to pay attention to God's presence and activity in everyday life, and he came to realize that his questions and doubts had found a welcome home in his own congregation. For Frank, it was more than simply acknowledging his deep spiritual hunger, it was also a process towards caring for his congregational community and the world. He recalls how he once had little concern for the needs of others outside his own internal angst. As he was able to explore the inner self without fear in a hospitable space, he began to open up to the voice of God calling him to pay attention to various social issues and to participate in God's mission for the world. Inner ferment gave birth to both formation and mission. Since those early meetings, Frank has participated in one-with-one and group spiritual direction, finding that these intentional relationships help to keep him on track in his spiritual quest.

While not everyone brings a deep inner angst to spiritual direction, Frank's story certainly exemplifies key features of the significance of spiritual direction for individuals and congregations. Recipients of spiritual direction are not all that different from pastors; they identify many of the same spiritually formative learnings as their pastors do. The findings of the research point to several areas of growth or change for participants including: (1) *an increased awareness of God's presence in everyday life*; (2) *bringing God out of the box*; (3) *a sense of belonging in the congregation*; (4) *discerning calls to ministry and service*; and (5) *nurturing action through prayer and reflection*.

Awareness of God's Presence in Everyday life

Without a doubt, one of the most profound changes that spiritual direction participants report is a deepened awareness of God in everyday life. Paying attention to God's presence or absence over the course of a day is a new experience for many who enter spiritual direction. For some, years of bedtime prayers and Bible stories, public worship and church participation have not fully prepared them to ponder the mysteries of personal experiences of God. Some say that reflecting on God's presence and activity on a personal level, especially sharing it with a spiritual guide or even a good friend, is beyond the bounds of the norm in their circles. One young woman suggests that growing up in her denomination has taught her the relationship with God ought to be a private, personal matter rarely shared with others. She has received the message that followers of Christ are best known by the 'fruits' of everyday living, rather than by their words. While she honours this concern for Christ-like living, she believes that learning to talk about her relationship with God helps her to live more faithfully as she pays attention to God's ongoing presence in her life.

According to one pastor who leads spiritual formation groups, participants sometimes say they do not have any experiences of God to share. He interprets this as code language for, 'I don't believe what is happening in my life is connected to God.' As individuals unpack their daily lives and respond to 'God questions,' they begin to view the possibilities of God's presence in new ways. Many participants easily rattle off the kinds of questions that feed the spiritual direction relationship, and these questions are surprisingly consistent across congregations. 'How is your relationship with God?;' 'What did you notice about God in that situation?' or 'What kind of call have you been sensing from God?' Numerous participants report that spiritual direction has given them two very important tools for communication: opportunities to listen for God and a language to reflect on personal experiences of God. These appear to be foundational for developing a greater awareness of God.[14] With practice, members of a congregation see that 'spiritual experiences' may actually be God-given and normal rather than something to avoid which could be paranormal or akin to 'voodoo.'

Many participants suggest that a heightened awareness of God's presence leads to a feeling of being close to God. As they comprehend that God is interested in the big and small moments of their lives, they experience a deepening of relationship with God and are increasingly aware that they are deeply loved by the One who created them. This kind of love seems to nurture what one participant describes as an 'honest' relationship with God because 'you can't fake it in spiritual direction.' She goes on to say that knowing God more also includes knowing oneself. Her comments echo the sentiments of many spiritual writers over the centuries who argue that the journey towards God is also a journey inward to self-knowledge.[15]

Paying attention to God is a process of discernment supported by many tools. One person described the journey as 'an expansion of prayer.' This kind of prayer commonly begins with learning to listen before God. In this regard, participants are not at all different from the pastors we have already discussed. Some noted how counter-cultural an intentional stance of listening for God seems within our 'noisy' society. One pastor who provides one-with-one spiritual direction describes it this way:

'What spiritual direction has begun to offer is a place where people can become still and listen to God – be with God – put down all of the things they are doing *outside* of God and *for* God long enough to pay attention to the movement of God in their

---

[14] These insights fit closely with descriptions in contemporary spiritual direction literature. For example, Barry and Connelly suggest Christian spiritual direction helps a person 'pay attention to God's personal communication to him or her' and 'to respond to this personally communicating God.' Barry and Connolly, *The Practice of Spiritual Direction*, 8.

[15] See, for example, Catherine of Siena, who suggested that we come to know God better as we know ourselves. This is especially true as we reflect on the goodness of God towards us. In self-knowledge, we come to recognize our dignity because we are created in the image of the Trinity, and our limitations because of our human frailty and propensity towards sin. Mary O'Driscoll, ed. *Catherine of Siena: Passion for the Truth, Compassion for Humanity.* New Rochelle: New City Press, 2005, 13–15.

lives. This offers them a way to grow in their faith and deepen that relationship with God, which I think is an incredible need because we live in an overworked society.'

This pastor goes on to say that we applaud hard work and accomplishments in the church just as we do in society.[16] She argues that if we ask people to serve in the church, we must also provide for silence and rest to create balance. One of the ways she strives to address the need for balance is to teach spiritual disciplines in one-with-one relationships, at retreats and in other congregational settings. Participants in the study frequently note that learning new spiritual disciplines has enriched their lives of faith. For those in spiritual direction, the opportunity to reflect on personal practices on a regular basis has been a significant help for paying attention to God.

Some participants recognize a connection between a growing awareness of God and godly choices made in everyday life.[17] For most, these are subtle differences noticed over time. Becoming more aware of God's presence seems to have some effect on how they live in light of this presence. For a few, the differences have been dramatic. One individual in particular described his experience of personal change. John did not regularly participate in church until later in life. He was first drawn to a congregation through a dating relationship with a church member. Slowly he began to discern that the church had something to offer that he was lacking. Participating

---

[16] Others share similar concerns about over-emphasizing action and accomplishments in the church. Brad Harper and Paul Louis Metzger argue that a missional church ought to be 'being-driven' rather than 'doing-driven'. Its purpose and activity actually 'flow forth from the church's identity, which is constituted through its communion with the Triune God.' See Brad Harper and Paul Louis Metzger, *Exploring Ecclesiology: An Evangelical and Ecumenical Introduction*. Grand Rapids: Brazos Press, 2009, 237.

[17] I say 'some participants' because not all described their experience of spiritual direction in terms of the ethical choices they make as a result of participation in the practice. Some clearly had more facility in describing the connections between an inward journey of encounter with God and the choices of daily living. Others would say that the experience was positive, but either did not know how to describe the connection with ethical living, or perhaps did not believe it had ethical significance, though none clearly stated that it did not. In the final analysis, many of those who were most interested in reflecting on spiritual direction theoretically commonly tied the *awareness of God* in all of life with the call to *live in a Christ-like manner* in all of life.

in several settings with the pastor/spiritual director and a community that consistently asks, 'What is God calling us to do?' caused him to reflect on changes needed in his own life. He once struggled with road rage, and he tended to evaluate his life in materialistic terms. Now he asks, 'Lord, is this important in the entire [scope] of life?' In light of questions like these, John has chosen to put aside behaviours and attitudes that no longer suit the person he believes God is calling him to be.

John keeps his focus on this new perspective by participating in a weekly prayer meeting and by serving in church leadership and on mission endeavours. The prayer ministry, in particular, is something John would never have imagined himself doing before. In his view, getting serious about God's presence in his life made a dramatic impact on everything else. John is not the only one who speaks of changes in everyday life. Another participant who faces several challenges in her family life suggests that the everyday difficulties do not seem insurmountable when in spiritual direction. She is able to notice that God is with her in the struggles and helps her to see people and situations in new ways.

Bringing God out of the Box

When the awareness of God expands, the older familiar ideas about God may no longer satisfy. Any parent knows that five-year-olds can no longer wear the clothes that fit them at age four. In a similar way, growing intimacy with God often means growing out of old percep- tions of God into slightly expanded perceptions that better fit developing images of God. More than one participant states that the God they thought they knew has 'come out of the box.' Several commented that their ideas about God and their sense of what God might do in their lives has developed dramatically. Some in the study talk about 'opening up to the Mystery of God' and 'relaxing about who God is for them.' Not that God is changing constantly, but rather that they are catching glimpses of new dimensions of God's character. This has been particularly important for some who have had a view of God as a firm disciplinarian with high expectations of people. Pastors are observing that these individuals are increasingly embracing the possibility of God's loving nature and unconditional acceptance of them exactly as they are.

When God comes out of a human-made box, participants talk about asking tough faith questions. Just as an active volcano cannot hold back its steam, so too hard questions are an out-pouring of the genuine spiritual quest. Spiritual direction asks questions about God's presence, but also about God's absence, about sin and about pain and brokenness. Because of this, the practice may not be a good fit for everyone, particularly those who are unable or unwilling to consider these kinds of issues. One participant noted that 'just about anyone could benefit from spiritual direction but it requires a willingness to answer tough questions honestly.' Several participants acknowledged that not everyone is willing to do that.

Spiritual direction sometimes dwells on the ambiguities of the life of faith. The 'God questions' may not result in clear and easy answers. One pastor reports that people are frequently surprised that the process is hard. They wonder:

> 'Why don't I believe what I used to believe?' And my response is, 'I don't know, but I do know that you can't go back to a Sunday School theology once you've been beyond ... Personally, that's one of the reasons why I initially was even interested in direction, because that's the kind of conversation I like to have ... I don't want to hang around with people who think they have all the answers.'

This pastor describes one directee from the congregation who does not seem ready to enter into the difficult dimensions of the spiritual journey. He believes their spiritual direction relationship has not been very helpful and he finds himself 'bored.'[18] He wonders if perhaps he was not the right choice for a director or if the timing is off. Regardless, the experience confirms for him that entering into

---

[18] The pastor has described this participant's journey of faith in light of James Fowler's stages. He suggests that she is in stage three, Synthetic-Conventional Faith. She does not feel drawn to asking or answering searching questions of faith. The pastor believes that most people entering spiritual direction are at stage four in their journeys, individuative-reflective faith. They are willing to explore and evaluate their own faith commitments and relate to God in new ways. It is much more likely that individuals who have moved into stage four and beyond will allow God to 'come out of the box.' In fact if participants who begin direction in stage three are able to relate to God in new ways, it might be a sign of the beginnings of faith at stage four. For a description of these stages of faith, see James W. Fowler, *Stages of Faith: The Psychology of Human Development and the Quest for Meaning.* San Francisco: HarperSanFrancisco, 1995.

dark places on the spiritual journey is a necessary part of spiritual direction that supports spiritual growth.

Just as directees are invited to hold the relationship with God with open hands, so too congregations that support spiritual guidance tend to characterize themselves as 'open.' One consistent finding across congregations in this study is a general attitude of openness to new ideas and new ways of doing things, including practices of other traditions. In over half of the churches, the actual make-up of the congregation is strongly ecumenical with new members often coming from outside the denomination. While leaders teach about key features of the particular denomination, participants involved in the study do not generally consider denominational identity to be the glue holding the congregation together. The congregations appear to be rooted strongly in their theological traditions, but there is also a general inclination toward eclecticism. Overall these congregations clearly show more interest in seeker spirituality than dwelling spirituality. This 'open' spirit makes it possible for them to explore practices like spiritual direction which do not arise out of their own traditions.

A Sense of Belonging in the Congregation

One important issue raised in this study is the impact of a practice that emphasizes the inward journey on the congregational experience of community. Sandra's spiritual direction relationship with Anna which resulted in Anna's return to the church is perhaps one of the most poignant stories of welcome and belonging. Other individuals comment that one-with-one spiritual direction with a pastor or lay leader gave them a sense of the love and care of the church for them personally. Of course, this impact is limited to those who participate. A much more widespread experience of belonging arises in congregations that used the tools of spiritual direction to create spiritual guidance groups.

One young woman reflected upon the plateau she had reached in her spiritual life. She had come to need respite from a chaotic life, and she desired a deeper connection to the church. She joined a spiritual guidance group led by the pastor/spiritual director and she finds that she experiences more peace with God now and has increased her participation in other church activities. She notes, 'at one time, I felt intimidated by the highly educated, intellectual people [in our congregation]. Now I recognize that people are just people; they feel and think the same things and have the same fears and wants.' She feels a greater 'sense of belonging' in the congregation even though she is in an ethnic minority. In this case, the intimacy of the group setting that invites honest reflection on one's relationship with God serves an equalizer for individuals coming from varied socio-economic backgrounds. When this young woman discovers she has much in common with others, she knows that she belongs. Her sense of belonging has drawn her to participate in the larger work of the church as well. In the case of spiritual guidance or formation groups, these pastors are reforming spiritual direction for their spiritual communities.

Small group ministries are not at all foreign to contemporary churches. When asked about the experience of the group, some participants noted that spiritual guidance/formation groups differed from other groups they had participated in because of an emphasis on *experiences of God* rather than *ideas about God*. While the Bible may be used in both kinds of groups, reflective listening in lectio divina is experienced differently from traditional forms of Bible study. Most participants are quick to say that all forms have important purposes, but what spiritual guidance provides is intimacy as they come to know the real stories of others. One group spoke almost exclusively about the power of listening to each other's stories. Watching for God in the lives of others has become transformative for them and created significant communal bonds. They may feel hesitant at first, but grow into the role spiritual care-giving. In the words of one participant, 'If you're doing what you're doing right, everyone kind of becomes a spiritual director for each other.' For some, receiving this form of spiritual care is the glue that binds them to each other and to this particular church.

Discerning Calls to Ministry and Service

One of the most common reasons given for beginning spiritual direction is the discernment of major decisions. In some cases, it involves a call to some kind of ministry or service. Participants point out that they find the practice helpful for attending to their desire to serve God and clarifying their gifts for ministry. Many feel an urgency to know what God is inviting them to do. In one congregation, the lay spiritual director has given significant attention to the discernment of major decisions and has extended her ministry to organizing related practices, such as a Quaker-style 'clearness committee.' A committee is comprised of discerning supporters who meet to listen and respond as an individual seeks clarity about an important decision. One participant talked extensively about the help he received from a clearness committee when he needed to make a vocational choice. The committee provided a source of confirmation and support at a critical time in his life.

Other participants talk about beginning spiritual direction to work on their own relationships with God and discovering a sense of passion for some kind of service along the way. Several church leaders commented that directees have often gone on to lead ministries in the church and the larger community. One directee now runs a program for kids with disabilities in her neighborhood. Spiritual guidance helped her tap into the passions of her heart as she became comfortable relating to God in a personal way. Over time, she developed the sense that God desired to do something in the world through her. Another directee experienced a change in focus during her time of spiritual direction. According to her pastor, she was a dynamic leader who employed a typical business management approach, yet something changed dramatically:

> 'She came to spiritual direction and was so moved by it that she went out and formed a home 'church.' She was very much a doer, and here she was creating this intimate group of women to come and pray and talk about their feelings, which was opposite of the way she was functioning in the life of the church beforehand.'

This example points to the impact of spiritual guidance relationships on the discernment of call. Other pastors have shared similar observations. One pastor notes that he no longer strives to shepherd all of the flock personally. He has become more intentional about training spiritual leaders to reach out into the larger congregation. The youth ministry now functions in the same way, giving older youth responsibilities to nurture younger youth spiritually. One unexpected result of this approach to leadership training is a relatively high number of individuals who have felt a call to pastoral ministry and are now training in seminary or serving as leaders in other congregations.

Nurturing Action Through Prayer and Reflection

One of the questions raised in this research is the relevance of spiritual direction for the congregation's participation in the mission to share the gospel of Jesus Christ. All the congregations included in this research actively participate in mission at home and abroad. Many have reputations in their denominations for a strong history of mission participation. There is no evidence to suggest that spiritual direction has hampered missional thinking in any way. Yet has the practice actually *supported* mission? These congregations were involved in mission work long before spiritual direction. Measuring the actual impact of spiritual guidance practices is quite difficult, but there are signs of a connection. Sometimes the effects are a tiny ripple in the pool of God's purposes and sometimes they make a splash.

The practice appears to support missional thinking most directly by providing: (1) an emphasis on discerning God's calls; (2) nourishment for those who are active in mission; and (3) tools for relationships with people on a spiritual quest. First, an emphasis on discerning God's calls can have a direct impact on the congregation's missional reach locally and globally. We have already discussed the role of spiritual direction in making individual life decisions, but there is more to say about the missional character of these decisions beyond the congregation. Discernment about a call to mission often begins with individuals, but it may also impact the larger ethos of the congregation. One pastor provided spiritual direction for a young woman who was not certain about her purpose in life. After several months, she grew clear about her desire to participate in peace and justice initiatives, and she joined a Christian peace-making organization in the Middle East. Her congregation has recognized the call and actively supported her in her work.

Another pastor who works to create a culture of spiritual guidance in his congregation reports that he hears individuals talk about living their faith in the workplace in new ways. One member who heads a large corporation has begun to pray silently during corporate meetings for his employees and for God's guidance in business decisions. Given the tendency for pastors to become like CEOs in congregations, this story holds a certain irony. The CEO of a corporation is drawing on the tools of a spiritual guide because of his belief that God is always present and interested in all of life, even boardroom decision-making.

Many other individuals in this congregation participate in various service organizations. The pastor believes there is a need for growth in programmatic approaches to mission, but organic missional thinking is already at work in the life of the congregation. This analysis tends to fit the concept that spiritual guidance is somewhat messy. When individuals seek God's call, they connect with God's desires for the world. Attending to personal spiritual growth often evolves naturally towards a desire to participate in something missional; a ministry beyond the self and even the local community. Yet the outflow may not be clearly obvious in typical congregational programs.

Second, individuals active in mission work sometimes seek nourishment in spiritual direction. Lay spiritual directors at a congregation with an emphasis on missional outreach note that several of those most active in service work also come for spiritual direction. They are fed by opportunities for silence and contemplation which energize them for action. There is a clear sense among spiritual directors and participants that contemplation and action work best when they flow in and out of each other. As one participant noted, 'We get our strength to serve others from our internal connection with God.' One lay spiritual director combines prayer and mission in everyday life. She provides spiritual guidance in various forms in her congregation, and she manages a local centre for an international Christian service organization.

Third, there is also evidence in this study that spiritual direction provides tools for relationships with people on a spiritual quest who are outside the church. The story of Jason and Thomas told at the beginning of the chapter is perhaps the best example of spiritual direction at work with spiritual seekers. Ben Campbell Johnson argues that evangelism may actually serve as the beginning of spiritual guidance in a person's life.[19] The simple language of spiritual direction enables individuals to overcome some of the communication barriers inherent in traditional theology. Thomas reports that conversations about God now come just as easily with agnostics as church members; he is comfortable having soul conversations with anyone, whether or not they are in the church. This is supported by a belief that the Spirit is already reaching out to individuals even before they become aware of it.

---

[19] Ben Campbell Johnson, *Speaking of God: Evangelism as Initial Spiritual Guidance.* Louisville: Westminster/John Knox Press, 1991.

While many of those interviewed connected spiritual direction and mission, some participants have not personally observed any specific impact for their congregations. A few who had never participated in spiritual direction were downright sceptical about the role of the practice within God's call to mission and service in the world. This is a significant issue that must be considered further. One woman wondered if spiritual direction is 'all talk' and 'no action.' She expressed having no interest if it is simply a psychological panacea involving digging deep inside the self instead of doing, serving, and acting as Christ modelled for his followers. This point of view must be considered, especially in light of the fact that spiritual direction as it is practiced in these congregations and described in contemporary literature relies on the agenda set by participants. They may choose to focus solely on the inward quest.

Conclusion

Congregations face the challenge of preparing an effective response to the quest culture we encounter. Reggie is one of many seeking answers that will bridge the divide between traditional church life and the spirituality of contemporary culture. This is a critical issue for discernment in many congregations as more and more people seek to go deeper into the spiritual life, both inside and outside the church.

★★★★★★★★★★★★★★★★★★★★★★

Spiritual Practice: Supporting Actors

In this chapter, we have heard stories of congregations and leaders who provide support for on-going spiritual formation. During this practice, you will reflect on the role of faith communities in your own spiritual journey.

Find a comfortable and quiet space and take a few slow, deep breaths. Invite God to be present with you and guide you through this time. Consider your life as a dramatic play made of various acts. You may choose to write down each act along a timeline.

Imagine yourself on stage. As you look around, you see that you're not alone. There are others playing supporting roles who have been an integral part of your life story and your spiritual development. As you look over your life, note any congregations that have been a part of your story. What has been your experience of the church? Are there specific individuals who were important in helping you recognize God? What did that person or persons say or do? How would you describe the spiritual guidance you have received? Do not hesitate to acknowledge painful experiences and/or relationships. These also impact our experience and understanding of God.

Take time to pray the Lord's Prayer slowly. Open yourself to confession and forgiveness of others as you consider any broken relationships in your life that hinder your spiritual formation.

★★★★★★★★★★★★★★★★★★★★★★★★★

Discussion Questions

- Do you think every pastor should have some kind of spiritual guidance relationship? Why or why not?
- How important is self-care in the lives of pastors? What tools can pastors draw upon to stay healthy in ministry for the long haul?
- Do you think spiritual guidance automatically leads to a greater commitment to mission and service? Why or why not?
- In your experience of congregational life, do you identify more with Joelle or Reggie? Is your current congregation open to 'new things'?
- Is there someone in your life who is a prayerful presence for you? How has this person made a difference in your spiritual formation?

Chapter 3

Looking over their Shoulders: Exemplary Soul Care in Scripture and History

M aria Frelinghuysen Cornell (1778–1832) started the first rural Sunday School in America in 1809 at a tiny Presbyterian Church in Allentown, New Jersey.[1] History books hardly mention her, but she was a pioneer and a truly remarkable woman. Maria was sixteen years old when her mother died and she took on the primary responsibility for raising several younger brothers and sisters, one of whom would become a U.S. senator. As a young adult, she married John Cornell, who accepted the pastoral assignment in Allentown which lasted twenty years. Their time in Allentown was a period fraught with difficulty and few obvious signs of success.[2] In spite of many challenges, the Cornells persevered.

---

[1] There were other Sunday Schools already operating in a few cities including Boston, New York and Philadelphia, but the Allentown congregation was probably the first to hold a Sunday School in rural America, which continues to run to this day. The story of Maria and her husband, John Cornell, is told in F. Dean Storms, *History of Allentown Presbyterian Church*. Allentown, NJ: Allentown Messenger, 1970, 81–105. The congregation has a plaque in the education wing which states, 'To the Glory of God and in the memory of Maria Frelinghuysen Cornell 1778–1832 who established here in the year 1809 one of the first Sunday Schools in America.'

[2] Despite being 'gentle, kind and scholarly' and a 'persuasive' preacher, John Cornell's years in ministry were filled with turmoil. He was poorly and irregularly paid, unfairly discredited several times by a congregational member, and saw very little growth in church membership over two decades of service. In spite of outward signs of discouragement, God accomplished something new. Ibid., 90–91.

In 1805, Maria joined together with a few others to begin the Allentown Sober Society, the first regularly organized temperance society in America.[3] This was only one of Maria's pioneering projects. In 1809, the same year John and Maria buried two of their children, she turned her attention to the Christian education of children in her community. In spite of terrible pain and anguish, Maria had the courage to start something new. She willingly took uncertain steps which would have long-term significance. Just two months before her husband left the pastorate in 1820, a building was set aside for Sunday Schools, Singing Schools and other religious meetings. Maria was determined to seek God's purposes in spite of grief and experiences of religious darkness. She once said to a friend, 'If God in Christ is the portion of my soul, surely I may rejoice in this valley of tears; and although billow after billow may be commissioned to roll over me, still I will rejoice. He can, and will say, 'Peace be still,' whenever the design of His providence is affected.'[4]

Just recently, the Allentown Presbyterian Church celebrated the two hundredth anniversary of the Sunday School, Maria's innovative idea. In a fitting tribute, sixty young children led the congregation in rousing worship. The guest speaker reminded listeners that God is always doing new things and we must watch for them.[5] We

[3] At that time, total abstinence was practically unheard of. Maria Cornell was probably motivated by conditions in her own congregation. Church records report several cases of discipline based on immoderate use of liquor around this time. The Allentown Sober Society is recognized by many historians as the first regularly organized temperance society in America. It was a forerunner of the great temperance movement that would sweep the country. Even after the Cornells left the congregation, the concern for temperance continued and a pledge to abstain entirely from liquor other than for medicinal uses is reported in session records. This kind of commitment to abstain from alcohol continues today in the Alcoholics Anonymous movement. We can observe Maria Cornell's willingness to address practical needs in her community and to try something different. She could not possibly have known the impact she would have. Historian F. Dean Storms reports that 'the fruits of her labours are felt here even to this day.' Ibid., 102–03.

[4] Ibid., 104.

[5] Dr. Freda Gardner gave a sermon entitled 'Body Building: A Habit for Humanity.' She is a pioneer in Christian education in the Presbyterian Church in her own right. She referred to Isaiah 43:19 in her sermon when she spoke of God doing new things.

often want to hang on to every old thing we are accustomed to, especially if what is new does not immediately please us.

This congregation displays an air of openness to testing what is new while cherishing many long-standing commitments like the Sunday School. There is a strong emphasis on spiritual guidance in this congregation with widely varied approaches. Today there are hundreds of young people from the community meeting in small groups with adult 'shepherds' on a regular basis. Essentially, the congregation offers a safe space for teenagers to receive spiritual care and guidance. Certainly Maria could not have imagined this future outcome when she began her Sunday School with just a few local children. Her willingness to follow God's call and try something different is a heritage this church celebrates. As we remember Maria, we are encouraged by her faithfulness to a call that must have seemed uncertain at times.

Looking over their Shoulders

My family went on vacation to the mountains last summer. As usual, our kids pushed us out of the door that first morning to search for the highest hill they could reasonably climb. To their delight, we found a rocky hillside with a cliff at the top and a beautiful view of the surrounding country. As I climbed the (very safe) steps provided for vacationers, the rest of my family was determined to get to the top the hard way. I caught my breath as I watched them climb over rocks and ledges with gusto. Fortunately, my husband went first and looked back over his shoulder, directing the young climbers by example and instruction on the safest spots to place a hand or foot. Under this watchful guidance, they were able to step carefully, and safely reach the anxious arms of their mother waiting at the top.

Over the centuries, the church has been composed of many experienced climbers who looked over their shoulders and provided examples and instructions. The spiritual guides we remember in this chapter had no idea how many would come to watch their spiritual journeys. They had little concept of the far-reaching influence of their practice and teaching. In this chapter, we are looking for evidence of spiritual guidance from among the crowd of witnesses, our foremothers and forefathers in the faith. In a few cases, we are looking for examples of spiritual guidance practices in Protestant communities that have not traditionally labelled their practice as spiritual guidance. This will give us insight into ways that we can reclaim or retool practices that are part of our own traditions.

In every historical moment, we focus on life and practice rather than on ideas alone. Our attention is caught by moments when the church engaged in forms of spiritual guidance that stand out as excellent – not perfect, but excellent. If we relate our search to theatrical improvisation, we might say that we are looking for occasions when all the actors play their parts in synch, creating a truly memorable moment for the audience. In this chapter, we are the audience watching the players exhibit their creativity and skill to the best of their abilities under the guidance of the Holy Director. We will view several scenes in which the people of God journeyed on their own spiritual quests in specific eras and cultures. As we consider each scene, we address the two main purposes of this chapter: (1) to gain insights about spiritual guidance from historical practice; and (2) to pay special attention to the integration of person, community and mission in each instance.

Scripture plays a special role in guiding the church through each scene of the Great Drama we call church history, and our first scene is a biblical example of spiritual guidance.[6] The apostle Paul's first letter to the Thessalonians stands out for providing guidance to an emerging church. We may not think of Paul as a traditional spiritual director, but his writings clearly reflect his call to spiritual guidance. We will pay attention to person, community and mission in Paul's soul care. After laying the foundation with a biblical example, we will look for characteristics of spiritual guidance in Julian of Norwich, Susanna Wesley, and Dietrich Bonhoeffer. In these three examples, we can identify a priority given to one formational concern: person, community or mission. Yet the other two dimensions are evident as well, sometimes unexpectedly. These women and men of faith teach us that a strong call to a personal, communal or missional life does not exclude the other two. They provide significant insight

---

[6] The book of I Thessalonians takes on a unique role in the historical stories we will consider here. In one sense, it is a letter from a missionary and spiritual guide (along with his associates) to a congregation they formed under the direction of the Holy Spirit. In another sense, it is the inspired word of God, worthy of teaching and preaching for the formation of God's people. Because of I Thessalonians' special role as Scripture and Paul's unique call to apostleship, this scene in the church's story will stand apart and can be used to bring special insight to spiritual guidance today and in every other historical period.

into the interconnected balance of all three in spiritual guidance and formation which is greatly needed in our time.

Paul's Letter to the Thessalonians

The first scene in our drama portrays the story of a young community of faith located in an urban center within Macedonia around the year 50.[7] At this time, they have already met Paul, an apostle for Jesus Christ, and they are convinced by his message. Paul and his companions have fled the area, most likely due to threats of persecution, but this community goes on to believe and live in radically new ways because they are now part of the church of Jesus Christ. Paul's first letter to the Thessalonian church is almost certainly the earliest of his surviving letters, and its authenticity is rarely questioned. The aim of I Thessalonians is clearly pastoral.[8] Paul worries that these new converts to the faith might abandon the gospel because they face significant opposition (1:6). Out of concern, he sends Timothy for a report on their circumstances (3:2). Paul rejoices at Timothy's return when he hears that the church is continuing on in faith and love (3:6).

Paul and his companions write the letter we identify as I Thessalonians to encourage and strengthen these new converts. The apostle reaffirms his relationship with the church and reminds them of the example he and his companions have set for them.[9] We hear the emotion in Paul's words. He cares deeply for this young church, and he longs to see them again. Paul and his companions are determined to share with the new believers 'not only the gospel of God but also our own selves, because you have become very dear to us' (2:8). The apostle lets the young church know that *they* have encouraged *him* by their commitment to the faith in spite of hardship (3:7–8). The letter reassures them that they are already living in a manner pleasing to God (4:1) and urges them to continue in loving and encouraging conduct toward each other and

---

[7] Jacob W. Elias, *1&2 Thessalonians*, Believers Church Bible Commentary. Scottdale, PA: Herald Press, 1995, 26–28.

[8] Victor Paul Furnish, *1 Thessalonians, 2 Thessalonians*. Nashville: Abingdon Press, 2007, 21–22.

[9] Alongside Paul, Silvanus and Timothy are named as joint authors of the letter (1:1).

in quiet diligence among those outside the faith (4:9–12). There is no need to be anxious about those who have already died or about the timing Christ's return, for they can trust the salvation that comes through Jesus Christ (4:13–5:11).[10]

Characteristics of Paul the Spiritual Guide

Paul maintains a special relationship with those he cherishes in the Thessalonian community, a relationship that might be characterized as spiritual guidance. We notice several features of spiritual guidance in this letter. First and foremost, Paul is clear that *he is not the true spiritual guide: the Holy Spirit is.* Paul is quick to give credit where credit is due. This does not mean that Paul's role is unimportant. He acknowledges that he is an apostle of Jesus Christ, entrusted with the task of preaching the gospel of God (2:4, 9). At the same time, Paul knows it is the Holy Spirit, not words alone, that brings divine power for conviction (1:5).[11] The Thessalonians have their own connection to God who has given them the Holy Spirit (4:8). Though Paul is the one to offer instruction on Christ-like living, it is God who accomplishes personal and communal transformation (5:24).

When a philosopher in Paul's day converted followers to a new teaching, they preached with passion and believed that their words

---

[10] Paul and his companions write this letter in the Greek paraenetic style which was generally used for moral teachings with the goal of encouraging personal improvement. Paul uses this form to provide basic instruction in Christian behavior (rather than doctrine, as in some of his other letters). Yet he also goes beyond moral teachings. Paul adapts the paraenetic style to describe the relationship between himself and his readers. He and his companions are examples, and watching them gives the new converts insight into the moral development Paul advises. Paul also uses their relationship to address the emotional condition of the Thessalonian church. The language of kinship is meant to provide a sense of comfort and security in the larger community they are now part of. If their anxiety extends to what they ought to be doing, Paul affirms them in their actions and encourages them to continue even more in what they are already doing. In this letter, Paul is attempting to meet the young faith community exactly in its current state and minister to them there. These features of Paul's soul care bring significant insight to contemporary ministries of spiritual guidance. See Abraham J. Malherbe, *The Letters to the Thessalonians: A New Translation with Introduction and Commentary*. New York: Doubleday, 2000, 85–86.

[11] Elias, *1&2 Thessalonians*, 43.

could bring about genuine change. Paul follows a similar pattern of conversion with one critical difference. He knows that his words cannot possibly alter the Thessalonians' lives; he is only preparing the way for the Holy Spirit who accomplishes the change.[12] God's role as the agent of change is absolutely fundamental for contemporary spiritual guidance. In the previous chapter, we described one pastor's recognition that *God* is the only one who brings transformation. Like Paul, the spiritual guide must trust that the Holy Spirit is already at work among potential converts.

A second feature of Paul's spiritual guidance is *his commitment to prayer and discernment*. Paul's prayers for the young church are ongoing (1:2) and include both thankfulness and intercession. He expresses gratefulness to God for their faith, hope and love (1:3) and asks God to strengthen personal piety (3:13) and nurture communal love for one another (3:12). In his prayers, he gives equal attention to personal and communal formation; both of these are necessary in a life that is pleasing to God. Paul's prayers are also instructive. Instead of simply noting that he prays for them, he explicitly lays out what he prays about. Later he directs them to model his practice of prayer and urges them to be discerning about the movements of the Spirit. A troubling situation may have arisen within the congregation, perhaps involving leadership and charismatic gifts.[13] Paul makes it clear that it is essential to seek the guidance of the Holy Spirit and test all things, holding on to what is good (5:19–22).[14]

Contemporary spiritual guides can learn from Paul's commitment to regular prayer and petition on behalf of those they minister to. We cannot underestimate the importance of prayers offered in private and in the presence of others. I spoke recently to a professor of spiritual formation, and was surprised to hear the extent of her prayer life on behalf of her students and her prayerful discernment of each aspect of her work. Perhaps this should not seem unusual, but on-going prayer and petition may easily slip away in the life of a busy professor or minister. Praying directly with others is also important. The experience of being named before God in prayer is

---

[12] Abraham J. Malherbe, *Paul and the Thessalonians: The Philosophic Tradition of Pastoral Care*. Philadelphia: Fortress Press, 1987, 29–30.

[13] Elias, *1&2 Thessalonians*, 227.

[14] Richard Robert Osmer, *The Teaching Ministry of Congregations*. Louisville: Westminster/John Knox Press, 2005, 41.

deeply encouraging and affirming to individuals. Regardless of what kind of spiritual guidance we provide, Paul shows by example that our ability to be in tune with what the Holy Spirit is doing hinges on our on-going communication with God.

A third characteristic of spiritual guidance in Paul's ministry is his *attention to God's presence in everyday life*. While we only hear about their relationship from one side, we can imagine that Paul might have offered informal spiritual guidance to the Thessalonians when he lived and worked alongside them (2:3–12). Paul watches for the presence of the Spirit and points to a specific moment when God was clearly with them in joy and inner conviction, a moment Paul witnessed in person (1:5). He goes on to describe how God has been speaking to and through them consistently, to the point that others have taken notice (1:6–8). Within their faith community, God has been communicating to them about their treatment of each other (4:9). Paul confirms that the Spirit is active and moving among them through the prophetic words of their peers (5:20).[15] The Thessalonians will know God's Spirit is present as they observe their own inward process of sanctification since God is the one who accomplishes this (5:23, 24). Paul also speaks generally about how God is active and moving in his own life and in the lives of all followers of Christ. He observes that God is present as God tests his peoples' hearts (2:4) and literally directs the travel decisions of those who seek the Spirit's guidance (3:11).

Contemporary spiritual guidance involves seeking the Spirit's presence in all of life in the same manner. Asking the 'God questions' of persons and communities may seem unusual in a congregation that has not been accustomed to discerning God's presence in this way. This kind of language and perspective about a divine being must have been somewhat foreign to the Thessalonians. Yet Paul provides an example for creating a culture of spiritual conversation in a community of faith. He helps them to notice how God is

---

[15] We do not know exactly what is meant in 4:9 when Paul suggests that they have been 'taught by God.' This may have been some kind of internal teaching or instruction coming from prophets among them, Jesus' teachings or Paul's own teaching under the direction of the Holy Spirit. Malherbe, *The Letters to the Thessalonians: A New Translation with Introduction and Commentary*, 244. Perhaps some or all of these contributed. Regardless of the method, Paul is emphasizing God's desire to communicate with the Thessalonians.

present with them, at times gently pointing out how God is active in ways they might not see on their own. Spiritual guides can nurture spiritual conversation by sharing their own stories of God's presence and inviting others to participate. This has happened in several congregations in the research where people with experience in spiritual guidance practices freely share moments when they noticed God's presence or sensed God's guidance.[16]

A fourth characteristic of Paul as a spiritual guide is *ministry rooted in Christian imitation*. Paul's letter to the Thessalonians attends to prayer and awareness of God's presence within the context of moral living. Paul invites the Thessalonians to remember his own witness, especially the manner in which he and his companions lived and worked alongside the people while sharing the gospel (2:9). Paul states that all are witnesses of 'how pure, upright, and blameless' the missionaries' conduct was towards the believers (2:10). He endeavours to live a Christ-like life before the God who has called him to life and service. Paul does this not only as a response to God's call on his life but also because it is an essential part of his witness to the gospel. In fact, he affirms the Thessalonians' *imitation* of the example he and his companions have provided during their sojourn in Thessalonica (1:6).

Paul understands his ministry to be more than preaching the gospel. He is also teaching by example the process of on-going formation toward sanctification or holiness in personal and communal life. We may wonder how Paul could possibly draw so many to his teachings. Was it his skill of persuasion? Perhaps a commanding physical presence? 1 Thessalonians 2 mentions proclamation of the gospel only briefly. The rest of Paul's description of their time together is filled with the missionaries' tender love towards them and their witness through upright living. The combination of Paul

---

[16] Within a culture of spiritual conversation, we are reminded by Paul of the importance of careful discernment about what we hear, holding fast to what is good (5:21). The word for 'test' here *(dokimazein)* is typically used by Paul for judging moral behavior (Rom 12:2; 1 Cor 11:28; 2 Cor 13:5; Gal 6:4). See Ibid., 333. The danger in a community that nurtures spiritual conversation is the possibility that experiences of God or messages from the Lord may be brought to the community of faith without careful discernment of the Spirit's presence. Word and deed must come together in the life of faith. Paul's letter to the Galatians is a reminder of the characteristic fruit that can be measured as evidence of surrender to God in a person's life (Gal 5:22,23).

and his companions' words and actions and the stirrings of the Holy Spirit awakened the hearts of the Thessalonians. We learn from Paul that spiritual guidance includes modeling Christ-like character.

Paul Copan writes about the apostle's spiritual guidance of the young faith community. He notes that Paul sets himself up boldly and intentionally as a model for those under his care.[17] This is an important insight for spiritual guidance. In contemporary spiritual direction literature, the impact of the director's lifestyle is given scant attention. Practical techniques have the lion's share of space on the printed page. This is unfortunate because 'the total shape of the life of the director is a key factor – if not *the* key factor – in the success of spiritual direction; effectiveness in spiritual direction is not to be found primarily in technique, but in the character and lifestyle of the one providing the direction.'[18]

William Barry and William Connolly, make a related observation in their seminal book on spiritual direction. They suggest that what spiritual directors bring to their directees at a most basic level is their membership in the Christian community and their sharing in the faith of this community.[19] Essentially, the most important qualities of an exemplary (not perfect, but exemplary) spiritual guide include the guide's own spiritual journey, their developing Christian character and their participation in the faith community. Spiritual guides in congregations may reside alongside those they minister to and exemplify living with a heart turned toward God.

While Paul invites the Thessalonians to imitate him, he is careful not to point to himself as the perfect model. Paul and his companions are actually seeking to follow *Christ's* model. Because they are imitators of Paul, the Thessalonians are also imitating Christ.[20] Spiritual guides in communities of faith can be models for the journey of faith but they must remember that they are always pointing to Christ, not

---

[17] Copan suggests that Paul's use of imitation in spiritual guidance would not have been unusual in this time and place. Paul draws upon a model common to Thessalonian culture and sets himself up as an example to be imitated. Victor A. Copan, *Saint Paul as Spiritual Director: An Analysis of the Imitation of Paul with Implications and Applications to the Practice of Spiritual Direction*. Milton Keynes: Paternoster Press, 2007, 80.

[18] Ibid., 1,2.

[19] Barry and Connolly, *The Practice of Spiritual Direction*, 122.

[20] Copan, *Saint Paul as Spiritual Director: An Analysis of the Imitation of Paul with Implications and Applications to the Practice of Spiritual Direction*, 104.

themselves. In the previous chapter, we considered the danger of one pastor who came to believe he had to be 'the God guy' before the young people in his pastorate. The inherent danger in this approach is stepping over the line and taking on the responsibility to resolve problems and save people. When spiritual guides take a healthy approach to ministry, the manner in which they journey with God and live their lives naturally draws people who hunger to know more. This worked in Paul's ministry and arises also in many other biblical, historical and contemporary examples, especially in the example of Jesus Christ himself.

Personal Experiences of God

The apostle Paul's letter to the Thessalonian church provides important insights about what it means to be a spiritual guide who attends to the formation of person, community and mission. We will consider each of these individually, beginning with specific dimensions of spiritual guidance for the person. Paul bestows a very important gift on the new community of faith right at the beginning of the letter. *He acknowledges the validity of a personal, inward experience of God.* As we read the letter, we have the privilege of hearing Paul's recollections of the Thessalonians' inward experience of God when Paul and his companions share the gospel. We learn that the Thessalonians 'received the word with joy inspired by the Holy Spirit' (1:6).[21] They experienced this joy *in spite of* persecution. A normal human response to suffering produced by persecution might be fear or anger. However, Paul specifically points to joy, a feeling that cannot be accounted for given their circumstances.

Perhaps Paul is responding to questions or doubts among the new converts. I wonder, did they ever question whether embracing the gospel was worth the difficulties? Did they question the presence of a God that Paul declares has chosen them and calls them 'beloved?' (1:4). Acting as a spiritual guide, Paul confirms that the joy spilling forth is not coming from them alone, but actually finds its source in the Holy Spirit. The inward emotion they have experienced is most definitely evidence of a personal encounter with God. Paul mentions God's action again when he speaks of the message they received. He

---

[21] Malherbe, *The Letters to the Thessalonians: A New Translation with Introduction and Commentary*, 115.

thanks God that they accepted it for what it really was – not a human word, but God's word (1:13).

Throughout the letter we hear Paul pointing to what the Holy Spirit accomplishes within them. As we have already noted, he speaks candidly of God's presence with them through the Holy Spirit (4:8). When they feel overwhelmed by all the changes that Paul asks of them, they can be reassured that it is actually *God* who will do the sanctifying. God will change the spirit, soul and body. The God who calls each of them and gives them inner joy is not like other fickle gods worshipped in various forms in the religions all around them.[22] This God promises to be present and active in their lives no matter what challenges they face.

It is probably difficult for most of us to relate directly to the Thessalonian experience of receiving the gospel. Yet we can all comprehend the experience of suffering in some form, whether or not it relates directly to our faith. What Paul does as a spiritual guide is very interesting. In the midst of difficult circumstances, he points to how God has been present with the people, and to the emotion they experienced when they heard the gospel. In a sense, he is urging them to remember. In our context, it is not uncommon for people to seek spiritual guidance when they are going through personal difficulty or God seems distant. Spiritual guides today have the same opportunity to support those who are struggling. Like Paul, a spiritual guide helps people recall that God has been with them in the past and remember what genuine experiences of God's presence felt like.[23]

Attending to inward emotions or sensations as a sign of the sacred is relatively distasteful to a materialistic, reason-oriented way of thinking. Many of us have learned to distrust emotion. We worry that if we rely on emotions, we will be led astray by our own reactions that are inherently untrustworthy. Too many hurts have been inflicted in God's name through misplaced passions. In our daily journey, it is difficult to tell if the feeling we have is from God or some subconscious reaction or just wishful thinking. I have

---

[22] Beverly Roberts Gaventa, *First and Second Thessalonians*, Interpretation: A Bible Commentary for Teaching and Preaching. Louisville: John Knox Press 1998, 86.

[23] Contemporary spiritual guidance often points to St. Ignatius as a principle figure who taught about the use of emotions in discernment. Ignatius' *Spiritual Exercises* is an important text that addresses this issue.

encountered several faithful people of God in my spiritual direction practice who are acutely suspicious of emotions, even positive ones. It is more than appropriate to question emotional responses because we are often unconscious of our true motives. Yet God created us with emotions, and they are a necessary part of our most basic desire to respond in relationship to God and others. We draw upon emotional responses alongside the witness of Scripture, the voice of the faith community, reasoned thinking and fruitful actions to make some sense of God's presence and activity.

What we learn from Paul is that emotions have a necessary place in our experience of God. It is not uncommon to find the Holy Spirit identified as responsible for joy in the New Testament (Luke 10:21; Acts 13:52; Rom. 14:17; 15:13; Gal. 5:22). As spiritual guides listen for signs of the Holy Spirit in the stories of others, they pay attention to emotions as evidence of God, including inner joy or other fruit of the Spirit (Gal. 5:22).[24] A part of the inward journey is remembering that God loves and has chosen us (1:4), and we may experience God directly with genuine emotion inspired by the Holy Spirit (1:6).

Spiritual Formation and Community Life

The new community of faith in Thessalonica was in a difficult situation. They had known joy at conversion, but living out their convictions was proving to be a test. Paul is well aware of this, and we can hear the depths of his concern for these dear ones (1:8).[25] In his letter, he outlines an approach to supporting their on-going faith formation. The role of relationships is critical, especially relationships with leaders and peers in the community of faith. One of the hallmarks of Paul's spiritual guidance ministry is his approach to team leadership. If Paul's teachings on mutual encouragement are any

---

[24] Paul explicitly reminds the people of the joy inspired by the Holy Spirit. Though Paul does not deal with it in this text, I believe that more 'negative' emotions also have a place in the church and in spiritual guidance relationships as a way of paying attention to what God is doing in the spiritual life.

[25] Paul is very concerned that the Thessalonian converts are experiencing 'the feeling that they had been forsaken, sometimes expressed by describing themselves as orphans.' Paul, too, feels like an orphan because of their involuntary separation, and Paul senses an urgent need to send Timothy to check on them (3:1–5). Malherbe, *Paul and the Thessalonians: The Philosophic Tradition of Pastoral Care*, 64.

indication (4:18; 5:11), he had a strong appreciation for the strength of a team with a shared vision. Part of the gift of Paul's team was the ability to send one team member out to minister on behalf of the others. The apostle allows Timothy to go to the Thessalonians to 'strengthen and encourage' them in the faith (3:2), a move that Paul hopes will make a difference at a critical point in the development of this young church.

The spiritual guide who is led by God can make a significant difference in a struggling community. When I was a young adult not yet in my twenties, I joined a mission organization for a year-long trip including formational training in the United States and service in a church in Mexico. The training period was a comforting season and a greenhouse of spiritual growth, and I was unprepared for the challenges of living and working in another country and culture while learning a new language. We did our best, but we struggled intensely as we tried to understand how to serve God in our new setting. The challenging external environment I experienced was combined with a sense of God's absence internally. These two factors created a genuine test of my faith.

A bright spot during that difficult year was a brief visit from the leader of the mission program. He had become a spiritual guide for me and others in our group, and I remember how important his visit was for our flagging spirits. I wonder if it was anything like the Thessalonians' experience of Timothy's visit. In those brief two days, I described my difficulties to a listening ear and sensed the love of God through the presence of our guide. After this experience, I found the courage to continue, and later observed some of the fruit of our work. Paul's approach to spiritual guidance reflects the importance of leaders for the encouragement of the community. A faith commitment made with joy will probably undergo testing at some point. The spiritual guide who has advanced a little further along the journey of faith becomes an anchor when the storm-driven waves are crashing. A wise approach to spiritual guidance includes gentleness and tender care founded on genuine love (2:7,8).

According to 1 Thessalonians, Paul and his companions are not the only ones offering spiritual guidance. Paul urges mutual encouragement among peers (4:18; 5:11). What he has shown by example he wants them to do for each other. He expects them to undertake their own nurture when he cannot be with them. They can comfort each other with words of hope, encouraging one another *(parakaleo)* and building one another up *(oikodomeo)*. This is what we might call 'spiritual friendship' or spiritual guidance among peers. Paul emphasizes the responsibility to care for one another, literally, 'one on one.'[26] Concern for individuals within the community is important to Paul: person and community both require attention and nurture.

Mutual care in the community of faith extends to admonition. Spiritual guidance includes mutual accountability. Paul reminds them to attend to the Spirit and to live holy lives. Moral formation and spiritual formation flow in tandem in Paul's teachings. The inner journey always influences the 'fruit' of outward living. The leaders have a special responsibility to admonish the congregation when necessary (5:12), and everyone is expected to admonish those who are idle. To admonish means to teach or nurture, which includes moral guidance.[27] Paul supports congregational discipline when applied with patience.

The spiritual guidance model Paul designs for the Thessalonians relies on relationships of spiritual formation at every level. Contemporary congregations learn from Paul that a variety of relationships are necessary to meet all needs. Spiritual guidance offered by leaders and peer-based spiritual friendships can provide on-going encouragement. Paul knew very well that it would be impossible for a leader to do it all. Instead, the community is taught to take care of each other. Part of their mutual care is also moral encouragement.

Spiritual direction practice faces an identity crisis on this issue today. Historically, the church has experienced significant variation in its approach to moral formation in spiritual direction. In some periods, acknowledgement of sin and obedience to the demands of the director took priority.[28] The pendulum has swung widely in our time and spiritual direction literature today rarely mentions moral formation or accountability. Is there a role for moral formation in contemporary spiritual guidance? How might Paul's teachings to the Thessalonians inform our practice? We must consider the contemporary relevance of Paul's example which includes moral encouragement as part of edification in a loving community of faith.

---

[26] Ibid., 79–81.
[27] Elias, *1&2 Thessalonians*, 217–18.
[28] Janet Ruffing, *Uncovering Stories of Faith*, 2–17.

Spiritual guidance practices are well suited to the kind of relationships of accountability that support moral formation. We will explore
these issues further in the next chapter.

From Spiritual Formation to Witness

One of the most striking things about the Thessalonian community
is the speed with which they have become a church witnessing to
the gospel of Christ. What started as joy in their hearts, an encounter
with the Holy Spirit and the knowledge that God has chosen them,
has expanded outward as a witness to the gospel. Paul observes that
they have become known near and far for their faith in God (1:8).
Undoubtedly, the Thessalonians have become an example to all
believers and the word of God has sounded forth from them, almost
like a trumpet blast. Reports of the Thessalonians' faith have spread
like ripples in a pond.[29] Paul does not even have to speak about them
because their faith speaks for itself. Beyond Paul's time and place, the
local context, the Thessalonian story has been read throughout the
centuries. Their lives of faith have provided insight for generations of
believers, far beyond what any of them could have imagined.

Genuine spiritual formation and spiritual guidance that relies on
the Holy Spirit and engenders all of the qualities already mentioned
captures peoples' attention. Participants exhibit significant change
– like a caterpillar to a butterfly. This is particularly true when communities of faith must suffer because of their commitments. Paul praises
the Thessalonians for their witness. Just as they have been taught by
his example, they are becoming an example to others. Contemporary
spiritual guidance in congregations has that same ripple effect. As
individuals experience the joys of a deepening relationship with God,
the interest expands outward. Some newcomers to congregations in
the study first visited because of the testimonies of others who have
already participated.

The rippling process also occurs in other ways. Participants are
concerned not only for their own formation. As they grow towards
God, they hear the beat of God's heart for the world. We can learn
from Paul's model of spiritual guidance the necessity of passing
on the good we have received. Genuine spiritual formation and
spiritual guidance practices necessarily lead outward. In many ways,

[29] Elias, *1&2 Thessalonians*, 46.

Paul provided an excellent model for spiritual guidance in the early church. By God's grace, he was not the first and not the last to have this vision. We turn our attention now to an unusual woman of God in unexpected circumstances.

Julian of Norwich: Anchoress and Spiritual Director

Imagine two children riding bikes down their street. They pass by a small house that appears closed up and forgotten. One of the children asks, 'Do you know who lives there?' Her friend responds, 'I think it's an old lady, but I'm not sure. I've never seen her come out. It's kind of strange, don't you think?' They keep going and soon forget this brief conversation. The elderly woman who has been shut in for some years peers out of her window. Her physical condition keeps her at home, but her heart and mind are actively attuned to what goes on in the outside world. She is a woman of deep faith who believes God has called her to intercede for her family, her church, her community and her country in these twilight years. The two children may not know her, but she names them before God every day.

This fictitious woman may be one of our closest contemporary comparisons to an anchorite. The medieval English anchorites were people of mystery; children would probably have considered them strange. Anchorites were women and men seeking a solitary existence who willingly entered small rooms typically attached to local churches. Anchorites never expected to leave their cells. They entered the space to remain forever buried with Christ and virtually dead to the world. What seems like a curious or even horrific form of incarceration to us was actually popular among those who wanted to live an ascetic life without risking the dangers of the wilderness.[30]

[30] See Anne Savage and Nicholas Watson, *Anchoritic Spirituality: Ancrene Wisse and Associated Works*. New York: Paulist Press, 1991, 16. The tradition of the solitary life in Christianity dates back to movements in the early church, such as the desert mothers and fathers who sought seclusion in Egypt and elsewhere. Guidance was typically given by a more experienced solitary to a disciple who would choose to live alongside the solitary for a time. In many cases, these desert ascetics fled to the wilderness to avoid an increasingly universalized Christian Church that they believed had softened the faith and caused the Christian life to be free from persecution. In essence, ascetics wished to become 'dead to the world' by embarking on individualized hermitical journeys and separating themselves from the larger

This enclosure enabled the anchorite to shut out the world and focus on communion with God. At the same time, the anchorite remained physically attached to the local church which was often located in the middle of town. The press of humanity on the anchorage and the anchorite's separation from the world must have been a strange paradox. Their physical and spiritual needs were attended to be the surrounding community and the church. Anchorites repaid their supporters through intercessory prayer, and many were known to provide spiritual counsel through a small window in their cells. A solitary anchorite may seem like an unusual choice for an exemplary model of spiritual guidance. Yet it is precisely the unexpected manner in which the anchorite takes on the role of spiritual counselor which is compelling. God can use the most unexpected people in unlikely situations to provide spiritual guidance. We consider one of these unusual choices here.

Julian of Norwich was an English anchorite in the medieval period (1342–ca.1416). We know little about the life of Julian beyond the

structured Christian community. The solitary life was considered a holy calling esteemed as the highest way to heaven. See Linda Georgianna, *The Solitary Self: Individuality in the Ancrene Wisse.* Cambridge: Harvard University Press, 1981, 34–36. Because of this, it is not surprising that the desert ascetics were sought out for counsel and wisdom. They accepted their obligation to direct others and they formed relationships with their disciples, offering specific advice about the inner life and various interior conditions, including consciousness of sin. See Patricia Ranft, *A Woman's Way: The Forgotten History of Women Spiritual Directors.* New York: Palgrave, 2000, 52. Those seeking the opportunity to engage in a solitary life of contemplation faced increasing challenges in the medieval period, especially in England. Significant population growth in the eleventh and twelfth centuries led to increasing numbers of small towns arising throughout the countryside. There were few places where one could go and be more than a day's travel from some kind of town. The solitary life was becoming more difficult to find. Some who desired to enter into a monastic community found that there were no opportunities available in established houses. An explosion of spiritual fervour was infiltrating catholic Europe during this time, and opportunities to express this heartfelt devotion to God through a lifetime of contemplation may have been few and far between. For these and other reasons, the numbers of people (mostly women) becoming anchorites grew to over two hundred in the fourteenth century at sites throughout England. See Ann K. Warren, *Anchorites and Their Patrons in Medieval England.* Berkeley: University of California Press, 1985, 20–21.

'showings' or visions she received on May 13, 1373.[31] Though Julian was an anchorite and lived the life of a solitary, she was also deeply concerned about the wider community. Julian came to believe that she had not received the visions for herself alone, and she recorded them so that others might receive them as if Jesus had sent every human being the showings personally. In her writings, Julian discusses many ideas about the spiritual life, including the experience of desolation and the insight that not all individuals benefit from the same kinds of experiences of God.[32] As a spiritual director, she struggles with her inability to communicate the truths of God more often with wisdom and insight.[33] Julian understands that God is the true Spiritual Director who reveals truth and wisdom. Though others may look upon Julian the anchorite with awe, she is clear about her responsibility to point them towards God.

Julian had become well-known for her excellent counsel on the spiritual life in surrounding communities, and Margery Kempe was a woman on a spiritual search who travelled to meet her. Margery reports that she shared with Julian her experiences of grace from God, her sorrow over past sins, the comforts of her devotional life and the revelations she had received. Julian was an attentive listener and she allowed Margery to unload a seemingly endless list of spiritual insights, not once mentioning the magnificence of her own revelations.[34] Margery reports that Julian prayed with her after hearing her story, and she thanked the Lord for his goodness and for Margery's visit.

While we cannot know what Julian thought of being inter-rupted in her solitude, Margery was convinced by Julian's sincere appreciation of her visit, and the anchoress' genuine compassion for Margery. Julian went on to advise Margery about remaining obedient to God's will, and 'carrying out with all [her] strength whatever prompting he put into [her] soul.' She is cautioned, too, that she must always discern her actions; that they not be 'contrary to God's glory

---

[31] It is not known when Julian entered the anchoritic life, but she is believed to have lived in a cell attached to the parish church of St. Julian in England. See Julian, Edmund Colledge, and James Walsh, *Showings*, Classics of Western Spirituality. New York: Paulist Press, 1978, 18.

[32] Ibid., 42, 191.

[33] Ranft, *A Woman's Way: The Forgotten History of Women Spiritual Directors*, 96.

[34] Margery Kempe, *The Book of Margery Kempe*. New York: Penguin, 1985, 73.

or to the benefit of [her] fellow Christians.'[35] Julian offers Margery the balanced wisdom of discernment of spirits and joy in God's revelations. In her spiritual direction, Julian is deeply concerned about encouraging actions that glorify God and benefit God's people.

Julian displays an interest in who Margery is and how she encounters God. She listens carefully and offers wisdom for the particular challenges Margery faces. Perhaps most important for Margery, Julian validates Margery's own individualized experience of God. Margery goes on to report that she stayed with Julian for several days. They spoke a great deal with each other and dwelt together on Christ. Julian's counsel was so memorable for Margery that she is careful to record it in her writings. Though Julian lived the solitary life of the anchorite, she made space and time for Margery. She was hospitable to a pilgrim on a spiritual journey, and she practiced the discipline that is often best learned in solitude: listening for God.

In spite of their isolation, anchorites in medieval England played an important role in the faith community. The term itself points to the purpose of this unique call. She is called an anchoress because she is anchored under a church like an anchor on the side of a ship 'to hold that ship so that waves and storms do not overturn it.' Her prayers and her example help to support the church as its members struggle with temptation and need spiritual guidance.[36]

What Julian offers to the community is a ministry of *prayerful presence.* She dwells among the people and reminds them of who they are called to be. She earnestly seeks to pray, live a godly life and be a comforting presence in times of turmoil. She puts aside her own life in community, including marriage and children, to serve the church with a commitment to be present; an anchor in the storms of life. She gives the gift of presence that is rarely found in the busyness of survival. Julian's ministry of presence frequently extended to spiritual direction. While her purpose was to forsake all others for intimacy with Christ, her location and her reputation as a holy woman caused others to seek her out for guidance in the Christian life. Ironically, the ones who most want to seek God on an inward journey are often the ones most sought out by others. John the Baptist is another example of this truth.

Julian of Norwich's spiritual journey was focused on the personal, yet she heard a clear call from God to reach out beyond herself. She

---

[35] Ibid., 74.

[36] Savage and Watson, *Anchoritic Spirituality: Ancrene Wisse and Associated Works*, 101.

provided spiritual guidance in the immediate community through personal spiritual care, and we could argue that she responded to a missional call by sharing her writings. Julian exemplified the paradox between the personal and the communal in anchoritic life. From the anchorites we learn that solitude does not preclude community. In fact, solitude which includes both self-reflection and reflection on God can produce deeply meaningful human relationships. The person who embraces solitude can more fully embrace community life that goes beyond the masks people so often wear. Being transparent with others often means learning first to be alone. Relationships in the church will be more effective if the paradoxical value of solitude is also cherished.

Looking at Julian as an example for contemporary spiritual guidance is certainly problematic. It would be unlikely to find a church today wishing to build an anchorhouse or a willing anchorite to fill it. But even if we do not commission anchorites in our congregations, is it possible to set aside some who have a special calling to pray for others and provide spiritual guidance? Are there prayerful people in congregations who seem to take on the roles of intercessor and spiritual guide naturally? In what ways might congregations acknowledge their gifts more fully and make space for them to use their gifts? Julian's life points to the possibilities of spiritual guides in congregations who may not be pastors or leaders, but who provide an important ministry. They are among us, yet we often fail to single them out in special ways as we do our board chairpersons or music leaders.

Spiritual formation in congregations benefits from calling out those who might offer a ministry of presence for others. You may recall the story of Joelle and Sonja from the previous chapter. Joelle's church has given Sonja a special role in their congregation to lead a prayer ministry, including intercession and anointing after worship services, an educational program in contemplative prayer, prayer shawls, and other responsibilities. Sonja credits the pastor of the church as a wonderful leader who 'knows how to get out of the way' and invite others to explore their sense of call. This congregation has made a commitment to call out the contemporary 'Julians' among them.

Susanna Wesley: Spiritual Guidance at Home

Susanna Annesley Wesley (1669–1742) is best known as the mother of John Wesley, the founder of Methodism. Yet there is much more to discover about this remarkable mother and spiritual guide than we encounter at first glance. Like Maria Frelinghuysen Cornell, Susanna was married to a minister who struggled in his career and was poorly paid. Susanna and Samuel had 19 children, but only ten survived past infancy. Raising a large family and enduring several crises, including failed crops and destructive fires, took a toll on the family's resources. They lived most of their years together in a remote region of England because Samuel was unable to find a position elsewhere. Susanna was a bright and inquisitive woman, and she and her husband did not always get along. He travelled on many occasions and she managed the home, including the spiritual formation and education of their children. This was no small task, yet she took it on with a great sense of purpose.[37]

In spite of the remote location and limited access to resources, Susanna trained her children with vigour. She gave significant attention to their education and development. Careful organization was emphasized in every dimension of the family lifestyle, from learning new subjects to mealtimes to moral expectations. The family studied for six hours every weekday, a schedule that rarely changed. Susanna opposed physical punishment, believing that the practice led to fear and lying rather than changed ways. She praised her children for acts of obedience and taught respect of others' property. Susanna was ahead of her time in the belief that girls should learn to read well before they were put to work. All the children waited until their fifth birthdays to learn the alphabet. Each child had an appointed day when Susanna took them aside and taught them to read letters. Other family members knew not to interrupt this dedicated process.

Susanna was able to create a fruitful environment characterized by order and well-developed methods. Her son, John, certainly found her approach memorable, and he requested a copy of the 'principal rules' by which she educated her children. When we consider Susanna's teachings, we recognize her influence on the methods that John Wesley initiated in his communities of faith. More than one

[37] While Samuel Wesley loved his children, he was taken up with writing and seeking out the possibilities of new employment. Susanna was left to take on the full responsibility of child-rearing. There are only a few recorded instances when Samuel interfered with Susanna's methods. Samuel J. Rogal, *Susanna Annesley Wesley (1669–1742): A Biography of Strength and Love*. Bristol, IN: Wyndham Hall Press, 2001, 33–41, 59.

historian has argued that Methodism did not begin at Oxford, but in the rectory at Epworth within the first two decades of the eighteenth century. [38]

Susanna's commitment to orderly education extended to the spiritual education and formation of her children. Her home was essentially a miniature monastery in which she served as a spiritual director. Susanna taught discipline and expected both confession and forgiveness. The concern for moral development was coupled with many biblical, liturgical and devotional practices to enrich the family's faith formation.[39] In spite of hardship, the Wesley home became a community of spiritual nurture.

We would expect few opportunities for any one of these children to spend time alone with a mother who was often pregnant, caring for babies and managing a large household. Yet this is where Susanna's story becomes truly extraordinary. Somehow, she managed to carve out a set time to meet with each child. She worked to create space in her busy life to have spiritual conversation with her children individually and in pairs on a regularly scheduled evening, from the tender age of four until adulthood. Even the young child's spiritual life was of great concern to Susanna. Each child's spiritual journey was so important that she gave attention to their particular spiritual needs as a one-with-one spiritual guide. When the children got older and moved on, she wrote letters to continue providing spiritual guidance. In surviving letters to John, she provides lectures and counsel, and to Charles she offers homilies.[40] She tells of her own joys and challenges in faith and she offers her constant prayers.

While Susanna focused on the formation of her children, she did not forget the surrounding community. During her husband's extended absence in 1711–1712, she expanded her small formational community to include the neighbourhood. People were invited to join the family for Sunday evening prayers. These gatherings grew from thirty or forty invited persons to some two hundred participants. Though she risked her husband's anger over this unconventional practice, Susanna honoured her sense of responsibility for spiritual care by leading the community in prayer and reading

---

[38] Ibid., 56–59.

[39] Jones, *The Art of Spiritual Direction: Giving and Receiving Spiritual Guidance*, 72.

[40] Rogal, *Susanna Annesley Wesley (1669–1742): A Biography of Strength and Love*, 156.

accounts of mission work to India. Without a doubt, Susanna Wesley carried within her a zeal for spiritual formation and a commitment to personal and communal spiritual guidance far beyond what was typical in her time.[41]

A woman in Susanna Annesley Wesley's situation should be forgettable. Perhaps we would know little about her if not for her famous sons. Yet what we discover as we consider her life is the power of creating a community of spiritual guidance within a home. While the family unit or 'community' is central, Susanna also gives priority to individual spiritual care and education for mission. In the Methodist movement John and Charles developed later, we find similar emphases on personal spiritual growth, communal spiritual guidance and missional concerns (or social holiness). These priorities were learned at home.

Susanna's story teaches us that there are many variations of spiritual guidance relationships we can draw on. The congregation is supported by other sacred starting points for spiritual formation. The family can become a source of spiritual guidance for its members. Many contemporary families expect to pass on faith to the next generation in two ways. First, most parents assume that the educational ministries of the church will provide their children with the support they need for spiritual formation. Adults with small children often return to church after a long absence because they want their children educated in the faith. Through Sunday School, worship and weeknight activities, kids are expected to learn about the faith and apply it to their own lives.

Second, a relatively smaller number of parents hope their children will pick up the important dimensions of faith by observation. As parents live according to the example of Christ, their children will learn what it means to be a Christian too. Both church participation and parental modelling are essential, but there is a third method that makes the first two more effective. This method has been in use from the beginnings of the Hebrew people for passing on faith from generation to generation. In order for families to be most effective in spiritual formation, they need to tell their faith stories to each other.

How can congregations provide parents with the tools and insights they need to become spiritual guides in their own homes? In the previous chapter, we considered the experiences of congregations

[41] Ibid., 27–29.

who create a culture of spiritual conversation. Congregations can teach parents to talk about their relationships with God so that they can share them with their children. Just as Susanna communicated the truths of faith and described her own spiritual journey with her children, parents today can be encouraged to talk to their children about what God means to them. This is a practice that must be learned. Family members begin by telling simple stories of coming to faith. As parents show that they are willing to talk about spiritual things, children will come with their thoughts and questions more easily. Young children are particularly open to these kinds of conversations, but it is never too late to start. Parents are the primary examples in the lives of children, and they have an enormous impact in forming the faith journeys of their children. The example of Susanna Wesley's influence in the lives of her children reveals that spiritual guidance can begin in the home.[42]

Dietrich Bonhoeffer: Spiritual Guide on a Mission

Dietrich Bonhoeffer (1906–1945) was born into an affluent German family. His father, Karl, was a neurologist and psychiatrist and his mother, Paula, was a licensed teacher who committed herself to their children's early education. Bonhoeffer grew up in the stimulating environment of Berlin's cultural and intellectual circles. His father was agnostic and the family did not attend church, but his mother introduced the children to the Bible and taught them prayers and hymns. The children experienced their father's attentions as a reward that had to be earned. Dietrich was desperate for his father's and brothers' approval, but he was often left alone and deeply lonely. It was not until young adulthood that he first experienced genuine friendship. The issues of person and community that arise in his writings likely have some roots in these early yearnings.[43]

In spite of his father's rejection of religion, Bonhoeffer chose to study theology. He was a bright young man who completed his doctoral thesis at the early age of twenty-one. Somewhere along

---

[42] For a contemporary discussion of parenting as spiritual guidance, see Betty Shannon Cloyd, *Parents & Grandparents as Spiritual Guides: Nurturing Children of the Promise*. Nashville, TN: Upper Room Books, 2000.

[43] Lisa E. Dahill, *Reading from the Underside of Selfhood: Bonhoeffer and Spiritual Formation*. Eugene, OR: Pickwick Publications, 2009, 21–24.

the way, the theologian also became a Christian, although he did not announce this change at the outset. Bonhoeffer had a passion for bringing the gospel to social issues including warfare and racism. He began work as a pastor and professor, and he spoke publicly against the rising power of the Nazi government and the compromises made by state churches. Under pressure from the Nazi party, Bonhoeffer left for London where he served in pastoral ministry and urged the churches to act against the political developments in Germany.[44] In spite of the danger to himself, Bonhoeffer returned to Germany and became the director of a clandestine seminary at Finkenwalde. During the seminary years, Bonhoeffer wrote *Life Together*, which reflects the spiritual atmosphere of the small community and describes the journey of individual and communal Christian formation. Bonhoeffer became increasingly frustrated about the lack of commitment among Confessing Church leaders to fight rising anti-Semitism. He pleaded for change but eventually left for America in discouragement.

During his brief sojourn abroad, Bonhoeffer acknowledged his mistake in coming to America. He wrote, 'I must live through this difficult period of our national history with the Christian people of Germany. I will have no right to participate in the reconstruction of Christian life in Germany after the war if I do not share the trials of this time with my people.' Bonhoeffer suffered an emotional parting from his sister's family to return to a war zone that would cost him his life. He became a double agent for the resistance movement and was ultimately captured and imprisoned. In the final two years of his life, Bonhoeffer continued to read, write, and provide spiritual care for fellow prisoners. On April 8, 1945, he conducted a prayer service and offered a meditation on healing and new birth in Jesus Christ. Guards came to remove him from the service. Before he was taken out, he had time to whisper to a friend that this was the end, but for him 'the beginning of life.' He was executed the next day at dawn.[45]

Bonhoeffer was a man on a mission. In spite of the personal cost, he was determined to do what he believed was right. He wrote many books and letters, urging the church to accept fully the call of Jesus Christ to stand up for the poor and defenceless. Bonhoeffer

[44] Geffrey B. and F. Burton Nelson Kelly, *The Cost of Moral Leadership: The Spirituality of Dietrich Bonhoeffer*. Grand Rapids, MI: Eerdmans, 2003, 7–18.
[45] Ibid., 26–34.

had a strong sense of purpose to guide the church in righteousness and justice for the oppressed. As a spiritual guide, Bonhoeffer was called to the missional edge, to the kind of discipleship that implores a nation to confess and begs the church to stand in solidarity with the oppressed according to the example of Jesus Christ. Bonhoeffer was known to have an intimate relationship with God. He was a man of prayer for whom God was very real, even in the context of filthy, demeaning prison life. Yet this closeness to God did not draw him toward a monastic existence or quiet university life. Rather than choosing to stay in the America where he could write and teach freely, he returned to the site of a great tragedy of the twentieth century. For Bonhoeffer, drawing near to the heart of God meant participating in the mission of God for the sake of the gospel.

While Bonhoeffer was deeply passionate about mission, he was also concerned with the pastoral work of spiritual guidance. *Life Together* tells of his efforts to nurture both the individual and communal life in the seminary at Finkenwalde. In his words, '*Let him who cannot be alone beware of community . . .* But the reverse is also true: *Let him who is not in community beware of being alone.*' As in the case of Julian of Norwich, we find the paradox of person and community in spiritual formation. Bonhoeffer is aware that God's call is personal. We all die and give an account of ourselves individually before God. At the same time, he recognizes the need for the community to help the individual struggle, bear the cross and pray. If we scorn the fellowship of God's people, we are also scorning Christ himself. We are members of a great congregation, even in death.[46] Healthy spiritual growth means nurturing both a personal journey with God and participating in genuine relationships within the community of faith. In *Life Together,* Bonhoeffer develops a practical guide for personal and communal practices that support spiritual growth.

Some of the most helpful dimensions of *Life Together* for contemporary spiritual guidance practices can be found in two small chapters entitled, 'Ministry' and 'Confession and Communion.' First, Bonhoeffer argues that Christians must learn to listen. Many people do not find a listening ear among Christians because we prefer to talk. Bonhoeffer warns that if we cannot listen to each other, we will soon cease to listen to God, which is the beginning of the

---

[46] Dietrich Bonhoeffer, *Life Together: The Classic Exploration of Faith in Community.* New York: HarperCollins, 1954, 77.

death of the spiritual life. If we forget to listen, nothing remains but pious words. Contemporary spiritual guidance requires this kind of listening that does not presume to know already what another will say. Instead the guide forgoes the anxious desire to fill the silence in order to be attentive to the heart of the other.

Second, Bonhoeffer identifies the importance of listening for the confessions of others. Bonhoeffer emphasizes the call to confession in the community of faith, something that does not have a significant role in most contemporary Protestant congregations. We hear this in his larger public indictment of the German Church and in the communal experience of the seminary. He gives contemporary spiritual guides a reason for inviting confession into the relationship. Sin creates separation, not just between humanity and God but also between human beings. A breakthrough to fellowship with each other is not possible until we remove false piety and admit our sinfulness. As the body of Christ confesses sin to one another (James 5:16), it is possible finally to break through the alienation and loneliness sin creates. We put aside lies and hypocrisy and participate in real community. Contemporary spiritual guidance relationships can function more deeply as real community when there is the safety and trust to offer and hear confession.

Third, Bonhoeffer speaks of the importance of bearing each other's burdens. This is certainly the work of the spiritual guide. Even in the other's weakness and oddities, the spiritual guide cares for the experiences of another and helps to carry burdens so that freedom can be found. Bonhoeffer states that this requires genuine love and a willingness to walk meekly with others. Bearing the burdens of others extends to the mission work of the church. This is a part of journeying in solidarity with those who are oppressed and mistreated. Bonhoeffer's teachings come full circle when we see how his care for those within the Christian community extends outward to those outside the church. Spiritual guides can walk with those outside the church just as they do with those within the church, and they can support individuals as they discern calls to live in solidarity with those who suffer.

Conclusion

We have explored several remarkable scenes in the history of the church. These moments remind us of the possibilities of spiritual guidance practices in congregations of any era. Thinking back to Julian's role as an anchor for the church, I am reminded that historical practices of the church can be anchors in a time when spirituality may mean many different things and take us in numerous directions. The biblical and historical scenes we have glimpsed become a kind of anchor that does not hold us back, but instead keeps us steady in confusing times.

★★★★★★★★★★★★★★★★★★

Spiritual Practice: Supporting Actors

As we have learned from Susanna Wesley, family members play critical roles in spiritual formation. During this practice, you will name the family members who have played significant formative parts in your spiritual autobiography.

Find a comfortable, quiet space and take a few slow, deep breaths. Invite God to be present with you and guide you through this practice. Consider your life as a dramatic play made of several acts. You may choose to write down each act along a timeline.

Imagine yourself on stage. As you look around, you see that you're not alone. There are others who have been integral to your life story and your spiritual development. As you look over your life, make note of the family members (the family of origin and others you have come to think of as 'family') who have played important supporting roles. Some people may have been genuine spiritual guides to you, caring for you and supporting you in your relationship with God. Take note of them. Some may have been influential in your life, but led you away from God. Their presence in your life may have engendered false ideas about God. Remember that some family influences are disruptive to the flow of the drama. As family members come to mind, ask God to help you see them as God sees them. Talk with God about them.

Read I Thessalonians 2:5–12 slowly and thoughtfully. Is there anyone God is calling you to provide spiritual guidance for? What would this guidance look like?

★★★★★★★★★★★★★★★★★★★★★★★★★★

Discussion Questions

- Paul has been described as a spiritual guide to the Thessalonians in this chapter. Are there other intentional relationships of spiritual guidance that you can identify in Scripture?
- Some people might argue that Julian of Norwich is an unexpected model of spiritual guidance because of her status as an anchorite. Are there other historical or contemporary figures who are also unlikely spiritual guides?
- What is the role of the parent in spiritual guidance? How can parents and congregations work together to support the spiritual formation of children?
- Dietrich Bonhoeffer beautifully reflects the intersection of person, community and mission in Christian living. Do you attend to all three in your life? Are any of these out of balance with the others?
- Are there any spiritual guides in your life who model excellence in their integration of person, community and mission?

Chapter 4

The Improvising Church: Spiritual Guidance in Protestant Theology and Practice

Dr Marcus Smucker first arrived at Associated Mennonite Biblical Seminary at the invitation of the president, Dr Marlin Miller, nearly thirty years ago. The seminary faculty was deeply committed to a theological education including Scripture, Ethics, Peace Studies, ministry skills and all things Anabaptist-Mennonite. Rooting theological studies in the Anabaptist tradition had become a critical dimension of the life and teachings of the seminary. At the same time, the president was aware of a deep spiritual hunger among seminary students and congregations that needed attention: a desire to *be nurtured* in a relationship with God alongside *doing* for God.[1] Marlin was convinced that the seminary could not assume incoming students had learned how to develop a life of prayer and a growing relationship with God before entering seminary. Marcus shared these concerns. After nearly burning out in pastoral ministry, he began to take an interest in on-going spiritual formation for himself and for the inner city congregation he served. Formational practices and contemplative retreats dramatically changed Marcus' own life and the lives of many in his congregation.

Yet Marcus knew that bringing intentional spiritual formation into a seminary would be an entirely different challenge from the

---

[1] Marcus Smucker and some other seminary leaders suggest that Mennonite communities of the past were closely knit and tended to provide on-going formational support through communal relationships. In our time, Mennonites have become increasingly transient and individualistic along with the rest of the western world.

111

congregational context. From the beginning, some faculty members were concerned that an emphasis on spirituality would result in a personal piety hampering communal life, peace concerns and ethical commitments. In short, this new 'spirituality' could introduce a wrong-headed theology founded on an individualistic personal piety at the expense of ethical living. Marlin and Marcus faced these issues head on. Instead of relegating spiritual formation to a course or two on campus for a handful of interested students, they sought to draw in the entire faculty. A spiritual formation program was a new thing for this community and patience would be required. Marcus began his work by developing a written proposal for spirituality at AMBS consistent with Anabaptist-Mennonite life and theology. After three years and many revisions, the faculty finally gave their approval.

Over the next decade, a cross-section of professors began to offer new courses in their fields including 'Spirituality and Peacemaking,' 'Biblical Spirituality,' and 'The History of Christian Spirituality.' Numerous spiritual practices from various Christian traditions became a regular part of seminary life. Not surprisingly, the interest in spiritual formation among faculty influenced students. A significant percentage of students received spiritual direction from newly-trained faculty and other directors in the community. Today, faculty and students welcome the spiritual formation emphasis virtually without question. In Marcus' perspective, spiritual formation brought renewed vitality to theological education by balancing love for God, love for oneself and love for neighbour.[2]

Learning to Improvise

At AMBS, faculty and students welcomed innovative ideas and practices that met the needs of the community without losing sight of a precious tradition and heritage. By working through a spiritual formation proposal as a community, professors were able to focus on biblical, historical and theological issues with specific attention to

---

[2] The information in this story is based upon my own research at Associated Mennonite Biblical Seminary and an interview conducted by Dawn Ruth Nelson with Marcus Smucker for her dissertation work. See Dawn Ruth Nelson, 'How Do We Become Like Christ? American Mennonite Spiritual Formation through the Lens of One Woman's Life and One Seminary 1909-2003'. Doctor of Ministry dissertation, Lancaster Theological Seminary, 2004.

Anabaptist-Mennonite convictions. Some professors have gone on to research historical Anabaptist spirituality and publish Anabaptist prayer books.[3] Others found ways to integrate spirituality into courses in their fields.

The metaphor of theatrical improvisation sheds light on the changes that took place at AMBS. Keith Johnstone writes: 'The improviser has to be like a man walking backwards. He sees where he has been but he pays no attention to the future. His story can take him anywhere, but he must still 'balance' it, and give it shape, by remembering incidents that have been shelved and reincorporating them.'[4] A primary work of the actor is to remember what has already happened and reincorporate these ideas back into the story. In the same way, the leadership at AMBS improvised in their context by looking to the past for what had been 'shelved' by their predecessors. By opening up to the possibilities of lost and neglected parts of various Christian spiritual traditions, including the Anabaptist-Mennonite heritage, the seminary is restoring these parts to a place in the contemporary story to meet the need for spiritual formation.

Spiritual Guidance and Jürgen Moltmann's Theology

In the last few decades, AMBS has trained hundreds of pastors in spiritual guidance. Thousands more have received training in schools and institutes in North America and around the world. While contemporary writers give some attention to the theologies of historical spiritual guides, such as Ignatius of Loyola, we are only just beginning to identify theologies that underpin contemporary practices. This is not surprising given the fact that the recovery

---

[3] See, for example, Marlene Kropf and Eddy Hall, *Praying with the Anabaptists: The Secret of Bearing Fruit*. Newton, KS: Faith & Life Press, 1994. Also: Arthur P. Boers, Eleanor Kreider, John Rempel, Mary H. Schertz, Barbara Nelson Gingerich, ed. *Take Our Moments and Our Days: An Anabaptist Prayer Book*. Scottdale, PA: Herald Press, 2007.

[4] Keith Johnstone, *Impro: Improvisation in the Theatre*. London: Methuen, 1981, 116. Samuel Wells draws upon the art of theatrical improvisation to enrich our understanding of Christian ethics. Some of the same metaphors and practices Wells finds helpful for ethics are useful for Christian formation. Wells points to this image of the man walking backwards in order to talk about the recovery of elements of the Christian tradition that are particularly fruitful for a moment in the present when the church is somehow 'stuck.' See Samuel Wells, *Improvisation: The Drama of Christian Ethics*. Grand Rapids: Brazos Press, 2004, 148, 182.

of spiritual guidance is still new in many contexts. In renewal movements, practice often precedes careful reflection on theological foundations. Perhaps we ought to take a lesson from the story of spiritual formation at AMBS. The recovery of ancient practices fits who we are and what we believe when we root these practices in the theological traditions we are committed to. Practice and theology are most effective when they inform each other.

In an earlier chapter, we noted the contemporary struggle between the cultural trend toward de-traditionalized eclecticism and a firm theological grounding. This chapter is based upon the assumptions that both are necessary in a vibrant contemporary congregation that engages culture. We can draw on an eclectic range of spiritual practices beyond our own traditions and discern how they ought to be formed and shaped in the light of our theological perspectives.[5] The goal of the chapter is to journey towards a Protestant theology of spiritual guidance that informs practice.

One influential Protestant theologian whose ideas are particularly well-suited to practices of spiritual guidance is Jürgen Moltmann. His writings in systematic theology are a great contribution to the church in our time. But Moltmann is much more than a gifted thinker, he is a man on a profound journey with God. Exploring his story briefly here provides a starting point for considering his theology. In Moltmann's autobiography, *A Broad Place,* we gain insight into the early factors that influenced the beginnings of his relationship with God, especially the tragedies of war. As a German youth in 1943, he was conscripted into Hitler's army. Just a few months later, he survived a terrifying battle which killed more than 40,000 people, including a good friend who perished right next to him. Through the night he found himself clinging to a plank in the water, and he battled tremendous survivor guilt. In these dark moments, he called out, 'My God, where are you?' Moltmann remembers this occasion as the first time he became a true 'seeker after God.'[6] He came to

---

[5] What I am describing here is the normative moment of practical theology in which we ask, 'What ought to be happening here?' In this chapter, we are identifying normative theological ideas and placing them in conversation with existing spiritual guidance practices. The norms help us to understand and shape spiritual guidance for contemporary congregations.

[6] Jürgen Moltmann, *A Broad Place: An Autobiography.* Minneapolis: Fortress Press, 2008, 16–17.

reject the German cause, especially after his father described the gruesome discovery of mass graves filled with murdered Jews.[7]

After the Germans were defeated, Moltmann became a prisoner of war in Scotland. The Scottish overseers and their families treated their former enemies with genuine hospitality instead of blame. Moltmann recalls that these relationships had a profound effect:

'We experienced a simple and warm common humanity which made it possible for us to live with the past of our own people, without repressing it and without growing callous. True, we had numbers on our backs and prisoners' patches on our trousers, but we felt accepted as people. This humanity in far-off Scotland made human beings of us once more. We were able to laugh again.'[8]

Moltmann's experience of renewed hope was fed by two things: the Scottish families and the gift of a Bible. Moltmann went on to get a PhD in theology, served as a pastor and a professor, and wrote several books on themes such as hope in the midst of tragedy, creation, the church and the Trinity. He built relationships with people at home and abroad. As we consider Moltmann's journey of faith, we recognize elements of his spiritual life that are evident also in his theology. This includes a personal, solitary journey with God, faith formed in community through healing relationships and a missional call to serve the local church and the wider world through theological engagement.

The triad of person, community and mission evident in Moltmann's own life is a central foundation for this dissertation. Diagram 1 offers one way to visualize the relationship between the three. While person, community and mission represent individual points on the diagram, all three are essentially inter-related. We can never completely separate one from relationship to the others. Yet this triad cannot function alone. The three are joined together through the presence and activity of the Holy Spirit. As we will soon see, the Spirit can be understood as the energy of life present in the world today, attending to personhood, creating fellowship in community and calling towards mission. Followers of Jesus Christ are invited to

[7] Ibid., 20.
[8] Ibid., 28–29.

move with the Spirit through all three points. There is no particular time or order in which any one or more may take precedence. As we explore each dimension of the diagram, we will draw upon the metaphor of theatrical improvisation, outline theological ideas and explore practical implications for spiritual guidance. We begin now with improvisation and the Holy Spirit.

The Great Drama

Some years ago, a popular television show called *Whose Line is it Anyway?* drew upon techniques of theatrical improvisation and stand-up comedy to entertain millions of people. What was truly unique about the show was the audience participation. One word from an audience member could move the dialogue in an entirely new direction. It was remarkable to see how the actors could take

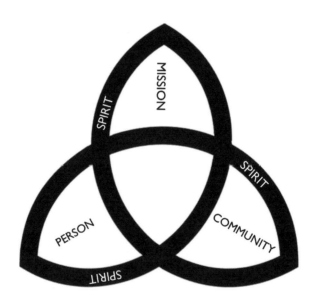

Diagram 1: Three Foundations of Spiritual Formation[1]

---

[1] Diagram 1 is a visual representation of three foundational concerns of spiritual formation. The theology of spiritual guidance we are developing here attends to each of these. Practices based upon this theology pay attention to how God is moving in our hearts in each of these areas. As we grow in one area, it influences our engagement in the others. The Spirit is the life and energy of God drawing our attention to these concerns and binding them together.

what they were given and generate humorous responses within seconds. Laughter and applause in the audience served to feed the antics of the actors. The method of improvisation in the show broke down what actors typically call 'the fourth wall.' A stage is bordered by three walls, one behind and two beside the actors. In most forms of performance, an imaginary fourth wall stands between the actors and the audience. The audience does not participate in the unfolding drama; they are simply present to observe the actions and interactions on stage. In improv, the rules change. The audience is critical to the success of the dramatic action. The actors cannot ever control how or what the audience members contribute to the performance.[9]

Some theologians have used the language of theatre to describe God's presence and interaction with human beings. The story of divine and human action is enacted throughout history in the great 'theo-drama.'[10] Sometimes the human 'actors' tend to imagine that God is in the audience behind the fourth wall. God may be watching us – perhaps judging our performance – but is certainly not involved in our daily lives in any way. In the art of improvisation, the fourth wall comes down and God participates actively in the story that unfolds. In fact, God may be viewed as an audience participant or even as a key player in the drama.[11] God's participation is critical, but God does not take complete control over the moment by moment action. God allows human beings the right to improvise by determining their own movements, something we usually call 'free will.' Ultimately, all of creation plays a full part in the drama.[12]

---

[9] Joseph M. Webb, *Preaching for the Contemporary Service*. Nashville: Abingdon Press, 2006, 23.

[10] Hans Urs von Balthasar is the theologian who has given the most attention to the concept of theology as drama. He explores the roles of each member of the Trinity in the great drama. The Father is the author of the drama, the Son is the actor, and the Holy Spirit is the director. Other actors include Israel, the nations, individual Christians, angels and demons. Balthasar's work covers five volumes from creation through the eschaton. See Hans Urs von Balthasar, *Theo-Drama: Theological Dramatic Theory*, 5 vols. San Francisco: Ignatius, 1988.

[11] Samuel Wells explores the possibilities of improvisation for understanding the relationships between God, human beings, the church and the world. He notes that it is not necessary to be too precise about who plays what part. We can imagine any one or more as actors, stage, and audience. Wells, *Improvisation: The Drama of Christian Ethics*, 69–70.

[12] Ibid., 53–57.

The God that Moltmann met on that horrible night during World War II is not a God who watches passively from behind the fourth wall. This God is present with people in their deepest suffering and in their highest joys. This God is so close, Moltmann describes him in the Hebrew way as *ruach*, or the Spirit who is the very breath of life and the power to live.[13] Moltmann's doctrine of the Holy Spirit is our starting point for developing a theology of spiritual guidance. Two features of his understanding of the Spirit are especially relevant for spiritual guidance practices: 1) the Spirit is God's presence and vitality in the world; and 2) the Spirit of God is both immanent and transcendent.

The Spirit of God: Presence and Vitality

First, the Spirit is God's presence and vitality in the world. In order to understand the role of the Spirit, we must take a step back and get a glimpse of Moltmann's view of God as a Trinity. He points out that the development of Christianity in the West has often emphasized the oneness of God at the expense of the unique presence and role of each member of the Trinity: Father, Son, and Holy Spirit. We generally think of the Spirit as subordinate to the Father and the Son. In other words, the Spirit is sent by the Father and by the Son into the world. This is certainly true but it does not provide a full picture of the relationships within the Trinity. The Spirit existed from the creation of the world and, together with the Father, also sent the Son into the world. The Spirit of God who hovered over the waters (Gen. 1:2) is fully equal to the Father and the Son. Traditional Christian theology identifies the Son in the word and the sacraments of the church. As a result, ministry comes first and then Spirit, and Scripture comes first, then faith. This tends to produce churches cemented in authoritarian institutionalism with little freedom to be led and guided by the Spirit.[14]

When I first received spiritual direction many years ago, I found myself facing a steep learning curve. I had been taught to look for God through studying God's work, worshipping with the faith

---

[13] Jürgen Moltmann, *The Spirit of Life: A Universal Affirmation*. Minneapolis: Fortress Press, 1992, 41.

[14] Jürgen Moltmann *History and the Triune God: Contributions to Trinitarian Theology*. New York: Crossroad, 1992, 58–59.

community and following Christ in life, which I believed were the most trustworthy routes to God. I still believe that these dimensions of the life of faith are absolutely critical for developing a relationship with God. Yet just as the rich, young ruler came to Jesus asking if there might be something more, I could not ignore an inner restlessness to experience God in a new way.

My spiritual director was a delightful Roman Catholic educator who fairly shimmered with energy. She had her hands full prying open the stubborn lock on my box of preconceived notions about relating to God, but I finally succumbed to her efforts. I began to acknowledge the role of the Holy Spirit as the presence of God in all kinds of life experiences, the Spirit who is our Teacher and Helper (John 14). Recognizing the Spirit as God's presence who guides people of faith does not in any way diminish the role of Jesus Christ as the Word of God who brings salvation to the world. Both are a part of the perfect fellowship of the Trinity. In a similar way, Moltmann wants to give adequate attention to the presence and work of the Holy Spirit without losing sight of the other members of the Trinity.

Moltmann also raises the concern that we risk depersonalizing the Spirit when we view the Trinity as a hierarchy (Father-Son-Holy Spirit). We lose a sense of relating to the Spirit, who becomes some kind of supernatural force sent by the Father and Son rather than a personalized presence. With this viewpoint, there is a tendency towards mistrusting the direct workings of the Spirit including inspiration, feelings, visions and dreams. Practices of spiritual guidance cannot possibly flourish in such conditions, which are all too common in congregations. Spiritual guidance is founded upon the idea that human beings may have direct, personal interactions with the Holy Spirit and can sense the nudgings of the Spirit through inspiration of all kinds which may include feelings, dreams or visions. As a result, it is necessary to develop a theology of the Spirit that can foster spiritual guidance. Moltmann's work assists us in developing this theology. Instead of the traditional hierarchy, he presents an image of the Trinity as 'persons-in-relation' who form an enduring unity in loving fellowship.[15]

---

[15] Moltmann and other theologians refer to this view of God as the *social doctrine of the Trinity*. The concept of *perichoresis* expresses the intimate indwelling and complete interpenetration of the persons of the Trinity. Ibid., 57–59, 86.

Within the trinitarian unity, each member, including the Holy Spirit, has a unique role to play in the great drama of divine and human history. Moltmann draws upon Scripture to explore the identity and activity of the Holy Spirit. The Hebrew word *ruach* is especially important for describing the Spirit's role as the presence and power of God in the world.[16] In the Old Testament, God as *ruach* is experienced as a storm or as a force in body, soul and nature. The Israelite people knew the *ruach* of God as a divine presence given to the community through judges, prophets and kings, and also as a presence that is known in the inward self. For example, in Psalm 51 the writer cries out to God in the most intimate way: 'Do not cast me away from your presence, and do not take your holy spirit from me.' God's *ruach* is the source of life itself. If God were to withdraw his *ruach*, it would mean the loss of life for the psalmist.

While the Spirit of God is often described as an inanimate force or presence in the Old Testament, we can also find references to the personhood of the Spirit. This is clearly evident in the *Shekinah* of God. The *Shekinah* originally meant God's 'tabernacle' or dwelling that travelled with the people and was present in the worshipping community. The *Shekinah* is not a divine attribute, but is the direct presence of God. God's Spirit is the gift of God's own self to the people. The doctrine of the *Shekinah* makes the personal character of the Spirit clear especially in God's identification with those whom he loves. The *Shekinah* participates with joy in the joys of humanity, and experiences suffering in the sufferings of the people.

The Spirit of God becomes the Spirit of Jesus Christ in the New Testament. The energizing power of the Spirit enables Jesus to drive out demons and heal the sick. This same Spirit is present in the suffering of the cross and in the celebration of resurrection. The indwelling Spirit 'brings the divine energies of life in Jesus to rapturous and overflowing fullness.'[17] The Spirit continues to be present in the world today. In fact, Moltmann argues that pneuma-

---

[16] Moltmann urges readers to forget the word 'spirit' as it is understood historically in western culture. He argues that the traditional western concept of spirit referred to something immaterial and supernatural. Our language for spirit tends to separate spirit and body which is foreign to the concept of *ruach*. Moltmann, *The Spirit of Life: A Universal Affirmation*, 40. This is an important distinction for spiritual guidance practices because they assume the presence of God in all of life, both the material and immaterial.

[17] Ibid., 61–62.

tology brings Christology and eschatology together. In other words, the Spirit is the personhood of God present with us now between the time of Jesus' physical presence on earth and the time when all God's purposes for the world are fulfilled.

We hear echoes of this description of *ruach* in Scripture in Moltmann's doctrine of the Spirit as the presence and vitality of God. When we speak about experiencing God's presence, we are talking about the ability of human beings to notice that the fourth wall has disappeared. The Spirit of God is actively participating in the great drama both within the human heart as the Psalmist declares and in all created things that cannot help but praise God (Ps. 65:12–13; Rev. 5:13). Humanity experiences the trinitarian God in the world through the presence and power of the Holy Spirit. When we encounter God in ourselves and in the world around us, we are encountering the Spirit. Moltmann is convinced that God is near every one of us even when it seems as though God is a distant mystery. We know so little of God's Spirit because God is too close, not because God is so far away.

The presence of God is characterized by life and energy. The Spirit is the living energy of the new creation of all things. In the nearness of God, life begins to vibrate. Life itself is dependent upon the presence of the Spirit. Without the life-giving energies of God's Spirit we would not exist. Moltmann sums up his understanding of the unique role of the Holy Spirit with the following definition: 'The personhood of God the Holy Spirit is the loving, self-communicating, out-fanning and out-pouring presence of the eternal divine life of the triune God.'[18]

Recognizing God's presence and vitality in the world is essential for spiritual guidance practices. When spiritual directors sit with directees, or pastors engage in pastoral care, they can do so knowing that God is directly present with them in that context. This presence is the *ruach* of God who is characterized as the very essence of life and energy. Every breath we take is evidence of the Spirit. Without it, we would cease to exist. In the chaos of a busy world, pausing to consider the basic components of our existence helps us to reconnect with God. Focus on our breathing enables us to pay attention to the fact that our very life is a gift from God. As we breathe, we recognize that God *is*; we are invited simply to *be* with God and put aside the

[18] Ibid., 289.

laundry list of needs we want to bring to God's attention. As we settle into God's presence, we may become aware of the qualities of the God who says 'I AM.' Moltmann suggests that one of the primary works of the Spirit is to draw us into doxology, or praise of God for God's own sake.[19] In doxology, we name who God is and reflect upon God's attributes. In the life of the church, praise of God is often left to a short section of our worship services. One of the gifts of a spiritual guidance relationship is the space simply to *be* with God in human community and to praise God for no other reason than that God *is*.

Moltmann suggests that we cannot live by the life and energy of the Spirit alone. Living things require a *living space.* In the creation story, the spaces of heaven, earth, land, water and air were created before living creatures. The world around us is often crowded with noise and activity. The demands placed upon us may leave us feeling that we have little room to move and be refreshed. Moltmann speaks of the Spirit as a broad place (Ps. 31:8) in whom we can breathe deeply and unfurl our potential.[20] The spiritual guide who moves in step with the Spirit creates a living, vibrating space for others.

In my experience, participants in spiritual direction often come to a session with a great deal of physical tension. There is a tightness to their posture which is evident in the way they sit and in the way they breathe. They are like racehorses wearing blinkers. Their horizons are narrow. It is difficult to see beyond a particular situation or issue for discernment. As they begin to focus on God and release thoughts and feelings, the blinkers come off and the possibilities of life expand; they can see beyond what is immediately at stake. Many a participant ends the session by saying, 'I can breathe again ...'. The ability to breathe easily often coincides with a deepened awareness of the *ruach* of God. While breathing is a natural human activity of which we are seldom conscious, it is a vital metaphor for the activity of the Spirit within and around us.

The Spirit also comes to us in personhood, a form that we can comprehend as a genuine 'Other.' We can communicate with the Spirit of God, and we can trust that the Spirit seeks to communicate with us. The Spirit of God is 'poured out' upon us as we go about our days. The evidence of this presence is not always obvious, but it

[19] Ibid., 301.
[20] Ibid., 277, 301.

is possible to gain brief glimpses into the way that God is moving. These moments can be as simple as a feeling of awe at the sight of a deer drinking from a stream, or a moment of inspiration and understanding while listening to a sermon.

Acknowledging God's on-going presence in all moments of life is the key for spiritual guidance. In spiritual guidance relationships, we work intentionally to prepare a place for God in our midst as we make space for silence. In the silence, we openly recognize that we are participating in a conversation that includes all those physically present plus the Spirit of God. In one-with-one spiritual direction, it sometimes helps to have three chairs, recognizing that we invite God to 'pull up a chair' with us. Some directors light a candle to symbolize Christ's presence in the room. In silence, we remember that every participant in our circle ought to have opportunity to speak. When we listen for God in silence, we are acknowledging that God is right there with us and we extend to God the same listening ear that we extend to others.

Acknowledging God's presence is especially difficult when the absence of God is keenly felt. Whether we have travelled down into a 'dark night of the soul' or have experienced a brief period of disconnection, we feel the loss. Yet Moltmann's theology presents us with an unexpected consideration. Perhaps we cannot recognize God's presence because God is too close, not too far away. Some years ago I entered a season when God seemed particularly absent in my spiritual journey. A wise caregiver prayed for me and then suggested that God was closer to me than my breath. This image stayed with me throughout that difficult season. Many times I stopped to pay attention to my breathing and I reflected on God's nearness, in spite of the fact that I could not sense God's presence in more familiar ways. Even when we cannot feel God, God is close. As we have already noted, the very fact that we breathe is evidence of God's constant presence. The Spirit is so close and yet hard to recognize.

At the same time, the Spirit is communing with the other members of the Trinity. The Spirit has been characterized by Moltmann as the 'Go-Between God.'[21] The Spirit reaches out to us in loving relationship, going 'in between' the Trinity and all creation. As a result, we are also able to relate directly to the Father and the Son. In spiritual guidance relationships, we seek to pay attention to

[21] Moltmann, *A Broad Place: An Autobiography*, 347.

God's presence. This presence can manifest itself in many ways. One of the gifts of trinitarian thinking is the possibility of relating to each Person of the Trinity. While God is certainly an independent being beyond human comprehension, human beings need language and images to understand and relate to God. At times, individuals may have difficulty connecting with one image of God or another. The doctrine of the Trinity helps us to recognize that we can experience God in more than one form. The Trinity is just a starting point for the ways we may describe God. Moltmann offers such metaphors for Spirit as mother, judge, energy, space, tempest, fire and source of light. The biblical text is a treasure chest of many more. These metaphors or images can help us find language for our experiences of God and assist in finding a new way to approach God.

The Spirit of God: Immanent and Transcendent

Moltmann provides a second foundation for spiritual guidance rooted in a theology of the Spirit. Discernment of God's presence centres in the belief that *the Spirit of God is both immanent and transcendent.* Moltmann explores this further by explaining that God is in the world and the world is in God.[22] Moltmann is pushing up against a western mystical tradition which gives greater attention to the search for God's presence within the human soul than in the world around us. He argues that the spiritual journey is outward as much as inward. God's Spirit fills the world and God holds together every created thing, both the visible and the invisible (Wis. 1:7; Col.1:17). It is therefore possible to experience God in, with and beneath each everyday experience of the world.[23] It is God's loving desire to reveal glimpses of God's own self in the created world.

Moltmann is careful to note that this does not mean all possible experiences have to be turned into the same thing or that each created thing reflects the same dimension of God. There is a creative variety in all that God has made. We must also recognize that finding God's

---

[22] Moltmann uses the term 'panentheism,' which means pan (all) – en (in) – theism (God) to describe this concept. This is not the same as pantheism which suggests that all creatures are part of the essence of God. Moltmann is not in support of divinization of creation. Rather panentheism speaks to evidence of God's presence in all things. See Jürgen Moltmann, *God in Creation: A New Theology of Creation and the Spirit of God.* Minneapolis: Fortress Press, 1993.

[23] Moltmann, *The Spirit of Life: A Universal Affirmation,* 34.

presence in all things is not the same as believing all created things are equal to God. Rather, we acknowledge that every experience encountered by a human being has a transcendent dimension. As a result, 'every lived moment can be lived in the inconceivable closeness of God in the Spirit.'[24]

What we glean from Moltmann's work is a theological foundation for human experience. In the scope of our world there is a transcendence which is immanent in created things and can be discovered by humanity. It is the infinite in the finite and the eternal in the temporal; experiencing *God in all things*. If we move from the other direction, we can also say that we are experiencing *all things in God*. We observe the finite in the infinite and the temporal in the eternal. Experiences of the world are considered in the light of the Creator God who is bound to all things and yet beyond.

Moltmann recognizes that no description of God's relationship to creation will be fully adequate, but he is attempting to point to the idea of reciprocal indwelling. This expresses an intimacy of relationship between God and his creation. It is intended to reconcile two seemingly opposite ideas that are both true. God is present in and with God's creation, the idea that God can be closer than our own breath. At the same time, God is infinitely beyond creation, a mysterious and unknowable divinity that transcends human understanding. With this foundation, it is possible to say that 'we are in God and God is in us wherever we are wholly and individually present. Moltmann suggests that this mysticism of everyday life is probably the deepest mysticism of all.'[25] We can also speak of a spirituality that cares deeply

---

[24] Ibid., 34–35. Many other Christian theologians and church leaders have noted that God is in all things. For example, Irenaeus, a second century father of the church spoke of creation coming out of the very 'substance' of God. In the same vein, the Celtic Christian tradition has long taught that the essential nature of creation continues to be born as sacred. See J. Philip Newell, *Christ of the Celts: The Healing of Creation*. San Francisco: Jossey-Bass, 2008, 36–39. Moltmann also points to John Wesley who taught that 'God is in all things.' Nothing is separate from God. To believe otherwise is a kind of 'practical atheism.' See Moltmann, *The Spirit of Life: A Universal Affirmation*, 317.

[25] Jürgen Moltmann, *Experiences of God*. Philadelphia: Fortress Press, 1980, 76. Moltmann makes this profound statement in a helpful little book that explores a theology of mysticism. While the term 'mysticism' is typically identified with an inward experience, Moltmann draws it out of that context so that it incorporates all forms of encountering God.

for the revitalization of all creation, including human beings, all living creatures and the earth itself. Our inability to notice God is a part of the brokenness of creation, a consequence of sinfulness.

Theologians have often felt the need to choose between the revelation of God in Jesus Christ and the experience of God as Spirit in everyday life. Moltmann suggests that it is possible to appreciate both the one time revelation and the on-going presence. This explicitly Christian spirituality finds God both in the incarnation of the Son and the indwelling of the Spirit in creation.[26] As we articulate an understanding of God's self-revelation in creation, it is important to keep in mind that this is just one form of God's loving decision to make himself known to humanity. The incarnation of Jesus Christ is the primary revelation of God's own self to humanity. Christ's passion and resurrection fulfilled God's redeeming purposes for the world. We can also know God through other gifts including the witness of Scripture, the history and community of the church and reasoned reflection. All of these forms of revelation are a part of the Spirit's work in our lives and are necessary for spiritual guidance practices.

In our world, spirituality is often separated from everyday life.[27] Most professions and workplaces do not incorporate reflection about the sacred. Even at home, we are often too busy managing daily responsibilities to give much thought to God. Our relationship with God does not enter easily into the lifestyle of work, shopping, childcare or entertainment. In my perspective, one of the most important reasons to practice spiritual guidance in our culture is to become aware of God's presence in everyday life.

In our world, we experience a drought of awareness of God. The concept of drought is very real to me. Growing up in a farming community, I was taught to be conscious of the weather. Rain was critical for survival of crops and, ultimately, our livelihood. Sometimes, even a week could be too long without rain. The normally soft black soil hardened and cracked, and the crops stopped growing. Farmers watched the skies and felt the wind. They often sensed the rain coming before checking the weather forecast. When a good rain finally arrived after a dry period, farmers scurried out to

---

[26] Ibid., 78.

[27] Moltmann challenges the theological trend that supports a 'not of this world' life in God. Moltmann, *The Spirit of Life: A Universal Affirmation*, 90.

their trucks, rushing to check rain gauges at every field. Rejoicing would commence in the coffee shops as farmers compared local rain amounts: 7 tenths, 9 tenths, 1½ inches! The amounts varied from field to field. Other concerns were equally important. How deep did the moisture go? Is it only in the topsoil or did it reach down to the roots? A much-needed rain was cause for celebration, perhaps taking the family out to eat or a special visit with friends.

Spiritual guides are a bit like farmers. We watch for the rains of the Spirit's life and activity around us. We know that God's presence is essential to our survival. Without the life-giving Spirit, we would cease to exist. We cannot make the Spirit come, just as the farmer cannot bring the rain. At times, we face significant drought and we pray for the rains of the Spirit to quench our thirst. The moisture will bring growth as it reaches the roots. In the same way, experiences of God only contribute to spiritual formation as they support the relationship with God at the root level of personhood, community and mission. As we focus on God, we learn to sense his presence and activity like the farmer senses the approaching rain. If we disconnect from God in everyday life, we mirror the unlikely farmer who gives no thought to rain, who does not even realize it is essential to his existence.

This earthy metaphor provides an entry into Moltmann's most important insight for spiritual guidance. His teaching about God's self-revelation through the Spirit's presence in all creation is absolutely fundamental for spiritual guidance. Many people on a spiritual search long to sense the rains of God's presence but they do not know where to look. Moltmann's theology points the way and spiritual guides take up the task. Spiritual guidance provides a space for exploring the Spirit's movement in the great variety of creation and in all kinds of experiences of life.

Many participants in the study spoke of spiritual guidance as a process that brought God 'out of the box.' What this means on a practical level is that they are able to notice God in new ways by reflecting on everyday experiences. A photographer is awed by a water droplet held within a single leaf. A parent is inspired by the inquisitive 'God questions' of a young child. A commuter experiences God's unexpected presence in the midst of road rage. A humanitarian worker senses God in the grateful smile of an injured earthquake survivor. These experiences deepen the relationship they already have with God and enrich their engagement in the community of faith, reading of

Scripture, participation in mission, and other places where the Spirit is drawing them. In spiritual guidance, we pay special attention to signs of the sacred in all things. Not only do we watch for them, but we listen for possible ways God may want to communicate through them. We may hear a call to repentance and greater faithfulness or we may hear God's love and affirmation. The possibilities are endless.

I was reminded some time ago of the wonder of God's presence in all creation. One of the directees I meet with is blind. She is a woman of fervent prayer and a gifted minister who lives an active life with the help of her guide dog, Tuck. In one of our session, she began to talk about noticing God's presence in Tuck. I must admit that I was surprised. Tuck is a beautiful dog with a keen intelligence, but I had never thought of him or any other dog as exhibiting the presence of God. She shared that Tuck seems to sense when people are praying. At least five times, Tuck has participated in a prayer circle. As the prayer begins, Tuck quietly leaves her side to stand next to the one being prayed for and lays a paw on the person's lap. After the prayer is over, Tuck returns to her. My directee noted with a laugh that she has begun to call it 'laying on of paws.' I was thunderstruck. Is such a thing possible?

As I watched Tuck resting quietly, I marvelled at the mysteries of God's presence resting on all creatures, even furry four-footed ones. Who am I to say that God could not be present and even communicate in the many gifts of love and companionship Tuck offers? Like Moltmann, I offered my thanks in doxology to the One who IS. Tuck reminds us that transcendence also means God is more grand and more mysterious than our God boxes might allow. As one pastor noted, the old ideas about God no longer satisfy. In spiritual guidance, it is often necessary to open up to the possibility that God moves in ways we have never imagined. God is a transcendent Mystery worthy of awe and praise.

As we meet God within the created world, we must address the historical western spiritual tradition that tends to separate the soul from the body and the natural world. Moltmann argues that this body-soul dualism engenders a spirituality of soul that searches for 'the other-worldly Spirit of the wholly other God.'[28] Our spiritual formation is stunted when we attempt to isolate the human soul from the human body. The soul is not some kind of ghostly, disembodied

---

[28] Moltmann, *A Broad Place: An Autobiography*, 349.

being like those represented in contemporary movies. Interacting with God's Spirit does not pull us away from the physicality of our world.[29] Rather the soul is the vitality of the body which is enlivened by God's Spirit. Moltmann invites us to reach back to a richer, Jewish spirituality which holds that the *ruach* of God breathes life into the human body and dwells with God's people as *Shekinah*. This same Spirit was also present in the physical form of Jesus of Nazareth, and was poured out on all flesh at Pentecost (Acts 2:1-21).

When spiritual guides accompany others on their spiritual journeys, they do so with a preconceived notion of where and how God may be found. If they rely solely on the spirituality of the soul, they may only give limited attention to God's presence in the created world including the physical, bodily experience. The 'God questions' of spiritual guidance might include wonderings about God in the world. The spiritual guide may ask: Did anything happen this week that reminded you of God's presence? Was there anything about this experience that reflected God's image or character to you? Was God communicating something specific to you in this experience? How would you like to respond to God? Spiritual guidance opens up to the mystery of God's movements when it is founded on a holistic doctrine of the Holy Spirit. Humanity encounters God's Spirit in body and soul, thoughts and emotions, alone and in community, in words and in created things. Moltmann suggests that the Spirit always comes from God to human beings, from above to below. The words and the actions of God for the sake of the world end in bodiliness. Spiritual guidance must be rooted in a spirituality of the senses and the body with a reverence for the earth.

One of the things my first spiritual director did was to teach me a body prayer. This was like no prayer I had ever offered and I had my doubts, but slowly I opened up to the possibilities. I found a living space where I could explore the prospect that God communicates through the body, the senses and the emotions. I am truly thankful to God for that first director who challenged me to see how much

---

[29] Osmer, *The Teaching Ministry of Congregations*, 232. Richard Osmer discusses the human-divine encounter in light of Moltmann's theology which holds body and soul together. Nancey Murphey provides a similar perspective from a philosophical point of view. She argues that we are 'blown by the Breath of God's Spirit; we are Spirited bodies.' Nancey C. Murphy, *Bodies and Souls, or Spirited Bodies?* New York: Cambridge University Press, 2006, ix.

broader and wider the holy space of the Spirit could be. A holistic foundation for spiritual guidance provides the resources to open up to God in many ways, both at the level of soul and at the level of body.

Person: Every Life wants to Grow

Constructing a doctrine of the Spirit for practices of spiritual guidance has been the focus of our theological explorations so far. Now we must go further to address briefly the three formational concerns of spiritual guidance we have identified. The diagram we considered earlier in the chapter gives a visual representation of the Spirit bringing life, energy, and direction to the formation of person, community, and mission. We want to give some attention to each of these now, beginning with personal spiritual formation. The role of each person can be described in terms of theatrical improvisation. Father, Son and Holy Spirit do not play out the dramatic action alone. In the true style of improvisation, each person is lovingly invited to participate in unique ways. We are not given a complete script to follow. In fact, we can choose to decline God's invitation altogether. Each person who elects to join in participates with God in a unique spiritual journey and contributes something to the shape of the developing plot. Moltmann provides a theological perspective which supports spiritual formation that is personal within the context of community.

The energy of the Spirit within every living being is an energy that is never stagnant. Every individual life that is born wants to grow, and no one life is exactly the same as any other. These are remarkable truths. In spite of the fact that billions of human lives have gone on before, every new human life reaches out again to understand and explore the world for him or herself. As we receive the Spirit's breath, we begin to move, feel, think and relate to others. As babies develop through their first year, they strive to do new things on a regular basis. From sitting to crawling to standing, babies have a need to explore their surroundings. They are curious about everything, and many unexpected objects find their way into a baby's mouth. Part of human development is also a growing sense of something or someone beyond ourselves.

Moltmann suggests that we come awake to the awareness of God; to the life that is vibrating through us. 'The beating heart experiences God's love, is warmed by it into love for life, and comes alive from its source.' Moltmann speaks of the process of spiritual formation as a 'rebirth' which is related to the biblical concept of being 'born again.' He draws on this concept to speak of personal growth in faith, in knowledge and in wisdom. As the confidence of our faith grows, we explore the depth and breadth of God's Spirit as our space for living.[30] The Spirit is urging each one continually towards formation so that we may become all that God imagines for us, to arrive at our own unique and proper form.

Moltmann paints a hopeful picture of personal spiritual growth, but he also recognizes the tragedies of evil and suffering, especially in *The Crucified God*.[31] A personal biography is not separate from a social history which may include a variety of catastrophic events. I would add that circumstances of abuse, other unhealthy environments, and forms of mental, emotional and physical illness may wreck havoc on the formational process. In these cases, continuous growth is impossible as individuals must struggle for daily survival. Suffering can crush people, but even those most desperately broken can hold out hope for God's redemption.

Moltmann's own story and those of so many others reveal that some difficulties can be turning points in the formational journey. They can even speed spiritual growth that has been languishing. Just as the athlete must rest a newly injured muscle and gently get it moving again, so too does an injured soul find a space for growth amid periods of relative calm, along with resources for processing difficulties. Whether in peace or struggle, spiritual growth is never forced upon anyone. Personal spiritual formation is freely chosen by every individual. At the same time, the Spirit is the source of all goodness who accomplishes the inner transformation with a passion for every uniquely created life, a passion that could only come from the Creator. Moltmann also notes that growth in faith does not mean sinless perfection, but rather a continual rebirthing of new life as we open ourselves to the Spirit. Ultimately, the eschatalogical hope for

---

[30] Moltmann, *The Spirit of Life: A Universal Affirmation*, 161.

[31] Jürgen Moltmann, *The Crucified God: The Cross of Christ as the Foundation and Criticism of Christian Theology*. Minneapolis: Fortress Press, 1993. Moltmann acknowledges the realities of human suffering and suggests that God suffers with the world through the suffering of Christ.

spiritual formation is the completion of the rebirthing process at the resurrection of the dead.[32]

Person: Practicing Spiritual Guidance

Of all church ministries, practices of spiritual guidance give the most intentional emphasis to personal spiritual formation. While other church practices such as preaching and teaching are concerned with spiritual formation, spiritual guidance practices make room for the one-with-one or small group experiences in which each individual's relationship with God is given top priority. Many of the pastors and congregations in the research have made a special effort to construct a space for the spiritual formation of individuals in congregations. These busy pastors set aside other responsibilities to support the spiritual formation of one person. As we noted in a previous chapter, one pastor talked about his deepened appreciation for the 'value of the individual soul' because every human being who crosses his path is deeply loved by God. The change he describes may be expressed in this theological conviction: if God has created every human life with a desire to grow and is continually drawing them along a path of spiritual growth, the spiritual guide will recognize the immense value of the hour spent with each individual.

The formational process of rebirthing described by Moltmann is precisely the focus of spiritual guidance practices. A key reason for attending to God's presence in everyday life, listening for God's self-communication and developing prayer practices is to support the personal spiritual growth that God has in mind for each one of us. Spiritual guidance is based upon the premise that God is continually inviting rebirth and providing moments of awakening throughout the joys and sorrows of life. Taking time to reflect on these and interpreting them in the light of what we know about God's character and purposes results in the fruit of formation.

Many of the research participants began spiritual direction when they faced intense faith struggles. Spiritual guidance provides one resource for processing these struggles. As participants listen to God, they may begin to see how God has been present in the midst of those struggles and how God might be inviting them to respond to specific circumstances. In a sense, the spiritual guide

---

[32] Moltmann, *The Spirit of Life: A Universal Affirmation*, 162–63.

is like the physical therapist treating the athlete's injured muscle. Gentle support and strengthening exercises get the athlete moving again. The spiritual guide provides an extension of the living space of the Spirit, where healing is emphasized and growth develops over time.

When we consider the personal process of spiritual formation, we cannot ignore the inward dimension. Moltmann differs here from a dominant western spiritual tradition when he says that 'the experience of God's Spirit is not limited to the human subject's experience of the self.' God is present both in the inner self and in experiences of nature and sociality.[33] Human experience has two references, an outward reference in the perception of what is happening to us, and an inward reference in the perception of how this 'happening' changes the self.

This interaction between the inward and outward is reflected in relationships. As children grow, they experience themselves according to the treatment they receive from others. Children who are loved and accepted grow in self-love and confidence. Children who experience rejection and mistreatment begin to hate themselves. 'Being human means being-in-relationship.'[34] In the formational process, the inward self may reflect upon what is experienced in the world, and this reflection has an impact on one's self-understanding. God is present on both sides of the process. God strives to communicate both through the Spirit's presence in all creation and within the depths of the individual as the love of God is poured into human hearts through the Holy Spirit (Rom. 5:5).

Recognizing inner change is often difficult, especially in a busy world. As Moltmann notes, those who are only committed to an

---

[33] Ibid., 34. Classical Christian spirituality has been deeply influenced by a tradition which posits that the inner being of the human individual reflects God more closely than any other part of the human self or any other thing in the created world. The individual experiences God and is formed spiritually by turning inward. On the spiritual journey, the route to God is inward and upward. Moltmann argues that this is too narrow. The spiritual journey does not *exclude* the experience of God in oneself, but *includes* experiences of God that are physical, bodily, social and part of the natural world. Richard Bauckham, *The Theology of Jürgen Moltmann*. Edinburgh: T&T Clark, 1995, 246.

[34] Moltmann suggests that we discover ourselves in relationship with others. 'It follows that our experience of ourselves and our empirical awareness of ourselves is always a "mediated" and never an "immediate" self-awareness.' No one can say 'I AM' as a being that does not depend on others for its existence except God. Moltmann, *The Spirit of Life: A Universal Affirmation*, 22–24.

active life often miss the changes taking place within themselves. Facing change is painful, but without it we will hardly experience life at all, much less be guided by the living, vibrating energy of the Spirit. We are reminded of the woman in the congregational study who was a dynamic lay leader and took a typical business management approach to her church work. Like many in our congregations, she was efficient and got things done. In spiritual direction, she learned the value of attending to the inward self. As she came to recognize God's voice in the inward places and watched for God's presence in those around her, she began to offer spiritual leadership to others in new ways that emphasized relationship with God and with others.

Community: Spiritual Formation in the Church

As we have already noted, God invites humanity to participate in the great theo–drama. Individuals freely choose to take up their God-given roles, but God knows they cannot adequately play their parts alone. The drama of human history is not a monologue. In theatrical improvisation, actors are carefully trained in theory and techniques so that they learn to act out of habit in a manner that is appropriate to each circumstance.[35] They are schooled in a tradition by actor-teachers with more experience. By observation and partici-pation, they learn to meet the ordinary and the unexpected with an improvised response.

In the same way, personal spiritual formation is absolutely dependent upon human community for developing the habit of spiritual practices. In our time, there are many places people can go to attend to their spiritual formation. From recovery support groups to retreat centres to individual spiritual directors, many individuals and organizations have taken up the call to support spiritual formation. Each one of these has a gift to offer, but in themselves they are not sufficient. Nor can the church rely on these individuals and groups to do the work it was created for. God has specifically designed the church, especially the local congregation, for the responsibility of providing education and support in the spiritual journey. The impro-vising church treasures historical spiritual practices and discerns their application in light of contemporary needs. This chapter rests on the

---

[35] Wells, *Improvisation: The Drama of Christian Ethics*, 65.

premise that the congregation is a key source for spiritual formation. Moltmann's work provides a theology of the church to back up the notion of congregation-based spiritual guidance.

Moltmann's ideas about the church begin in the Trinity. The unified fellowship of Father, Son and Holy Spirit is not a closed system. The persons of the Trinity open up their fellowship with the most treasured invitation ever received, an invitation to all creation to participate in their divine fellowship. As we have already discussed, God gave human beings a relational nature. We cannot come to maturity without the companionship and support of human community. In this sense, human beings are made in the image of God. While we reflect God's image in our individuality, the isolated self falls short of the fullness of God's image in humanity. The image of the divine Trinity, or *imago Trinitatis*, is most fully found in human beings as they participate in community.

The social relationships in the godhead are certainly not the same as the social relationships people share, but there is a correspondence between the Trinity's patterns of fellowship and patterns of genuine human fellowship. At our best, we strive to model our communal life after the perfect love and self-giving nature of God as Trinity. Of course, we cannot get far on our own. God reaches out to us in relationship, enabling us to extend ourselves in a loving and respectful manner to other people and to all creation. For Moltmann, Jesus' prayer in John is a singular representation of what God has in mind for the church, that we may be one in fellowship with God and each other, even as Jesus and the Father are one (John 17:21).[36]

According to Moltmann, the church is a 'messianic fellowship.' It is the community of Jesus Christ, made up of Christ's brothers and sisters who uphold and sustain the hope of God in this world. The church remembers the sacrificial life of Christ and looks forward to fulfilment of Christ's world when all is made new. 'The community of Christ stands between the Christ who sends and the Christ who awaits.'[37] Along the way, the church draws upon the teachings of Christ and the whole body of Scripture as a part of its on-going communal and personal faith formation. One key task of the Spirit is to empower the church to create a messianic fellowship. Congregations are made up of different charismatically-endowed

---

[36] Moltmann, *The Spirit of Life: A Universal Affirmation*, 217–21.
[37] Moltmann, *A Broad Place: An Autobiography*, 203.

people who have the potential to create a community that is a source of life for many. In fact, Moltmann notes that every dimension of a person's ability and potential can become charismatic through the person's call if they are used in Christ.[38]

While there are many gifts intended to support the mutual exhortation and on-going spiritual formation of the whole community, there is only one Spirit. This one Spirit has the good of the entire community in mind, and the congregation is responsible for discerning this good. When the church participates in the initiatives of the Spirit, it becomes a sign of the new order of all things associated with God's kingdom. Moltmann speaks of the responsibility of the community to live according to the 'rule of Christ.' This rule is not based on hierarchical structures; rather, it is concerned with liberation from the violence and pressure exerted by the powers of this world.

One of Moltmann's most helpful insights for spiritual guidance is his description of the church as a community of voluntary friendship. He expands the traditional offices of Christ to include friendship:[39]

> 'Friendship unites liking with esteem, love with respect. A friend is someone who likes you and someone you like to be with. A friend is always there, but can also leave you in peace. There is no need to make oneself sure of a friendship every day, because one has no need to worry about it. One can pour one's heart out to a friend, without having to keep up appearances. Friendship joins freedom with faithfulness and dependability.'[40]

Jesus is called 'friend' in two places in the New Testament: he is a 'friend' to tax collectors and sinners (Luke 7:34) and he calls his followers 'friends' for whom he sacrifices his own life (John 15:13ff.) Moltmann views the church as a community of friends because a friend is someone who loves in freedom. As friends in Christ's

---

[38] Jürgen Moltmann, *The Church in the Power of the Spirit: A Contribution to Messianic Ecclesiology*. Minneapolis: Fortress Press, 1993, 293–297.

[39] Moltmann recognizes the traditional offices of Christ including prophet, priest and king. He suggests that two offices of Christ which ought to be recognized include friendship and transfiguration. Ibid., 114–21.

[40] Jürgen Moltmann, *A Broad Place: An Autobiography*, 210.

church, we voluntarily offer our commitment and self-giving love for the benefit of others.

Moltmann argues that the church will not be able to address its present crises through the reform of ministries or administration of sacraments. It must occur through the rebirth of practical fellowship recovered from the grass roots of the church.[41] Moltmann's insights about friendship stand in contrast to church structures that emphasize authoritarian control and obedience. The language of domination common to hierarchical structures moves from the top down. Communities of voluntary friendship emphasize the equality of the Spirit and the ability of everyone in the congregation to minister to every other one using the gifts of the Spirit. This view of the church is especially appropriate for congregations that want to reclaim communal practices such as spiritual guidance. Spiritual communities of voluntary friendship will also appeal to those contemporary seekers who reject authoritarian religious structures.

Community: Practicing Spiritual Guidance

Spiritual guidance is founded on the theological perspective that growth in faith is not just individual, it is wholly communal. Socialization and individuation are two parts of one operation in the work of the Spirit. This challenges the notion that spirituality is primarily an individualized search for God. If we hold to a communal theology of the church, we must draw on the life and giftings of others to continue growing in relationship with God. Practices of spiritual guidance directly emphasize the value of the communal relationship. More than anything else, it is the experience of loving human community that makes spiritual guidance a fruitful ministry.

If we follow Moltmann's thinking, we model spiritual guidance relationships after the kind of fellowship the Trinity shares and offers to us. Spiritual guides who value another human being so much that they listen deeply with loving hospitality offer a tiny glimpse of the image of God in human community. This image is also reflected in the kind of access to God that all participants in spiritual guidance share. The Trinity reaches out to every human being in relationship. While pastors and others who provide spiritual guidance may have

---

[41] Moltmann, *The Church in the Power of the Spirit: A Contribution to Messianic Ecclesiology*, 314–17.

roles of authority, they never serve as mediators between God and people. The term 'spiritual direction' may suggest that directors tell directees how to relate to God. Instead, the spiritual guidance relationship provides an opportunity to approach God together as a community which is God's desire for the people of faith. Moltmann's theology assumes that all have equal access to God and all are welcome to fellowship directly with God. We are the messianic community as we trust the words of Christ, that where two or three are gathered in his name, God is there with them (Matt. 18:20).

Faith communities that practice congregation-based spiritual guidance can do so knowing that God intends the congregation to employ its Spirit-inspired gifts for the benefit of the community. God has provided the church as a place to pass on the practices of faith and to encourage the deepening of spiritual life. Yet we find many people going outside the local congregation to address their spiritual questions and yearnings. If the Spirit has called the congregation into existence and gifted it to pour out the Spirit's life and hope, then the congregation ought to be the epicentre of the search for a deeper spiritual life.

When a natural disaster occurs on land, the epicentre is the place rescue workers begin to search. We can think of the congregation as a kind of epicentre of the Spirit. While the Spirit's presence and activity is found beyond the church in all creation, the church has a special responsibility to train people in faith and to participate in Christ's messianic mission.[42] It is not so much about a physical place, or a dwelling-oriented spirituality, but about *relationships* among those calling themselves brothers and sisters in Christ. Spiritual guidance practices ought to provide relationships within the congregational context that make room for pondering the Spirit's presence and activity. The influence of spiritual guidance practices opens the congregation up to contemporary spiritual questions and yearnings.

This brings to mind Ryan's story from chapter two. He struggled with a deep spiritual angst and believed that if the leaders knew what he really thought, they would want to get rid of him. To his surprise, the opposite was true. Through spiritual guidance with his pastor he discovered that genuine questions and yearnings were welcome there. Spiritual guidance is also valuable for the church on a communal

---

[42] Moltmann makes it clear that the church is one element of the Spirit's work and power. Ibid., 64–65.

level. Leaders who are spiritual guides help congregations watch for what the Spirit is doing within their communities and beyond. Spiritual guidance is giving them a practical handle on the notion that the institution of the church is guided by the Spirit, not the other way around.

Spiritual guidance practices are well suited to congregations that are communities of voluntary friendship. Based on this theological perspective, spiritual guidance relationships ought to be freely chosen and function out of self-giving love and respect. Few acts of self-giving are better suited to a culture of noisy activism than time spent listening for the soul of another. Spiritual guides must love in freedom. They do not accomplish their purpose by demanding certain practices. They are often reluctant even to give any kind of homework. While suggestions for practice or study may be offered, recipients are equal members in the community of faith who freely choose how they will relate to God. Margaret Guenther suggests that spiritual guides are like teachers who expect commitment and hard work but never coerce or motivate by fear. The accountability in the relationship is mutual, reflecting the equality of each partner in the relationship with God. Spiritual guides offer personal attention, discretion and prayers, and participants honour this gift of time by taking the relationship seriously and bringing their truest selves to the work.[43]

As we consider the future of congregation-based spiritual guidance, the grass roots concept of communities of voluntary friendship may be most clearly reflected in spiritual friendships. This is a growing form of congregational care which we will explore in the next chapter. The spiritual guidance relationship is fully equal as individuals draw upon the gifts of the Spirit to provide spiritual guidance for each other. The accountability in the relationship is mutual. As these friends share their joys and struggles in the spiritual life, they experience the respect and affirmation of a friend in faith who makes room for an honest spiritual search. Within the scope of the whole congregation, spiritual guidance helps to create a culture of spiritual conversation and reflection. These practices teach communities of faith the language and skills for accompanying one another on the spiritual journey. Along the way, participants learn to

---

[43] Guenther, *Holy Listening: The Art of Spiritual Direction*, 63,75.

be reflective about God's presence in life as they develop a language for experiences of God and participate in various spiritual disciplines.

In some congregations, a culture of spiritual conversation and reflection has become the fibre of congregational life. In these settings, it is possible to catch a glimpse of the free and open spiritual formation that Moltmann describes. In our efforts to create communities of genuine friendship, we may ask: What is it about the friendship of Jesus Christ that we are drawn to? We notice that Jesus walked with his disciples through their questions and struggles. He loved them unconditionally, always giving them the freedom to stay or to go. Jesus offered forgiveness and absolute commitment, serving them in the ways they most needed. These features are a training ground for us as we strive to fulfil our roles in communities of voluntary friendship under the lordship of Christ.

Sin and Spiritual Guidance

One of the theological foundations for spiritual guidance we have not yet discussed is the doctrine of sin. Sin does not fit neatly into personal or communal categories. Historically, the Roman Catholic tradition has often tied spiritual guidance to sin and confession. The spiritual director one visits for personal guidance might also be a priest who hears the confession of sin. Unfortunately, there have been periods when sin and confession were over-emphasized in spiritual direction. Contemporary spiritual guidance tends to separate itself from this regrettable past and focuses on freedom of conscience and the responsibility of personal choice.[44] This fits well with a theology of personal spiritual formation incorporating free will. At the same time, we need a theological foundation that addresses the human failures that de-form us. Reflecting on the meaning of sin and the need for restoration is critical to understanding the Christian journey. With person and community in mind, we will explore sinfulness and restoration.

For Moltmann, sin is understood as a choice to turn away from relationship with God. The created ones reject the goodness of the divine life, becoming anxious and acting destructively to get what they want for themselves. Sinfulness pervades individuals and communities. Moltmann makes it clear that sin is not just what one

[44] Ruffing, *Uncovering Stories of Faith: Spiritual Direction and Narrative*, 2–17.

person does and another person suffers. There are structural sins that destroy what God has created. The stark reminders of Auschwitz stay with Moltmann as a symbol of the sinfulness of human systems bent on stealing the life that is birthed by the Spirit. Other structural sins are less obvious but still destructive, making the rich richer, the poor poorer, and leading to ecological death. People are easily caught up in social and structural evil that gets out of hand. While the guilty are hard to pinpoint, behind these larger structures lie individual human choices: structures are created by people. God is not indifferent to what is wrong. The Spirit is not just a feel-good God, but also a judge. God speaks in the guilty conscience to bring restoration that is only possible through the atoning power of Christ. Without God's intervention, there is no hope or peace.[45]

Many North Americans have an active appreciation of the concept of restoration. For some it involves old houses that reveal untold treasures of architecture and workmanship underneath years of dirt and wear. Others can't wait to get their hands on historic furniture, paintings or aeroplanes. My husband has a passion for restoring old cars. Where I see a dilapidated gas-guzzler sadly lacking in the easy comforts and sleek lines of the modern automobile, he sees a gem in the rough that has had a 'hard life' but deserves to be useful again. He derives great joy from rediscovering the value and purpose of something most of us would gladly send to the junk-yard. We have a God with a passion for restoration. By God's grace, we have not been left to rot in the junk-yard. God is about the work of sanctifying every human life which is by nature holy and priceless. Though the exterior is dented and the interior is torn and dirty, God chooses not to abandon us. God is painstakingly at work to repair and renew us from the inside out.

Moltmann describes this restorative process as a journey of growing into the image of God. This is what Moltmann means when he speaks of 'life in the Spirit.' Human beings are adopted into the loving relationship shared within the members of the Trinity. They are gradually transformed by God into the *imago Christi,* the image of Christ. 'To become an *imago Christi* is to be transfigured into a visible image of the self-giving love of God. With this transfiguration human beings attain their messianic destiny; they glorify God the Father with the Son and Holy Spirit, and become themselves

---

[45] Moltmann, *The Spirit of Life: A Universal Affirmation*, 138–43.

the glory of God.'[46] For Moltmann, restoration is also replicated in sociality as people mirror the image of the Trinity, *imago Trinitatis*, in loving fellowship. The creatures actually become what they were intended to be both individually and socially. Christ is the firstborn of the new creation and believers are to become like him through a life of discipleship. This discipleship is more than passive acceptance of divine intervention. It acknowledges the self-determination of God's people who choose to enter into covenant with God and who recognize the joint responsibility shared by God and people in the work of restoration.[47]

Contemporary spiritual guidance literature gives limited attention to sin and restoration.[48] Some concept of sin is certainly assumed. Sin may sometimes be related to experiences of the absence of God and we find clear reference to sin in historical texts such as the Exercises of Saint Ignatius. Yet we are also immersed in a culture that avoids talk of sinfulness. Just the other day, my young son commented on something he had observed and said, 'that's a sin.' It was so completely unusual that it took me by surprise. When I asked him about it later, he acknowledged that it felt 'weird' to say it. Though we hold a theology of sin, it may not be an explicit part of our language or our reflection in spiritual guidance relationships.

I want to propose that spiritual guidance may benefit from becoming more explicit about a theology of sin and restoration. I make this suggestion tentatively, knowing that any discussion of sinfulness must be done with great care, always incorporating the more-than-sufficient grace of God. Let me suggest a few reasons for

---

[46] Joy Ann McDougall, *Pilgrimage of Love: Moltmann on the Trinity and Christian Life*. New York: Oxford University Press, 2005, 124.

[47] The metaphor of restoration is helpful, but not completely adequate for spiritual formation. It represents the journey of change but does not acknowledge the role of human beings who participate in the change. The classic car does not participate in its restoration; it is completely passive. In addition, experts in restoration generally attempt to restore an object to its original condition. This describes the original goodness of all that God has created which is consistent with Moltmann's theology. Yet the spiritual formation process is also a work of personal growth that is not a recovery of some past state but involves ever-deepening levels of maturity.

[48] Some spiritual guidance theorists choose to speak about sin using other kinds of language, such as resistance. However, resistance tends to be more broadly understood to include resistance to the spiritual guidance relationship or to an encounter with God.

this inclusion. First, spiritual guides know that the Spirit is at work in the guilty conscience. Exploring the source of the guilt may help participants to release the burdens that they carry. At times, coming alongside in prayer and sharing the truth that God forgives those who earnestly repent brings a sense of relief. The spiritual guide is not mediating forgiveness, just standing alongside, recognizing what God is already doing.

Second, the more obscure dimension of sinfulness is the reality that it is not always as simple as one person directly injuring another. Sin is a larger structural issue that catches people in a sticky web. For example, the employee of a corporation that establishes profitable but damaging practices may feel guilty but not know what to do about it. Spiritual guidance offers a safe place to name destructive practices as sinful and seek God's guidance for how to participate in the restoration that God desires to bring. Third, as we explore images of God in spiritual guidance, we may discover a God who can get angry. Far too many people identify God as an angry judge who is out to punish wrongdoing. Yet the popular Santa Claus God who is only happy and generous is not an accurate picture of God either. As we consider the character of God, we must recognize that God does get angry about sin and disciplines those he loves for the purpose of formation towards maturity in Christ. As we own up to our sinfulness and our complicity in the larger sinful structures of the world, we may also freely accept the healing of forgiveness and a renewed connection with God. If spiritual guidance is about the process of restoration in relationship with God, then it must also attend to the obstacles that stand in the way of the relationship.[49]

Mission: Participating in Transformation

Mission is the final formational concern of spiritual guidance that we will address. We will consider how spiritual guides participate

---

[49] While Moltmann addresses some relational dimensions of sin, he gives limited attention to sin overall in the larger corpus of his work. He writes very little about the wrath of God or the demand for substitutionary atonement for human sinfulness. In my perspective, this is inadequate. I do not dispute God's unending love or the overall tenor of hopefulness, but we need to attend also to the anger of God and to the utter devastation we cause individually and communally when we commit sinful acts. A hearty doctrine of sin is necessary if we are to speak with any conviction of a call to confession and repentance in spiritual guidance.

directly in the mission of God and how spiritual guidance practices support the missional work of congregations. Moltmann's understanding of mission is founded upon God's interaction with the broken state of the world. As we have already seen, the Spirit has a dynamic relationship to all created things. But it is not only the created ones on which this relationship has an impact. God's shared fellowship with creation extends fully to the point that God can rejoice or suffer pain with the earth and its inhabitants. God's love relationship travels in two ways: he *affects* his creation and he is *affected by* his creation. God is moved by our experiences of the absence of divine life. Moltmann calls this 'suffering under the dark side of God, his hidden face.' As we have already noted, Moltmann experienced his own dark journey through the horrors of World War II and the reality of mass genocide. He recalls the moment in 1944 when his military unit was shipped to the war zone in a cattle car and passed another train on the journey. Through the slats he perceived the pale faces of people wearing the striped clothing of concentration camps. The guilt and burden of recognition that his own people created the catastrophe of Auschwitz led him to write *The Crucified God.*[50]

It is hard to comprehend how a transcendent God dwells in the experiences of suffering. What Moltmann discovers is a very human reality in the story of God's interaction with the world. Every person of the Trinity is present in the suffering of the cross and the agony of forsakenness. Because of this, it is possible to believe that a suffering God accompanies his own creation in its suffering. The suffering God is so close to his creation that his heart aches for them in their pain and anguish. As we grow closer to the heart of God, we find that God hurts with us and draws our attention also to the hurts of others. Moltmann suggests that God is on the side of the most vulnerable creatures.[51] Jesus took special note of the poor, imprisoned, and oppressed that he came to free (Luke 4:18). Along with liberation theologians, we call this God's 'preferential option for the poor.' The church is invited to join in solidarity with the oppressed and to work for justice.

There is a promise of hope in Moltmann's theology. The Spirit of God is present with creation in suffering now and is moving all things towards future healing and transformation. Through his

---

[50] Moltmann, *A Broad Place: An Autobiography*, 189–91.
[51] Moltmann, *The Spirit of Life: A Universal Affirmation*, 129.

mission and resurrection, Jesus brought the kingdom of God into the history of humankind. The Holy Spirit is present with a creative love in the world, actively drawing all things towards a future in which God *will* finally be all in all. Healing and transformation will be complete.[52] This is the great theo-drama's conclusion, a grand finale already promised. But before the drama reaches its end, the Spirit invites God's people to get on stage and improvise. The church has a special responsibility to discern how the Spirit is moving and to participate in what the Spirit wants to do. The gifts of the Spirit are not for the gathered community only but are to be employed as the members are scattered out into the world.

The Spirit is also working in the world beyond the community of faith in many ways, including the 'kingdom of God work' accomplished by all kinds of action and support groups that work for justice, peace and the integrity of creation. Jesus reached out beyond religious institutions to the outcasts. The fellowship of the Spirit must be sought at the place where distraught people experience Jesus, both inside and outside the congregation.

Mission: Practicing Spiritual Guidance

As we consider the Spirit's movement in the world, we must attend to the interaction between divine life and aching woundedness. Moltmann's theology of the suffering God has important implications for spiritual guidance. God remains intimately involved in the creation he gives life to. This does not change when the earth or its inhabitants act in destructive ways. God suffers along with his creation in this devastation. Spiritual guidance often becomes a place of personal and communal brokenness. God is present directly with the one who suffers and indirectly in the compassion of spiritual guides who participate with God by opening up to the suffering of others. As we learned from the stories of pastors in the research, it is common to want to 'fix' what is wrong, to make the bad stories not be bad any more. These pastors know from experience that serious burnout awaits spiritual guides who cannot separate themselves from the hurts of those they care for.

Instead, we remember that those who suffer are not alone. God is already present with them in their pain. Part of the spiritual guide's

---

[52] Moltmann, *The Church in the Power of the Spirit: A Contribution to Messianic Ecclesiology*, 189–96.

work is to listen and pray in solidarity with the hurting as they struggle to identify God's presence and then to release them to the Spirit who is closer to them than they could possibly know. This is an act of humility for the spiritual guide who recognizes God alone can bear the burden. Intentional prayers of release after spiritual guidance sessions symbolize the guide's trust that God is especially present to the wounded.

Because God is deeply concerned with the healing and redemption of creation, spiritual guidance must go beyond an inward journey for the purpose of self-fulfilment. God's purposes always reach beyond the individual to life in the community and in the world. Connecting with God's call beyond ourselves is a journey. Some will need time before they can ask missional questions. Others begin guidance because they have a yearning to participate in God's work in the world and need a place to figure out how their God-given gifts best meet the world's needs.

Spiritual guidance can support the church's mission through discernment of individual calls. This involves both an inward journey of recognizing the passion God places within the individual and a growing awareness of the possibilities that exist for engaging that passion. The spiritual guide provides prayer support and directs the conversation about the nature of the call. The participant who responds to God's missional call need not fear the unknown, because God is already present and active in the world. It is the Spirit's responsibility to bring all things to final transformation. Spiritual guidance keeps the possibilities open, even watching for God's presence within groups not organized by the church. For those already active in mission, spiritual guidance provides a place to be nourished and encouraged to continue in the work.

Conclusion

We have explored some possible avenues of a Protestant theology of spiritual guidance with the help of Jürgen Moltmann. One of the greatest gifts Moltmann offers as a systematic theologian is his deep integration of theology and spirituality. In his writings, he shares his own yearning for the God who is both immanent and transcendent in a profoundly intimate way. One night Moltmann was reading Augustine's Confessions and he was inspired to write a prayer to respond to Augustine's question: What do I love when I love

God? Augustine had a written a prayerful response to the question which emphasized the wonder of God's presence in the inward self. Moltmann was drawn to find God beyond. I invite you to reflect with me on this poetic prayer that provides a delicious taste of a theology for spiritual guidance.

> 'When I love God I love the beauty of bodies, the rhythm of movements, the shining of eyes, the embraces, the feelings, the scents, the sounds of all this protean creation. When I love you, my God, I want to embrace it all, for I love you with all my senses in the creations of your love. In all the things that encounter me, you are waiting for me.
>
> For a long time I looked for you within myself and crept into the shell of my soul, shielding myself with an armour of inapproachability. But you were outside – outside myself – and enticed me out of the narrowness of my heart into the broad place of love for life. So I came out of myself and found my soul in my senses, and my own self in others.
>
> The experience of God deepens the experiences of life. It does not reduce them. For it awakens the unconditional Yes to life. The more I love God, the more gladly I exist. The more immediately and wholly I exist, the more I sense the living God, the inexhaustible source of life and eternal livingness.'[53]

★★★★★★★★★★★★★★★★★★★★

Spiritual Practice: Presence of God

In this practice, you are invited to attend to God's presence and activity in the story of your spiritual journey. God can play many roles in the dramatic action, including actor, director and audience. Today we remember that God is the true creative Director of our drama and has been part of the story's development since before our conception.

Find a comfortable, quiet space and take a few slow, deep breaths. Keep in mind that God is *ruach*, the breath that gives you life. As you breathe in, remember that the Spirit of God is with you. As you breathe out, release any tension, anxiety or concern that you want

[53] Moltmann, *A Broad Place: An Autobiography*, 349–50.

to lay aside during this time. Invite God to be present with you and guide you through this practice. Consider your life as a dramatic play in several acts. You may choose to write down each act along a timeline.

Pay attention to life events that were central to your spiritual formation (these events could have been positive or negative experiences). Where did the dramatic action bring significant growth? Choose one or more of these events and ask, How did I notice God in that time and place? What was God like? How did my relationship with God change? How did my relationships with others change?

Notice any periods of time when your spiritual formation seemed to be particularly slow or stagnant. Choose one or more of these periods and ask, Did God seem present or absent? How would I have characterized God in that time? Has my relationship with God changed since then? Has this experience changed me in other ways?

Read Colossians 1:15–20 a few times. Take a balcony view of the drama and talk with God about how you have noticed God's presence and absence. Offer any thanksgiving you wish to and/or requests for greater awareness of God's presence in your life. Close with Moltmann's prayer at the end of this chapter.

★★★★★★★★★★★★★★★★★★★★★★★★★★★★

Discussion Questions

- As you think over Moltmann's story, what strikes you about his life?
- How do you respond to the idea that we can experience God in all things and all things in God? Has this been your experience?
- This chapter identifies person, community and mission as foundations for spiritual formation. What foundations would you identify?
- Could your congregation be described as a 'community of voluntary friendship?' Why or why not? Do spiritual friendships emerge naturally in your community? What could your congregation do to support the development of a culture of spiritual friendship?
- Are there people in your life who you trust to provide a source of accountability or a place to confess sins?

Chapter 5

Relationships that Form: Toward a Congregation-Based Model for Spiritual Guidance

An Uphill Battle

I visited Gerald's congregation in the middle of winter. The church is located in a small town in the country surrounded by farmland and the wide open spaces of the midwest. While it was cold outside, inside the congregation I encountered a warm welcome. Several members shared enthusiastically with me about their experiences of spiritual direction. What they know about the practice they have learned from their pastor who is recognized among area church leaders for his ministry as a spiritual director inside and outside his congregation. This was not always the case. In Gerald's first few years in this congregation, he experienced a deepening hunger for personal spiritual formation. A colleague suggested that he might try spiritual direction, so he went to see a Roman Catholic sister at a nearby monastery. When the opportunity came to train in the practice through a local seminary, he jumped at the chance. In the years since training, spiritual direction has become a significant part of his spiritual journey and his pastoral work. He offers individual spiritual direction and intentionally employs the lens of spiritual guidance for all he does in ministry.

While Gerald appreciates the difference spiritual direction has made in his congregation, he also acknowledges difficulties and frustrations. The more he practices spiritual direction, the more people come asking for it. While the congregation sets aside time for him to practice, he cannot keep up with the demand so he only commits to one year per member. Those wishing to continue must find an alternative. Even with this limitation, he cannot fulfill all requests. Gerald has other questions and concerns. He wonders if spiritual direction reaches over into pastoral counselling at times. He wants to be clear about the distinctions, but boundaries are sometimes fuzzy in a profession that requires so many different tasks. While Gerald encourages members to consider many kinds of informal spiritual guidance relationships, he regrets not giving participants much training. He hopes to offer more educational opportunities and will encourage a few interested lay people to begin taking a spiritual direction class. These goals are important but will require many safeguards, including adequate supervision. Gerald is not sure how he will fit these responsibilities into an already busy schedule. He is passionate about spiritual direction, but recognizes that there are significant challenges ahead.

Linda's experience as a spiritual director in her congregation is quite different from Gerald's. She serves as a lay director in a small, urban church on the west coast with strong interests in social justice and peace concerns. Linda first received spiritual direction from her pastor and quickly became hungry for more of the contemplative tradition. The practice opened her up to the unconditional love of God which she embraced wholeheartedly. The kind of listening inherent in spiritual direction was a strong draw for Linda. She soon found herself training in a local program. The congregation recognized the value of Linda's gifts and commissioned her to work as a spiritual director for the church. Linda enjoys the mix of two passions in her life: congregation-based spiritual direction and part-time work with a Christian service organization.

Linda's spiritual direction ministry is generally well-received, but she has faced a number of bumps along the way. When a new leading pastor came to the congregation, he did not understand how Linda's role fit in with his own responsibility as the spiritual leader of the community. There were a few misunderstandings before the issue was resolved. The leading pastor was not the only one wondering about this structure. A few members reported that they would rather seek spiritual guidance from a pastor than a lay person; this seems to be a more natural fit for their understanding of the minister's leadership. One of the biggest challenges is a general ignorance about the nature and purpose of spiritual direction. Many note a lack of communication within the congregation about what Linda does and who it is best suited for. Linda herself wishes that her ministry were better publicized but she seems uncertain about how to accomplish this. She does not want to push her agenda on to the congregation. Several people express profound appreciation for the gifts that Linda offers to the congregation, but drawing the practice into the mainstream life of the congregation is still an uphill battle.

What insights can we offer to Gerald and Linda? Developing a practical strategy for spiritual guidance in congregations is easier said than done. In previous chapters, we have addressed Scripture, history, theology, sociology and empirical research from local churches. These are important foundations for developing meaningful practice, but they are not enough without a pragmatic model and concrete ideas to help us imagine the possibilities for our contexts. I do not pretend to offer a comprehensive prototype for spiritual guidance that will suit each congregation. Every pastoral leader and community of faith has a unique character and quality. I seriously doubt that God would desire a cookie-cutter answer for each context. If that were the case, we would never need to do the hard work of seeking and listening for God's direction for our communities.

Instead, we will explore a variety of approaches to spiritual guidance ministries that Gerald, Linda and their congregations might consider as they prayerfully discern the way ahead. In this chapter, we develop a vision for spiritual guidance in community by following several steps: (1) reviewing the key issues and insights we have uncovered so far; (2) articulating a model of practice for spiritual guidance; (3) developing various types of spiritual guidance relationships; (4) bringing spiritual guidance into pastoral ministry; and (5) addressing the challenges and pitfalls that may arise along the way.

Key Issues at Stake for Congregations

This book began with reflection on the widening gulf between traditional religion and contemporary spirituality. Many Americans are keenly aware that they have spiritual longings, but they feel free to look outside of traditional religious organizations to satisfy their spiritual quests. Religious institutions no longer monopolize the spiritual marketplace. As the church's influence weakens, some congregations and their leaders wonder how they can respond faithfully to the spiritual climate. They raise concerns about the nature of contemporary spirituality which seems to accentuate an inward journey that ends in the self. How can Christians engage the spiritual hunger of our time while remaining rooted in theological traditions that emphasize community and mission? Our sociological reading of culture raises the possibility that congregations can improvise creatively in their contexts by drawing upon historical spiritual practices. Some congregations are doing just that in the recovery of spiritual guidance.

Simply borrowing from traditional Christian practices is not enough. As participants in our culture, we are still in danger of turning spiritual guidance into an inward journey that loses sight of other dimensions of holistic Christian spirituality. In my perspective, a faithful recovery of spiritual guidance practices must attend to three key concerns: person, community and mission. We have considered several excellent examples of spiritual guidance relationships in biblical, historical and contemporary life. As we look them over, we notice common themes including awareness of God in everyday life, intimacy and belonging in community, the intermingling of personal and communal forms of spiritual practices and the combination of action and contemplation.

What so many people have known through experience is articulated in Jürgen Moltmann's theology of the Holy Spirit. We affirm that God is beyond us in Holy Mystery and yet closer than our very breath. Because God is in all things and all things are in God, we are able to grow in our awareness of God through reflection on everyday experiences. Here again, person, community and mission are all tied up in God's work of restoring us towards the image of Jesus Christ by the power of the Holy Spirit to the glory of God the Father. The community of the Trinity is extended to all of us who are willing to participate.

A Model of Practice: The Heart of Christian Spirituality

Just as a chemist carries out many tests on one substance to understand its properties and uses, we have 'tested' spiritual guidance from many perspectives with the ultimate purpose of engaging in faithful practices. The model of practice I suggest here is hardly profound and it has been both implicit and explicit in every chapter. Yet I believe it is helpful now to work at distilling the mass of insights we have explored so far to get down to the heart of Christian spirituality. These are essential building blocks for practical approaches to spiritual guidance.

First and foremost, the heart of Christian spirituality is relationship. God's own being as a Trinity is relational; this is an integral part of God's essence. The human being's relational nature is a core feature of what it means to be made in God's image. Because God is relational, we are relational. We are always in relationship with God, with other people and with all creation. Our need for companionship is God's precious gift to humanity which God recognized from the very beginning (Gen. 2:18). Our relational nature is also a fundamental part of what makes it possible for us to change and grow. God has created human beings to be formed and to develop through our experiences of relationship. Any kind of human growth, including the physical, emotional and intellectual, requires participation in relationships. Our spiritual lives are no exception.

The Christian faith is not primarily based on a list of doctrines and decrees. It is a relationship with God that impacts our relationship with all of God's creation. Even our efforts to answers God's invitation to relationship is deeply affected by what we learn from others. We may choose to live under the illusion that spiritual formation is primarily an inward journey that we can travel alone towards the hidden self. But why go on the journey at all if God is not the source and destination? How will we know how to begin if we have not been given some suggestions from others who are on the journey ahead of us? Christian spirituality and spiritual formation develops in and through participation in divine and human relationship. With the cornerstone of relationship in place, we can build the formative process with attention to person, community and mission.

Second, individual persons are invited on a spiritual journey with God. The key concept here is God's incredible love, commitment and investment in each one of us as uniquely created persons. Holistic growth in a personal relationship with God moves us in two directions: inward and outward. The Spirit offers a restorative relationship to each one of us through inward experiences of God and outward recognition of God's presence in the world. Both are necessary. As we have already discussed, western spiritual traditions tend to direct those who desire spiritual growth to undertake an 'inward journey.' While we must be cautious about any spirituality that ends in the self, the notion of an inward journey does describe a natural part of how human beings have been designed by God. As individuals look inward, they come to some understanding of their own frailty and sinfulness. In the light of this frailty, they may recognize the need for something or someone to change and fill them.[1]

Growth in relationship with God and change toward Christlikeness does not happen in one brief encounter. Instead it is a life-long process that develops continually, a journey. We hear echoes of the inward recognition of Christ in Revelation 3:20. As a child, I was shown a picture in Sunday School depicting Jesus knocking on a door. I was told this door was my heart. Jesus would come and eat with me and I with him if I would only answer the door. I suspect many children have received this message in Sunday Schools over the years. This may appear very simplistic, but it speaks to the nature of the inward journey. When we respond to Jesus' knock, we are embarking on an inward journey that leads to a place where God is present, seeking to commune with us. This involves personal choices to draw toward or away from God. Others cannot make these decisions for us. Jesus brought the good news that the kingdom of God is within us. The inward journey really means an encounter with God as we grow to know God and know ourselves. Spiritual guidance practices focus directly on the inward journey in a way that few other practices do.

The inward journey is only one side of the spiritual pilgrimage with God. As we move inward in reflection, we also encounter God through all kinds of experiences of life. Jürgen Moltmann has helped us to understand how we grow spiritually through our encounters with God when we are out engaging with the world around us, including all the life that God has created. We recognize the inherent goodness of what God has made, in spite of the broken and destructive forces that fill the world. When we catch glimpses of God in creation, we are reminded again who God is and how God seeks to communicate with each one of us. As we notice the work of God in the world, we need an internal process to help us make sense of what we see. The inward, reflective process helps people to identify signs of God's presence. True spiritual formation is enriched by the on-going interaction of the inward self with the world around because God is reaching out to us in both places. Practices of

---

[1] While this is generally true for most people, I recognize that there are others for whom this process may not result in a clear sense of one's own frailty or sinfulness. Some psychological conditions and/or very difficult life experiences may make it impossible to pursue an inward journey or come to a realization of personal brokenness.

spiritual guidance work to bring together these two dimensions of the experience of God.

Third, the journey of spiritual formation requires a community characterized by nurture and accountability. We have already described how we cannot grow without participation in relationship. We must clarify here that not just any kind of relationship will do. The quality of communal relationships is absolutely critical to the potential for spiritual formation. The community must create an ethos for spiritual formation that comes directly from the Spirit's participation among the people. God has given us a model for what relationships ought to be like; they are characterized by self-giving love and compassionate fellowship. As we grow towards God's image, we begin to exhibit the same quality of love in our human relationships.

An ethos that supports spiritual formation requires both nurture and accountability. Nurturing spiritual relationships shape us like the potter gently shapes the mouldable clay. Communities must nurture their participants in a manner that encourages and holds them up so that they can pay attention to God who is doing the formative work. One of the primary ways communities do this is through numerous kinds of practices that are done together over time. Yet practices (including spiritual guidance) can lose their value if we come to think that it is the practice or the experience that will form us. Practices taught in spiritual community are only tools for growing our faith. Loving relationships with God and each other are the true backbone of formation. People will know our love because we listen to them, recognize God's fingerprint in their lives and aid in providing for their needs. This helps to create the fertile ground out of which God grows beautiful things.

Formation in community is more than acts of love and compassion, it also incorporates education and imitation. We learn something about a personal relationship with God from our interaction in the human family. The path will be somewhat different for each of us, but we cannot learn to communicate at all – not with God or people – unless we are taught to do so. From the Scriptures we read to the words we use to pray, we learn from those who have gone long before us and from those who sit beside us in church on Sunday morning. Jesus taught his followers to pray and showed them how to develop a personal relationship with the God he called 'Father.' So, too, we learn something about our own path to spiritual formation by watching how others pay attention to God's work within them.

God communicates with us directly, but God has also given us the community of believers to instruct and guide each other.

Various kinds of relationships of spiritual guidance, especially in communal contexts, provide opportunities for learning from the journeys of others. We need the support and insight of the community to climb the next hill or traverse around the next bend. Ultimately, the inward journey of one person can have significant impact upon a community's formation. As we grow in relationship to God, we will hear an invitation to care for our brothers and sisters in the faith.

Spiritual formation also requires accountability. This is often painful because we are frail and broken. Like the child who grows a few inches each year, we need the steady process of formation and development. At the same time, we need accountability for the transformation and change of our existing condition. Scripture reminds us that the work of the Spirit is to transform us from one degree of glory to another towards the image of Jesus Christ (2 Cor. 3:18). It helps to have others with us when we embark on the spiritual journey and acknowledge the effects of sin on our lives.

Spiritual guidance offers a relationship of accountability for facing failures and keeping the commitments we want to make to become more like Christ. Few people experience this kind of compassionate challenge in a relationship of unconditional love. We are steeped in a world that avoids naming or correcting personal sinfulness. Our culture has trained us to prize tolerance and to avoid direct confrontation with our peers regarding issues of lifestyle. Even if we recognize sin in others, we have probably heard more than one sermon on passing judgment. How dare we point to the speck in another's eye when we probably have a giant log in our own (Matt. 7:4)? Each of us has a shadow side and a tendency toward self-deception. On the spiritual journey, we need to give permission to other loving and compassionate souls who have the courage to walk alongside and help us give an honest account of the marred scenery we pass by. At their best, spiritual guidance relationships serve as a compassionate source of accountability.

Fourth, the spiritual journey connects us to the heart of God where we hear the call to serve the world. Both calling and service are a part of spiritual formation. We could also describe this as the intertwining of reflection and action. Determining our sense of call from God draws upon the inward spiritual journey as we reflect on our gifts and passions. This is the part of a call to mission that is about 'me.' Each of us has a purpose for living and special tasks we are especially well suited for. As we continue on the inward journey, we may gain glimpses of God's heart for the world and grow increasingly aware of the brokenness around us. The compassion of Christ fills us and we turn our ears to hear how God desires to mesh our gifts with the world's great needs. A genuine inward journey that grows the relationship with God can never be separated from participation in God's work in the world. Even if our contributions seem small and insignificant, we are participating in the fulfilment of God's purposes to bring redemption and wholeness. Spiritual guidance relationships can help us discern the whispers of the Spirit and identify our role in responding to the concrete needs of others.

We are also formed spiritually through concrete acts of service that meet the needs of others. Here we turn our attention from ourselves and on to others. The Spirit's presence is evident in compassionate caring that mirrors the actions of Christ who came to meet the needs of the poor and imprisoned (Lk. 4:18). We have the potential to grow in Christ-likeness as we serve by Christ's side. In the spiritual journey, engaging in mission may not actually begin with discerning a specific call. In fact we may participate in self-giving acts first, and only later reflect on how God is filling us with compassion for a particular kind of service. This is often the case among young people and adults who go on mission trips or service assignments and return to discern a call to further service.

Regardless of how our awareness of the call to mission begins, a deepening spiritual journey is marked by the on-going cycle of action-reflection. Spiritual guidance practices help us with the reflection side so that we can be more effective on the action side. Reflective relationships are especially important when we find ourselves so busy with service that we forget about the call. Many pastors and missionaries can probably relate to that experience. Progressing along the spiritual journey requires an inward and outward flow – attending to self and to others – as we listen for the heartbeat of God.

The Congregation is the Primary Home of Spiritual Guidance

There are many kinds of relationships that can support the Christian spiritual formation I have described above, but I am convinced the congregational community ought to be the starting point. Churches today often feel the loss of their role in providing the spiritual guidance that people seek. Many people who are spiritually hungry but have never been to church would not consider it as a place to meet their needs. Others may attend church services but then look elsewhere to address the deepest emptiness of their souls. What is wrong with this picture? The congregation is called by God to provide exactly what the model of practice includes: relationships that incorporate inward and outward awareness of God, nurture and accountability, along with discernment of calling and opportunities for service. Congregations are designed to provide these things in ways that other spiritual providers in the marketplace cannot. The spiritual director with an office down the street cannot begin to offer all the core features of spiritually formative relationships.

Having said this, I want to be clear that there is a place for formative resources outside the church. While the congregation may be the primary home of spiritual formation and guidance, it is not the only source. Families, friends, small groups, spiritual directors and a myriad of other relationships have critical roles to play which may or may not be part of congregational life. Beyond this, we must recognize that congregations cannot pretend to be everything to everyone, and some congregations have a long way to go to develop a spiritually formative ethos. There are good reasons for seeking spiritual guidance elsewhere. However, we must not give up on the congregation as the primary home for the spiritual quest, even when cultural influences suggest otherwise. We are left to wonder, then, how leaders and lay people can give a little more attention to the work of spiritual formation in their midst. The remainder of this chapter will offer some practical possibilities, beginning with forms of relationship.

Forms of Spiritual Guidance Relationships

As congregations grow interested in spiritual guidance, they begin to consider what structures fit their contexts best. Most pastors or lay leaders in the congregational study entered spiritual direction training without realizing the future impact upon their ministries. When they brought spiritual guidance practices to their congregations, they were only beginning to imagine the best ways to implement them. Training programs typically seem to give little attention to spiritual guidance in congregational life. If we look at each of these congregations individually, we note that all of them employ some forms of individual and communal practices. The communities with pastors that have reflected more extensively on spiritual guidance tend to move their congregations towards communal practices which incorporate more participants. Yet they still articulate the importance of individual spiritual guidance. We will explore three forms of spiritual guidance relationships that can be based in congregations. There is no right or wrong choice. One or more of these forms may be appropriate for each congregation.

One-with-One Spiritual Direction

One-with-one spiritual direction gives special attention to the individual. I use the term 'direction' here instead of 'guidance' because this relationship most closely resembles the historical form of practice. Spiritual directors typically set aside a full hour for directees to work through their own issues of faith. This provides them with a rich space to attend closely to God's presence in their lives. Sometimes individuals are more comfortable sharing personal details with one person than with a group of people.

Pastors can serve as spiritual directors. This may be most successful when the congregation grows to support spiritual direction as an important ministry and recognizes it as one of the pastor's responsibilities. Pastors who provide one-with-one spiritual direction must carefully consider what fits well into their schedules. One way to manage time is to offer spiritual direction over limited time frames, such as an hour each month over one or two years. After this point, pastors can refer participants to other spiritual directors if necessary. If possible, it is important for pastors to advertise this service adequately so that more will know what spiritual direction is and be able to participate, even if it is not with their own pastor.

Lay spiritual directors are a good addition or alternative to this approach. Congregations often have a few people with interest and willingness to attend a training program and make this a part of their service to the church. They can share the load. If a few spiritual directors are trained, it is possible for each one to take a handful of directees. This provides directees with options since not every director is the right fit. One possibility is training at least one male and one female director. This teaches the congregation that the practice is suitable for both genders and helps new directees who may prefer to see someone of their own gender.

A clear structure is necessary to define the lay director's role and any reimbursement. Is this a voluntary assignment like other lay roles in the church or will the church or participants pay for costs? Congregations may or may not choose to subsidize spiritual direction. Large congregations with more resources may provide spiritual direction as a separate entity. One congregation I know does this as part of a pastoral care centre connected with the church. It is very important that the leadership openly endorses the work of the lay spiritual director and communicates with the congregation periodically about the role and purpose of the spiritual director and the availability of services.

Small Group Spiritual Guidance

Another meaningful approach to spiritual guidance is the small group. This format reaches more people more quickly. While it cannot achieve the same level of depth with each individual as the one-with-one model, it creates a true spiritual community within the larger congregation that is a lifeline for many people. The group teaches the principles of spiritual guidance to participants and instructs them in ways to care for each other. Groups can allow each individual to share briefly during each meeting or give full attention to one person during a meeting. Some groups may consider reading a book together as a part of the discussion. Others incorporate spiritual practices such as lectio divina.

Regardless of the method, the primary focus is prayer, silence and reflection on experiences of God. This is not the same as a Bible or book study group where participants analyse the text and give opinions for personal application. Trained leadership is absolutely critical, especially at the beginning, as groups learn ways of being together that are very different from other social relationships in their world. Groups must keep commitments to confidentiality and accountability in order to succeed. Leaders may emerge from the group who can receive further training and become spiritual directors themselves.[2]

---

[2] There are books available on group spiritual direction that would be helpful for congregations, for example, Rose Mary Dougherty, *Group Spiritual Direction: Community for Discernment*. New York: Paulist Press, 1995.

The group model can extend into the life of the congregation in unique ways. Some congregations offer retreats which create space for silence, teach spiritual practices and introduce techniques for listening to God. Congregational retreats are a greenhouse of growth for people as they pull away from other responsibilities for a short time and focus on being with God and others. These settings help to create spiritual guidance relationships that may continue long past the original event. Group spiritual guidance may also form out of adult Sunday School. This is a prime opportunity for spiritual directors to gently introduce spiritual practices and key principles about listening for the soul. Groups may form out of these classes.

Spiritual guidance is not limited to adults. Younger age groups can use the principles of spiritual guidance for their small group contexts. Groups can also draw upon other practices in their meetings, such as the Quaker clearness committee, that is used for discernment of specific decisions. As a pastor or lay leader introduces spiritual guidance to a congregation, it is not necessary to use a particular title or name. The language of 'spiritual formation' or 'accountability' or 'covenant' group may be more accessible for some.

Spiritual Friendships

One of the most interesting forms of spiritual guidance that has significant potential for congregations is spiritual friendship. This kind of relationship can be used for two (or even three) people who want to create a peer relationship of spiritual guidance. On a scale between formal and informal, one-with-one spiritual direction with a trained director is a more formal relationship which focuses solely on the life of the directee. Spiritual friendship is a peer relationship on the informal side of the scale in which each person shares equally. Not everyone needs a trained spiritual director. Many receive adequate support through a peer relationship. Spiritual friendships give intentional time at regular intervals to the same kinds of questions and reflection used in more formal relationships. Friends offer each other dedicated space to reflect on their lives and hold back the impulse to give opinions or compare what they hear with their own experiences. They try to restrain themselves from comments like, 'Something like that happened to me the other day,' or 'How about you try this idea …'. They ask questions about God's presence and reflect back what they hear. A common method is to break the time in half, giving a dedicated part to each friend.

Learning to communicate in these ways requires education and practice. Spiritual guides can begin to offer some basic training in congregations and provide guidance for questions or issues that arise along the way. In one congregation in the research, the pastor estimates that at least 25 per cent of members participate in an intentional spiritual friendship. Many relationships developed naturally as friendships and became intentional over time. He supports these relationships by encouraging them from the pulpit and in personal conversations. Even so, the pastor believes there is room to do much more. Congregations can nurture spiritual friendships by teaching about the concept and facilitating their formation. Everyone who desires to grow spiritually ought to have a spiritual friend.

Spiritual friendships can be built around a variety of activities. For some, going out for coffee or meeting in a home is the best choice. For others, a more active approach makes conversation easier. This may be especially true for some men who find it easier to talk about their lives during physical activity. For example, one pastor runs with his spiritual friends. These relationships can also develop over a particular interest or need. Support groups can help to create spiritual friendships that arise out of crises. Congregations can draw upon all kinds of existing relationships to encourage the development of intentional spiritual friendships.

Spiritual Guidance in Pastoral Ministry

Typically, a varied mix of spiritual guidance relationships does not easily spring up in a congregation on its own. An ethos of spiritual formation does not create itself. Leadership is critical, and the pastor is the most likely link. In the introduction to this book, I talked about spiritual guidance as a ministry of companionship in which Christians support one another in their Christian formation by helping each other to notice God's presence and activity in their lives. Regardless of a pastor's training or experience in spiritual direction, *every pastor serves as a spiritual guide*. It is the very nature of the work that people look to a pastor for support to recognize how and where God is moving.

Whether they know it or not, pastors offer spiritual guidance in all kinds of settings and circumstances. This does not mean that pastors must think of themselves as *representing* or *speaking for* God. There is too much pressure and expectation bound up in that. We do not need to return to the model of the Old Testament prophets; all of us have direct access to the Spirit. Instead, people are looking for companionship on the spiritual journey and the pastor is a natural choice. Every pastor will serve in this role to some degree and will help develop an ethos of spiritual formation as they understand that this is an essential part of their work. Some pastors will be especially drawn to this work and will sharpen their guiding skills through spiritual direction training and practice. This is what Gerald chose to do, and his efforts have borne fruit.

Spiritual Guidance is a Lens for Ministry

One of the most astounding results of the research is the way pastors use spiritual guidance as a lens for all the tasks of ministry. In chapter two, we considered how pastors like Gerald have reoriented their approaches to ministry in the light of spiritual direction training. It was not that their instructors spent time teaching them to do this, but rather that it came to them naturally. About a decade ago, Howard Rice suggested that spiritual guidance can serve as the 'organizing principle' for ministry.[3] What this means is that spiritual guidance does not become just another thing pastors do in ministry. While they may serve as one-with-one and group spiritual directors at times, all that they do is a part of their spiritual guidance of the congregation. This lens helps pastors to stay connected with their passion while they engage in the ministry tasks of the pastorate. Using the lens strengthens pastors as they seek to stay rooted in the reasons they got into ministry in the first place. We will take time now to explore the implications of a lens of spiritual guidance for a few of the pastoral tasks: pastoral care and counselling, preaching and teaching, worship, and administration and congregational discernment.

The work *of pastoral care and counselling* is closely related to spiritual direction. In fact, pastoral care can be seen as an overarching umbrella for many forms of care-giving, including spiritual direction. The separation between spiritual direction and pastoral counselling is not always obvious. One way to understand the difference is to view pastoral counselling as a ministry that deals with personal crises and

---

[3] See Howard L. Rice, *The Pastor as Spiritual Guide*. Nashville, TN: Upper Room Books, 1998.

helps the parishioner solve problems. Spiritual direction may address similar issues, but it does not seek strategies for problem-solving.[4] When pastors who are spiritual guides engage in any kind of pastoral care, they come with a certain perspective and technique in mind. First, they listen carefully for God's presence in the struggle or conflict. There are many big and small challenges in people's lives that seem overwhelming. People come to the pastor for answers. How can I deal with my teenager who won't listen? Should I marry my boyfriend? How do I help my mother realize that she can no longer take care of herself?

Before strategies can be identified, the pastor encourages parishioners to slow down and reflect on signs of God's presence. Pastors communicate that God is genuinely with parishioners. God cares for them and is intimately involved in their lives even in details they may tend to shrug off as inconsequential. What have they been grateful for in the troubling relationship? When was the last time they experienced peace about this situation? Pastors can draw on the same kinds of 'God questions' that are part of spiritual direction, but use them in ways that address crises and conflicts. These questions are really an extension of the examen, a spiritual practice in which we pay attention to our experiences of God's presence and absence. Recognizing the unconditional love of God in a crisis helps people to remember that they are never alone, even when they feel isolated or that everything is falling apart. When God's loving presence is recognized, it is easier to identify feelings and develop strategies for dealing with challenges.

Recognizing God's presence in a crisis is a great help to the pastor as well. Instead of being overwhelmed by the pain or grief of others, pastors remember that God is intimately close. As we discussed in

---

[4] More could be said about the differences between spiritual direction and pastoral counselling. Hamilton-Poore and Sullender suggest that pastoral counselling and spiritual direction may actually differ in the fundamental understanding of human nature. Spiritual directors tend to listen with a 'hermeneutic of trust' that God is speaking to the directee, even if the meaning needs to be sorted out carefully. Pastoral counsellors listen with a bit more suspicion, knowing the self-deceptive nature of the human soul and the unconscious motivations that drive human beings. For more on this topic, see Samuel Hamilton-Poore and Sullender R. Scott, 'Psyche and Soul: Dialogue at the Crossroads of Pastoral Counseling and Spiritual Direction,' *Presence: An International Journal of Spiritual Direction* 15, no. 1 (2009): 29.

chapter two, no pastor can 'fix' what is wrong in the lives of others, turning the bad stories into good ones. Taking this approach is a downhill race to burnout. The pastor can draw on many spiritual guidance techniques to keep perspective about *who* really accomplishes healing. In times of intercession or prayers during counselling, it helps to imagine those who are hurting and see God embracing or encircling them. As we acknowledge that this is what God is actually doing, we can offer our petitions to God and trust them into God's care. In the counselling setting, it may even be appropriate to share the image with the client.

One of the gifts of spiritual guidance is recognizing that God is present in all kinds of moments in everyday life. The pastor who is a spiritual guide recognizes that opportunities for pastoral care arise when we least expect it. In conversations with people through the course of our days, we have opportunities to really listen to them. This is based upon the premise that God invites us to be genuinely present with others. We do this because of the fundamental value of every human soul, even those souls that sometimes rub us up the wrong way. We listen for what we hear under the words that are spoken. How is God moving? Is there something going on that I ought to ask a question about? Sometimes these conversations open up the opportunity to pray with someone. Offering this kind of care requires that we cannot allow ourselves to become too busy to listen. If we are distracted and preoccupied, running from one event to another, we may miss the opportunities God provides for us to be genuinely present with others, one of the most important gifts we can offer.

Spiritual guidance also has important implications for *preaching and teaching*. Of all pastoral tasks, these may be the ones that reflect a Protestant approach to spiritual guidance most directly. When Protestants turn a sermon or an educational class into a form of spiritual direction, they are borrowing a practice from another tradition and revising it for their own contexts. There are several ways pastors attend to spiritual guidance in the work of preaching and teaching. First, spiritual guidance begins in the preparation. Planning for sermons and classes is a sacred task and a weighty responsibility. Pastors are best prepared for preaching and teaching when they spend significant time attending to their own spiritual formation. This enables them to express the passion that God has given them in the public sphere.

Sermon preparation typically begins with Bible study. Spiritual guidance teaches pastors to listen to Scripture not only for *information*, but also for *formation*. This could mean practicing lectio divina with the text for a few days before looking at biblical commentaries. Prayerful reflection on the text makes room for the Spirit to draw our attention to a word or idea. We explore the meaning of the text for ourselves first, but this may extend to a word for the community. We ask: What is God inviting me to do or to be through the text? What is God inviting our congregation to do or to be through the text? The insights might be similar or completely different. Throughout the process, plenty of space for silence helps the pastor to listen carefully.

Second, the sermon serves as a form of spiritual guidance for the congregation. This happens when pastors explore key sermon material including Scripture, theology and current events alongside topics that are common to spiritual guidance practices. Pastors address themes of God's presence and absence, noticing God's activity in the world, creating relationships of spiritual friendship and discerning how God calls to mission. The sermon is an opportunity to encourage parishioners to draw closer to God and to educate them about the journey of spiritual formation.

One of the most important things the pastor models is how to ask questions. Instead of giving all the answers in a sermon, pastors wonder about important issues and ask 'God questions' during the sermon. This communicates to the congregation that they can approach God directly with their own questions. Pastors encourage personal and communal spiritual formation when they willingly share stories of how they have sensed God's presence or give examples of the significance of spiritual companionship in their own lives. The topic of the sermon can extend to other personal testimonies in worship.

Providing spiritual guidance through a sermon is not limited to certain topics. A sermon on poverty, justification or baptism can end with questions about God's invitation for persons and communities. In several congregations in the study, the sermon has been a powerful tool for introducing spiritual guidance to the congregation and creating a culture of spiritual conversation. More than one person involved in spiritual direction first participated because God nudged them in some way through a sermon. Pastors and other congregational leaders lay the foundation for spiritual guidance relationships as they address these concerns through instruction and by example.

Spiritual guidance in the classroom setting shares many similarities with sermon preparation and delivery, but there are some additional features to consider. Teachers have opportunities to engage with participants more interactively. This begins with a willingness to listen carefully to the comments of participants just as we do in spiritual direction sessions. Sometimes this involves asking follow-up questions such as, 'Why did that idea seem important to you?' or 'How does God seem present in the situations we are discussing?' Spiritual guidance requires flexibility mentally to put aside the next point we want to make and listen prayerfully to the comments we hear. In this way, we create a hospitable space and we are intentionally listening both to God and to participants. Classes that begin or end with prayer practices of some type help teachers and participants to stay connected to God during the teaching time. In this way, we remember that God is present with us in every class and is the true source of all knowledge and insight.

Spiritual guidance also extends beyond the sermon to the entire experience of *worship*. It is not hard to tell when a worship planner values spiritual guidance. Periods of silence, extra attention to prayer times, various kinds of spiritual practices and the prayers and stories of the congregation may be included. The spiritual guide can make space to respond to God after the sermon through a period of silence or a guided prayer. Any part of the service might include a pause for reflection, recognizing that we have a hard time hearing God speak when we are doing all the talking. One congregation makes room for conversation at the end of a service, specifically inviting questions of faith. Another congregation emphasizes the prayers of the people, sharing prayer requests and offering them up to God at the end of worship. A third congregation invites individuals to bring something to share in word or song that God has drawn their attention to in the previous week. You might hear a lay person say during worship, 'This is what I felt called to sing.' The worship service is an opportunity to listen for God and to offer our response to God in doxology.

Worship is a sacred space where we can share what we are discovering about God with each other. Drawing on the gifts of God's people for worship is also an essential part of spiritual guidance. In chapter two, I recounted the story of the woman who saw an image in a spiritual direction session that turned into powerful dramatic pieces long remembered by the congregation. The pastor as spiritual guide helps the congregation to discern wise and orderly ways to make use of their gifts in a manner that honours God and encourages the community of faith.

The spiritual guide views *church administration and congregational discernment* very differently from a typical CEO. Many pastors have grown weary of dealing with church management. Is there a way to attend to the human need for organization while nurturing the spiritual lives of church leaders? The answer to the question begins with clarity about the relationship between the purpose of the church and administration. Regardless of the mission statement, church administration is always about serving the congregation's purpose. The nuts and bolts of church management must take a secondary role to God's call. Pastors accomplish this in several ways. First, church leaders can create meetings for both worship and work. In every meeting, leaders may invite participants to hear Scripture, to pray, to reflect on a spiritual reading or to listen for God. In one congregation, board meetings always incorporate some form of support and prayer for one another, a second congregation begins church-wide meetings with a ringing bell to indicate a reflective minute of drawing attention to God. A third congregation limits the amount of church business done in one meeting in order to create space for prayer and reflection. The pastor encourages members to stay focused on how God is calling rather than getting too bogged down in the details of tasks. Giving priority to prayer, reflection and silence reminds us that we are more than a community that *does* things. We are a community that cherishes relationship with God and with each other.

Second, congregations make decisions through discernment processes that grow out of the grass roots of congregations. Church leaders do not assume that God is only whispering in *their* ears. God may tug upon the heart of any member who is open and willing to notice. Pastors must create open spaces or forums that invite the people of the church to come forward with insights about how God appears to be moving. This requires structures for discernment. Sometimes the pastor can serve in this role, gently encouraging and redirecting when necessary. At other times, a small group of leaders can help with this task. Decision-making is a work of discernment. Thoughtful prayer is required, followed by an opportunity to share the sense of direction within a community format. In one congregation, decisions are made by asking how God is calling the congregation rather than by a more conventional vote. The language encourages individuals to set aside their own agendas and focus on God's purposes. This model of decision-making must be taught. It is very different from the political and business processes that rule the rest of life. Instead, pastors teach the process of discerning God's purposes, and encourage individuals to practice it in their own lives. In this way, the culture of spiritual conversation is deepened and expanded to include practices of discernment.

The issue of discernment in congregations is not an easy one to deal with. How can we be certain we are hearing from God? What if different individuals or groups believe they are hearing different things? There is no obvious solution to this issue. Teaching a language of spiritual conversation in a congregation may result in the unexpected difficulty of determining how God is really leading when there are competing perspectives. Along the way, we need to keep a few things in mind. First, anytime we communicate that we believe God is leading in a certain direction, we *must always do so with a spirit of humility.* We always use language that communicates that we think God *may* be leading in one direction or another. In many decisions, we can never know for certain. We do our best to listen and then take steps forward, willing to turn around or head in another direction if it seems necessary.

Second, we draw upon other *sources of authority.* John Wesley valued human experience of God in the pursuit of knowing God's will, but he balanced this with three other sources of authority: Scripture, tradition and reason. These sources make just as much sense today. We discern God's calls alongside the truths we find in Scripture, the teachings of the Christian tradition over time and God's gift of the ability to reason, which has just as much value for seeking God's will as feelings and experiences. Third, we recognize that *God often invites us to participate in the decision-making.* Sometimes it seems that life would be easier if God would just make clear what God wants for our lives. That would take the guesswork out of it. But Jesus reminds us that we are no longer called servants. We are friends with God (John 15:15). Friends who grow in intimacy learn to trust each other. We need to consider the possibility that God invites us to participate in our discernment as co-labourers for the kingdom. When we draw upon all these resources in a spirit of humility, together with the community of faith, we will have a greater possibility of discerning wisely.[5]

Every Pastor Needs a Spiritual Guide

If pastors are going to acknowledge their role as spiritual guides, they will need spiritual guidance themselves. *Every pastor needs at least one spiritual guidance relationship.* This was a key point to learn from Kathryn's story which we explored in the very beginning. Like so many others, Kathryn entered ministry with a desire to walk with people in their faith journeys. What she found herself doing was attending numerous meetings, hurriedly preparing sermons and managing congregational crises. Kathryn was slowly losing sight of the work she was once truly passionate about. So many leaders who accept a pastoral call to care for the souls of people become CEOs of church structures. Some pastors feel torn as they strive to meet demands in order to fulfil a wide range of expectations or to stem the tide of declining membership. Others struggle to portray a personal piety they believe their communities expect of them, even if it means covering up their true selves. When they get up to preach on a Sunday morning, they worry about how the message will be received and what opinions will pass along the grapevine in the coming days. Clearly this is a pessimistic view of congregational life. There are many loving, compassionate people in churches today who understand their pastors' limitations and free them up to do the work that is most needed. Yet so many pastors somehow lose a sense of who they really are along the journey of congregational ministry.[6] Spiritual guidance addresses these issues in a pastor's life.

When it comes to reflection on spiritual formation and leadership, Parker Palmer is a helpful, contemporary voice.[7] Much of what he says about teaching applies directly to pastoral life. In the work

---

[5] One fine resource for congregational discernment written by a pastor and spiritual director is: Graham Standish, *Becoming a Blessed Church: Forming a Church of Spiritual Purpose, Presence and Power.* Herndon, VA: Alban Institute, 2004.

[6] Rice, *The Pastor as Spiritual Guide*, 16.

[7] I have chosen to reflect on Parker Palmer's work here because he develops some helpful ideas about the spiritual growth of a leader that are valuable for pastors. Palmer is not a theologian as Moltmann is, but his work in education and spirituality sheds some light on the importance of spiritual guidance for pastors. See Parker J. Palmer, *A Hidden Wholeness: The Journey toward an Undivided Life.* San

of ministry, the question pastors most commonly ask is the 'what' question. What programs should we invest ourselves in? What are the truths we are teaching? When we probe a little deeper, we ask 'how' questions. How do we best communicate the gospel? On occasion we may look at our callings at an even deeper level, asking 'why' we are engaged in ministry. Or we may ask deeper questions of faith: 'Why does God allow pain and suffering?' Seminary students ask the 'why' question quite often. Experienced pastors may return to this question when they are on the verge of burning out or when some form of ministry is not working.

The one question pastors seldom ask is 'who.'[8] Who is the self that ministers? Is my true self reflected in the way I relate to my congregation, my family and friends and my God? How often do we consider the inner landscape of the ministering self which is intimately connected to God and to others through the presence of the Holy Spirit? What does God have to say about who I am? Have I lost myself in my pastoral work? What will help me to remember who God is making me to be? Asking the 'who' question opens up the inner landscape of the self God created and loves deeply.

Palmer suggests that all of us are on a spiritual quest for connectedness. Pastors want to be connected to God, to the people they serve and to the world God has created. For the reasons noted above and many others, pastors may lose sight of their true selves and operate out of a false self that they believe ministry requires. They lose connection with the personal identity God has designed and the community of creation has helped to shape. They lose heart and are too weary to live by an integrity that reflects who they really are.[9]

Francisco: Jossey-Bass, 2004. and Parker J. Palmer, *The Courage to Teach: Exploring the Inner Landscape of a Teacher's Life.* San Francisco: Jossey-Bass, 2007.

[8] Palmer, *The Courage to Teach: Exploring the Inner Landscape of a Teacher's Life*, 4.

[9] Palmer suggests that identity and integrity incorporate those dimensions of ourselves that include both strengths/potential and shadows/limitations. He writes, 'By *identity* I mean an evolving nexus where all the forces that constitute my life converge in the mystery of self: my genetic makeup, the nature of the man and woman who gave me life, the culture in which I was raised, people who have sustained me and people who have done me harm, the good and ill I have done to others and to myself, the experience of love and suffering – and much, much more. In the midst of that complex field, identity is a moving intersection of the inner and outer forces that make me who I am, converging in the irreducible mystery of being human. By *integrity* I mean whatever wholeness I am able to find within that nexus as its vectors form and re-form the pattern of my life.

According to Palmer, all of us have true and false selves. Serving in pastoral ministry requires vulnerability. Every time pastors speak about the things they care about, they are vulnerable before those who listen. Pastors live in the challenging space between public and private, between professional ministry and a personal life dedicated to Jesus Christ. If pastors fear judgment or indifference, they may take steps to protect themselves.

When we live in fear, we put on the false self like a mask and project that false self to the world. We hide our true identity and disconnect from the community of faith. We may even fool ourselves to the point that we believe the false self is who we truly are. I spoke with one former pastor some years ago who admitted that she did not really know herself during her years in ministry. She worked hard to please others – she learned to give people what she thought they wanted. Many good things happened during her tenure at the church, but she felt relieved to leave the pastorate. It was only later that she began to recognize the illusion of the mask she had been wearing.

When we live out of identity and integrity, we are finally able to bring the inward self together with the self we project to the world. Palmer calls this living 'an undivided life.'[10] Our inner and outer worlds are never in perfect harmony, but we are not created to tolerate extremes between the true and false selves. If I draw on both Palmer and Moltmann here, I can argue that living an undivided life means to find our centre in the trinitarian God, a centre that is external to the institution of the church. We are willing to take steps of vulnerability, communicating out of who we truly are and genuinely connecting with others. Though fear threatens, '*no punishment anyone lays on you could possibly be worse than the punishment you lay on yourself by conspiring in your own diminishment.*'[11] As we live the undivided life, our passion for the call of God, whatever it may be, is restored.

Integrity requires that I discern what is integral to my selfhood, what fits and what does not, and that I choose life-giving ways of relating to the forces that converge within me: do I welcome them or fear them, embrace them or reject them, move with them or against them? By choosing integrity, I become more whole, but wholeness does not mean perfection. It means becoming more real by acknowledging the whole of who I am.' Ibid., 13.

[10] Ibid., 167.

[11] Ibid., 171.

Learning to live an undivided life is a central component of the life-long process of spiritual formation. We cannot possibly live the undivided life alone. We need others who join with us in welcoming the Spirit to construct a sacred space. Spaces crafted to welcome the soul and provide support for the inner journey are relatively rare. This sacred space is generated by a 'circle of trust' that opens the door to the elusive soul and helps it recognize deforming influences that cause it to hide behind the false self. 'In a circle of trust, the powers of deformation are held at bay long enough for the soul to emerge and speak its truth.'[12] Essentially, this is a part of the accountability I described earlier. We are invited to adapt our lives to the shape of the true soul that is yearning for Christ-likeness. Palmer notes that a circle of trust knows when to sit quietly with others, waiting for shy souls to show up. The community is not pushy or confrontational, but compassionate. The community knows that God is speaking in the inward self and in all of creation to remind each one who they were made to be. With the guidance of the Spirit and the support of the circle of trust, it is possible to grow spiritually.

We draw on the insights of Parker Palmer to emphasize again this very crucial point: *pastors absolutely must have some kind of circle of trust.* This community may be one other individual, such as a spiritual guide or the spiritual friendship of a peer, or a small group that provides on-going spiritual guidance. Regardless, it is absolutely critical that every pastor have a safe place to reconnect with their own true selves and identify the forces and tendencies in their lives that cause them to live a divided life. They need relationships where they can be themselves without fear of judgment or external expectations. Pastors need places where there are no expectations. They simply watch for the presence of God and reflect on how God is communicating. If pastors want to be effective in ministry for the long haul, they must recognize that they are not immune to the influences that de-form their souls. They cannot be lone rangers and stay healthy in ministry. Relationships providing spiritual guidance help us to keep growing in relationship with God and reconnecting with the God-given passion ignited by the breath of the Spirit.

---

[12] Palmer, *A Hidden Wholeness: The Journey toward an Undivided Life*, 58–59.

Watching for Challenges and Pitfalls

I want to close this chapter by offering a few insights on challenges and pitfalls that may occur as congregations develop spiritual guidance practices. The challenges we consider are real issues that have arisen in congregations that participated in the research. They incorporate the struggles Gerald and Linda face, and several others. These congregations have graciously agreed to share their difficulties as well as their victories. We can learn a great deal from watching their journeys as we continue to follow our own.

First, individuals and congregations often wonder who should practice spiritual direction and how it should function in a church context. In four of the six congregations, pastors offer one-with-one and/or small group spiritual direction. Many of those who participate in the practice comment that they would not have considered it if they did not already know and trust their spiritual directors and see them functioning in ministry. This is a crucial factor that supports the concept of congregation-based spiritual guidance. But there are pitfalls too. Pastors have limited time to devote to such practices, a factor raised by all leaders who participated in the study. Gerald is not the only pastor who has turned some people away because of time constraints. In two congregations, lay leaders provide spiritual direction. They may have more time, but not everyone sees them as spiritual leaders who are best suited to provide guidance. As in Linda's case, confusion arises regarding authority in the church. Role ambiguity that raises questions among leaders filters down. When pastors are unsure about the role of the lay spiritual director, they are less likely to encourage parishioners to participate. Rather than deal with the issue directly, the entire practice is left on the sidelines of communal life. Spiritual direction is likely to fail in a congregation if it is not supported by the pastors. Congregational leaders need to be clear about the role of spiritual guides and communicate this to the congregation.

Second, boundary issues may surface among spiritual direction participants. In one case, a participant in a spiritual direction group began to talk with another participant about difficult personal issues outside of regular meetings. This created a challenge for all members of the group and fundamentally changed the experience of spiritual direction. Ultimately the group disbanded. While such circumstances appear to be unusual, the roles of participants inside and outside the group can create problems, especially when the director is not explicit about roles from the beginning. The spiritual director must be attentive to the various kinds of relationships shared among members of a group and help the group understand that they put on different relational hats in different settings.

Third, some spiritual direction participants are better served by going outside the congregation to find the support they seek. This is especially true when pastors are accountable for their work to particular lay leaders in the congregation. Many pastors made it clear that they would hesitate to provide spiritual direction to someone serving on a church board that they are responsible to. This is another boundary issue that could create a serious conflict of interest. It might be difficult for the lay person to be honest about their experience of spiritual life in the congregation with the pastor. Other church members speak of the refreshing experience of receiving spiritual direction from a practitioner outside their own faith tradition who teaches them something new. Still others have specific hurts related to life in their faith communities or they feel that they do not mesh well with the particular personality of the spiritual director who is available. Discerning the right fit in a spiritual direction relationship is not always easy. At times it may be best to look outside the congregation. Churches with spiritual guidance practices need to be clear that spiritual guidance relation- ships can also be sought outside the congregation. Having a list of local spiritual directors that are committed members of other congregations is a useful resource.

Fourth, spiritual direction flies under the radar. One key reason for this has already been mentioned: busy pastors have limited time to practice spiritual direction. In one congregation, the pastors have not started any new spiritual formation groups recently because of their own busy schedules. They announce spiritual direction opportunities infrequently and selectively to limit the number of participants. They suspect that if they offered the experience openly to all, they would be overwhelmed by the interest. In many congregations in the study, a large percentage of members are not involved in spiritual direction because of the time constraints of their pastors.

Pastors are not the only ones who keep silent about the spiritual direction experience. Some participants feel that the personal faith concerns they address in spiritual direction are so private, they are reluctant to share the experience with their friends. Others are willing to share, but the topic does not come up easily in conversation. Joan is unlikely to say to Pamela, 'By the way, the other day I had a fascinating experience of God and talked to my spiritual director about it.' Many congregations are still learning to develop a comfortable language for experiences of God. While church practices and programs often flourish through word of mouth, this approach is not very effective for current spiritual direction structures. As a result, a significant amount of ignorance surrounding the ministry of spiritual direction still exists in each setting.

During my visits to congregations, I spoke with several individuals who were completely unaware that spiritual direction is even available. On one Sunday morning, I sat next to an elderly man in worship who had heard I was conducting research in the congregation. He asked if I had come for the music. I should have expected a question like this, especially since he came to church carrying his own hymnal with the song numbers already marked. When I replied that I came to learn about spiritual direction in the congregation, he seemed at a loss and our conversation ended. After this conversation and many others, I have come to the conclusion that many people do not know spiritual direction is practiced in their congregations, and they do not have a clear understanding of what the practice actually is. Because pastors have limited time, they choose to downplay a practice they are otherwise passionate about. As a result, spiritual direction tends to fly under the radar for most church members. The mystery surrounding spiritual direction does not help those who find the language of spirituality ambiguous. There are considerable challenges ahead for congregations to educate people that a messy practice like spiritual direction can support the cognitive, active and communal dimensions of the church that they hold dear.

In these circumstances, it may be wise for pastors to begin educating parishioners more explicitly about Christian spiritual formation and spiritual guidance. When pastors are overwhelmed by interested participants, other forms of spiritual guidance, such as spiritual friendships, can be introduced. Many more could be involved in some kind of spiritual guidance without the direct contact of the pastors. In addition, other lay people can become trained spiritual directors. Sharing stories of spiritual direction is also important. Space can be made in worship and educational classes for participants to communicate their experiences. As people begin to talk about their own spiritual journeys, developing a language for spirituality will come more easily.

Fifth, it seems clear that traditional spiritual direction is not the work of every pastor. Several pastors observed that spiritual direction training may not be the right fit for every leader's gifts and temperament. It is only one approach to growing as a spiritual guide for the congregation. Becoming a recipient of spiritual direction is also not the right fit for every individual. Participants must be willing to ask difficult questions of faith and live with some doubt and uncertainty. Not everyone is ready to do this. Timing is important. Certain periods in one's life are better suited to spiritual direction than others. One congregational member made his perspective on spiritual direction clear: 'I'm not interested in all of this. I have my childhood faith. I want to cling to that faith that has supported me my whole life.' Others may struggle to see the benefit in contemplation and silence. Spiritual direction represents a particular stream in spirituality and these spiritual directors believe there are other streams that can also nourish the soul. They make it known that the practice ought to be voluntary, never forced. Some will never participate. The key to finding the right place for spiritual guidance in a community of faith is discernment.

Conclusion

There are many opportunities for developing spiritual guidance ministries in congregations. What pastors must take to heart is an understanding of their role as spiritual guides for the community of faith and their own need for spiritual guidance relationships that protect the undivided life. There are no definitive models for how this must occur, but the riches of the historic Christian tradition can help to open up the possibilities.

★★★★★★★★★★★★★★★★★★★

Spiritual Practice: Discerning the Call

In this practice, you are invited to look to the future, the scenes of the play that have not been written yet. You will borrow skills from improvisation as you watch for the movements of God in your life and discern God's call about where to go from here.

Find a comfortable, quiet space and take a few slow, deep breaths. Invite God to be present with you and guide you through this practice. Begin by reading John 15:12–17 slowly twice. Close your eyes and imagine yourself walking in a peaceful place outdoors: it might be a beach, a quiet path in the woods or another location that helps you to relax ... Become aware of the sights and sounds of the place ... Pay attention to the wonder of God's creation ... As you go, you notice someone coming toward you. It is Jesus. He calls out to you, 'Friend! Let's walk together!' As you go, Jesus invites you to tell him what is in your heart. Take some time to tell Jesus about your deepest desires for your own life, for your relationships, and for the world ... After you have shared for a bit, ask Jesus what *He* imagines for you. What is He calling you to do or to be? Take time to listen in Jesus' presence ... After a while, Jesus says it is time for him to go, but before He does, He reminds you that He has made you for a purpose – to bear fruit that will last ... The two of you embrace in whatever way seems right and head back on your own.

When you are ready, consider the following questions prayerfully: Is God calling your attention to anything in your inward self? Are you living out of your true self? Is God calling your attention to anything in your relationships or your community of faith? Is God calling your attention to any specific way he is inviting you to serve his purposes in the world?

★★★★★★★★★★★★★★★★★★★★★★★★★★★

Discussion Questions

- In this chapter, we considered some of the pitfalls of spiritual guidance in congregations. Are there any that concern you in particular? Are there others you might add?
- How do you think spiritual guidance might impact the tasks of pastoral and lay ministry?
- In your experience, what makes for effective congregational discernment? What are the pitfalls to watch for in congregational discernment?
- Do you believe that every pastor needs a spiritual guidance relationship? Why or why not?
- Why are people at risk for living out of the false self instead of the true self? In what ways do you wear a mask before the watching world? In what ways do you reveal your true self?

Epilogue

In these chapters, we have explored the marvellous encounter between God and humanity and addressed a congregational response to the contemporary spiritual search that relates to person, community and mission. What we cannot do is create a standard program that fits the wonderings of each spiritual seeker. In fact, the more we pursue understanding of how we grow in relationship with God through practices like spiritual guidance, the more we realize the fluid and inexplicable nature of encountering God. A humble attitude towards God means accepting that we are not in control of how God chooses to be known by us or how God is present in the world. The call of the Christian faith is a path of surrender. Yet by God's grace, we also have moments when we catch a glimpse of who God *might* be and who we are becoming as we continue on the spiritual journey.

The prophet Elijah has one of the most fascinating encounters with God in all of Scripture. In 1 Kings 19 we find Elijah running for his life and hiding in a cave. In the midst of this scary turning point, God asks him an important question, 'Why are you here?' Elijah states the obvious, 'They're after me, God. Everyone else is gone and I'm the only one left.' The response is very interesting. Before God lays out an immediate plan of action, God offers presence. Elijah discerns that this presence does not come in the power of a strong wind, earthquake or fire, but in the slightest little sound – a whisper. Elijah ventures out from his hiding place to encounter God. Many of us hide in the cave with Elijah today, confused about our passion for ministry, struggling to succeed and bogged down with things that seem to pull us away from the passion for soul care we once felt. We wonder how God is calling us to respond to the spiritual searching of our time. With Elijah we recognize God in the whisper – a whisper that breathes revitalizing life, energy, and purpose into us. May this renewing breath of God give us courage to engage the contemporary spiritual quest.

Bibliography

Alcoholics Anonymous: The Story of How Many Thousands of Men and Women Have Recovered from Alcoholism. 4th ed. New York: Alcoholics Anonymous World Services, 2001.

Arnett, Jeffrey Jensen. *Emerging Adulthood: The Winding Road from the Late Teens through the Twenties*. Oxford: Oxford University Press, 2004.

Augustine, and Henry Chadwick. *Confessions*. New York: Oxford University Press, 1991.

Balthasar, Hans Urs von. *Theo-Drama: Theological Dramatic Theory*. Vol. 3. San Francisco: Ignatius, 1992.

———. *Theo-Drama: Theological Dramatic Theory*. 5 vols. San Francisco: Ignatius, 1988.

Banks, Robert J. *Reenvisioning Theological Education: Exploring a Missional Alternative to Current Models*. Grand Rapids, MI: Eerdmans, 1999.

Barry, William A. *Spiritual Direction and the Encounter with God: A Theological Inquiry*. Rev. ed. New York: Paulist Press, 2004.

Barry, William A., and William J. Connolly. *The Practice of Spiritual Direction*. New York: Seabury Press, 1982.

Bass, Diana Butler. *The Practicing Congregation: Imagining a New Old Church*. Herndon, VA: Alban Institute, 2004.

Bass, Dorothy C. *Practicing Our Faith: A Way of Life for a Searching People*. San Francisco: Jossey-Bass, 1997.

Bauckham, Richard. *The Theology of Jürgen Moltmann*. Edinburgh: T&T Clark, 1995.

Boers, Arthur P., Eleanor Kreider, John Rempel, Mary H. Schertz, Barbara Nelson Gingerich, ed. *Take Our Moments and Our Days: An Anabaptist Prayer Book*. Scottdale, PA: Herald Press, 2007.

Bonhoeffer, Dietrich. *Life Together: The Classic Exploration of Faith in Community*. New York: HarperCollins, 1954.

Clebsch, William A., and Charles R. Jaekle. *Pastoral Care in Historical Perspective*. New York: Jason Aronson, 1983.

Clinebell, Howard J. *Basic Types of Pastoral Care & Counseling: Resources for the Ministry of Healing and Growth*. Rev. ed. Nashville: Abingdon Press, 1984.

Cloyd, Betty Shannon. *Parents & Grandparents as Spiritual Guides: Nurturing Children of the Promise*. Nashville, TN: Upper Room Books, 2000.

Copan, Victor A. *Saint Paul as Spiritual Director: An Analysis of the Concept of the Imitation of Paul with Implications and Applications to the Practice of Spiritual Direction*. Milton Keynes: Paternoster Press, 2007.

Dahill, Lisa E. *Reading from the Underside of Selfhood: Bonhoeffer and Spiritual Formation*. Eugene, OR: Pickwick Publications, 2009.

Dintaman, Stephen F. 'The Spiritual Poverty of the Anabaptist Vision.' *Conrad Grebel Review* 10 (1992): 205–08.

Dougherty, Rose Mary. *Group Spiritual Direction: Community for Discernment*. New York: Paulist Press, 1995.

Drane, John William. *Do Christians Know How to Be Spiritual? The Rise of New Spirituality and the Mission of the Church*. London: Darton Longman & Todd, 2005.

Elias, Jacob W. *1&2 Thessalonians*, Believers Church Bible Commentary. Scottdale, PA.: Herald Press, 1995.

Finger, Thomas N. *A Contemporary Anabaptist Theology: Biblical, Historical, Constructive*. Downers Grove, IL: InterVarsity Press, 2004.

Flick, Uwe. *An Introduction to Qualitative Research*. 2nd ed. Thousand Oaks, CA: Sage Publications, 2002.

Fowler, James W. *Stages of Faith: The Psychology of Human Development and the Quest for Meaning*. San Francisco: HarperSanFrancisco, 1995.

Furnish, Victor Paul. *1 Thessalonians, 2 Thessalonians*. Nashville: Abingdon Press, 2007.

Gaventa, Beverly Roberts. *First and Second Thessalonians*, Interpretation: A Bible Commentary for Teaching and Preaching. Louisville: John Knox Press 1998.

Georgianna, Linda. *The Solitary Self: Individuality in the Ancrene Wisse*. Cambridge: Harvard University Press, 1981.

Guenther, Margaret. *Holy Listening: The Art of Spiritual Direction*. Cambridge: Cowley Publications, 1992.

Hamilton-Poore, Samuel and Sullender, R. Scott. 'Psyche and Soul: Dialogue at the Crossroads of Pastoral Counseling and Spiritual Direction.' *Presence: An International Journal of Spiritual Direction* 15, no. 1 (2009): 25–30.

Harper, Brad and Paul Louis Metzger. *Exploring Ecclesiology: An Evangelical and Ecumenical Introduction*. Grand Rapids: Brazos Press, 2009.

Holifield, E. Brooks. *A History of Pastoral Care in America: From Salvation to Self-Realization*. Nashville: Abingdon Press, 1983.

Johnson, Ben Campbell. *Speaking of God: Evangelism as Initial Spiritual Guidance*. Louisville: Westminster/John Knox Press, 1991.

Johnstone, Keith. *Impro: Improvisation in the Theatre*. London: Methuen, 1981.

Jones, W. Paul. *The Art of Spiritual Direction: Giving and Receiving Spiritual Guidance*. Nashville: Upper Room Books, 2002.

181

Julian, Edmund Colledge, and James Walsh. *Showings, Classics of Western Spirituality*. New York: Paulist Press, 1978.

Kelly, Geffrey B. and F. Burton Nelson. *The Cost of Moral Leadership: The Spirituality of Dietrich Bonhoeffer*. Grand Rapids, MI: Eerdmans, 2003.

Kempe, Margery. *The Book of Margery Kempe*. New York: Penguin, 1985.

Kropf, Marlene, and Eddy Hall. *Praying with the Anabaptists: The Secret of Bearing Fruit*. Newton, KS: Faith & Life Press, 1994.

Leech, Kenneth. *Soul Friend*. San Francisco: Harper & Row, 1980.

Leslie, Robert C. 'A History of Pastoral Care in America.' *Journal of Pastoral Care* 37, no. 4 (1983): 302–13.

Malherbe, Abraham J. *The Letters to the Thessalonians: A New Translation with Introduction and Commentary*. New York: Doubleday, 2000.

———. *Paul and the Thessalonians: The Philosophic Tradition of Pastoral Care*. Philadelphia: Fortress Press, 1987.

Martens, Paul. 'Discipleship Ain't Just About Jesus: Or on the Importance of the Holy Spirit for Pacifists.' *Conrad Grebel Review* 21, no. 2 (2003): 32–40.

McDougall, Joy Ann. *Pilgrimage of Love: Moltmann on the Trinity and Christian Life*. New York: Oxford University Press, 2005.

———. 'The Return of Trinitarian Praxis? Moltmann on the Trinity and the Christian Life.' *The Journal of Religion* 83, no. 2 (Apr., 2003): 177–203.

McNeill, John Thomas. *A History of the Cure of Souls*. New York: Harper, 1951.

Moltmann, Jürgen. *A Broad Place: An Autobiography*. Translated by Margaret Kohl. Minneapolis: Fortress Press, 2008.

———. *The Church in the Power of the Spirit: A Contribution to Messianic Ecclesiology*. Minneapolis: Fortress Press, 1993.

———. *The Crucified God: The Cross of Christ as the Foundation and Criticism of Christian Theology*. Minneapolis: Fortress Press, 1993.

———. *Experiences of God*. Philadelphia: Fortress Press, 1980.

———. *God in Creation: A New Theology of Creation and the Spirit of God*. Minneapolis: Fortress Press, 1993.

———. *History and the Triune God: Contributions to Trinitarian Theology*. New York: Crossroad, 1992.

———. *The Spirit of Life: A Universal Affirmation*. Minneapolis: Fortress Press, 1992.

———. *Theology of Hope: On the Ground and the Implications of a Christian Eschatology*. London: SCM Press, 1969.

Moltmann-Wendel, Elisabeth. *Rediscovering Friendship*. London: SCM Press, 2000.

Moon, Gary W., and David G. Benner. *Spiritual Direction and the Care of*

Souls: A Guide to Christian Approaches and Practices. Downers Grove, IL: InterVarsity Press, 2004.

Murphy, Nancey C. *Bodies and Souls, or Spirited Bodies?* New York: Cambridge University Press, 2006.

Nelson, Dawn Ruth. 'How Do We Become Like Christ? American Mennonite Spiritual Formation through the Lens of One Woman's Life and One Seminary 1909–2003.' Doctor of Ministry dissertation, Lancaster Theological Seminary, 2004.

Newell, J. Philip. *Christ of the Celts: The Healing of Creation*. San Francisco: Jossey-Bass, 2008.

O'Driscoll, Mary, ed. *Catherine of Siena: Passion for the Truth, Compassion for Humanity*. New Rochelle: New City Press, 2005.

Osmer, Richard Robert. *Practical Theology: An Introduction*. Grand Rapids, MI: Eerdmans, 2008.

——. *The Teaching Ministry of Congregations*. Louisville: Westminster/John Knox Press, 2005.

Palmer, Parker J. *The Courage to Teach: Exploring the Inner Landscape of a Teacher's Life*. San Francisco: Jossey-Bass, 2007.

——. *A Hidden Wholeness: The Journey toward an Undivided Life*. San Francisco: Jossey-Bass, 2004.

Pettit, Paul, ed. *Foundations of Spiritual Formation: A Community Approach to Becoming Like Christ*. Grand Rapids: Kregel, 2008.

Ranft, Patricia. *A Woman's Way: The Forgotten History of Women Spiritual Directors*. New York: Palgrave, 2000.

Reiser, William E. *Seeking God in All Things: Theology and Spiritual Direction*. Collegeville, MN: Liturgical Press, 2004.

Rice, Howard L. *The Pastor as Spiritual Guide*. Nashville, TN: Upper Room Books, 1998.

Rizzuto, Ana-Maria. *The Birth of the Living God: A Psychoanalytic Study*. Chicago: University of Chicago Press, 1979.

Rogal, Samuel J. *Susanna Annesley Wesley (1669–1742): A Biography of Strength and Love*. Bristol, IN: Wyndham Hall Press, 2001.

Roof, Wade Clark. *Spiritual Marketplace: Baby Boomers and the Remaking of American Religion*. Princeton, N.J.: Princeton University Press, 1999.

Roof, Wade Clark, and American Academy of Political and Social Science. *Americans and Religions in the Twenty-First Century*, Annals of the American Academy of Political and Social Science, V. 558. Thousand Oaks, CA: Sage Publications, 1998.

Ruffing, Janet. *Uncovering Stories of Faith: Spiritual Direction and Narrative*. New York: Paulist Press, 1989.

Savage, Anne, and Nicholas Watson. *Anchoritic Spirituality: Ancrene Wisse and Associated Works*. New York: Paulist Press, 1991.

Schumacher, Julie. 'A Support Group Is My Higher Power.' *New York Times*, July 6 2008, 6.

Showalter, Richard. '"The Spiritual Poverty of the Anabaptist Vision": A Critical Assessment.' *Conrad Grebel Review* 13 (1995): 14–18.

Smith, Christian. *American Evangelicalism: Embattled and Thriving*. Chicago: University of Chicago Press, 1998.

Smith, Christian, and Melinda Lundquist Denton. *Soul Searching: The Religious and Spiritual Lives of American Teenagers*. Oxford: Oxford University Press, 2005.

Snyder, Arnold. 'Modern Mennonite Reality and Anabaptist Spirituality: Balthasar Hubmaier's Catechism of 1526.' *Conrad Grebel Review* 9 (1991): 39–51.

——. 'Revisiting "the Spiritual Poverty of the Anabaptist Vision".' *Conrad Grebel Review* 13 (1995): 1–22.

Standish, Graham. *Becoming a Blessed Church: Forming a Church of Spiritual Purpose, Presence, and Power*. Herndon, VA: Alban Institute, 2004.

Steere, Douglas. *Gleanings: A Random Harvest*. Nashville, TN: Upper Room Books, 1986.

Storms, F. Dean. *History of Allentown Presbyterian Church*. Allentown, N.J.: Allentown Messenger, 1970.

Volf, Miroslav, and Dorothy C. Bass. *Practicing Theology: Beliefs and Practices in Christian Life*. Grand Rapids, MI: Eerdmans, 2001.

Wadell, Paul J. *Becoming Friends: Worship, Justice, and the Practice of Christian Friendship*. Grand Rapids, MI: Brazos Press, 2002.

Warren, Ann K. *Anchorites and Their Patrons in Medieval England*. Berkeley: University of California Press, 1985.

Webb, Joseph M. *Preaching for the Contemporary Service*. Nashville, TN: Abingdon Press, 2006.

Wells, Samuel. *Improvisation: The Drama of Christian Ethics*. Grand Rapids: Brazos Press, 2004.

Winnicott, D. W. *Playing and Reality*. New York: Routledge, 2005.

Wright, Nigel. *Disavowing Constantine: Mission, Church and the Social Order in the Theologies of John Howard Yoder and Jürgen Moltmann*. Carlisle, U.K.: Paternoster Press, 2000.

Wuthnow, Robert. *After Heaven: Spirituality in America since the 1950s*. Berkeley: University of California Press, 1998.

——. *The Restructuring of American Religion: Society and Faith since World War II*. Princeton, NJ: Princeton University Press, 1988.

——. *Sharing the Journey: Support Groups and America's New Quest for Community*. New York: Free Press, 1994.

Yungblut, John R. *The Gentle Art of Spiritual Guidance*. New York: Continuum, 1995.

Zaporah, Ruth. *Action Theater: The Improvisation of Presence.* Berkeley, CA: North Atlantic Books, 1995.

Index

John the Baptist 40, 41, 100
Johnson, Ben Campbell 78
Johnstone, Keith 113
Julian of Norwich 12, 84, 97–100,
    107, 110
journey inward 22, 38, 48, 74, 93,
    100, 146, 151–4, 156–7

Kempe, Margery 99

lectio divina 54, 75, 160, 166

McNeill, John 20
Mennonite 9–14, 49, 111–13
missional
    church 22, 71, 77, 78, 115, 144
    focus 9, 36, 38, 77, 78, 84, 101,
    104, 146
Moltmann, Jürgen 12, 113–48, 152,
    154, 170, 172
Moral Formation 95–6

normative task 11n. 14, 114n. 5

Palmer, Parker 170–3
pastoral care ix, 1, 20–3, 56n. 9,
    59n. 10, 60, 87n. 12, 93n. 25,
    121, 128, 160, 163–5
pastoral limitations 55–6, 170
Paul, the apostle 12, 84–97
pluralistic culture 24, 34
practical theology x, 11n. 14,
    114n. 5
pragmatic task 11n. 14, 12, 151
Presbyterian 43, 44, 49, 81, 82
Protestant 15–16, 20–2, 29, 39,
    49n. 2 51, 61n. 12, 83, 108,
    146, 165
    Theology 12, 111, 114

Reformation 39, 49
Roof, Wade Clark 12, 18, 23, 26, 36
ruach 118, 120–2, 129, 147

sacred space 7, 27, 167, 173

sanctification 92, 141
secularization viii, 3n. 2
self-actualization 22
self-knowledge 70, 70n. 15
seminary 7, 9–10, 18, 21, 49, 50, 52,
    63, 68, 76, 106–8, 111, 112
Shekinah 120, 129
simplicity 13
Smith, Christian 12, 18, 34, 36
Smucker, Marcus vi, 14n. 17, 111,
    112n. 2
sociology viii, 12, 18, 23, 27, 40,
    151, 161
spiritual climate 20, 33, 37, 43, 152
spiritual conversation 14, 14n. 17
    culture of 63, 88–9, 89n. 16, 103,
    105, 139–40, 166, 169
spiritual direction training 44, 46, 49,
    52–4, 60–5, 67–8, 162–3, 177
spiritual diversity 26, 27
spiritual friendships 9, 95, 139,
    161–2, 176
spiritual formation
    and calling 101, 158, 178
    foundations diagram 115
spiritual guidance
    and accountability 14, 139, 156
    161
    and freedom 139–40
    and healing 20, 133, 165
    and inward journey 38, 146,
    151–4
    criticisms of 10, 22
spiritual leaders 76, 134, 174
spiritual/religious marketplace 6–7,
    23, 30, 151, 58
spiritual seeker 29, 32, 78, 179
support groups 6n. 8, 134, 145,
    162,

theological convictions 9, 18, 25,
    27, 64
Thessalonians 84n. 9, 85–96,
    109–10
transcendence 125, 128

vision 7, 11–12, 35, 41, 51–2, 61,
   66, 94, 97, 99, 112, 119, 150
vocation 8, 17, 53n. 7, 55, 76

Wesley, John 21n. 5, 101–2, 125n.
   24, 169

Wesley, Susanna 12, 84, 101–9
wholeness 6, 38, 157, 170n. 7, 171n. 9
wilderness 97
witnesses 83, 89
Wuthnow, Robert viii, 6n. 8, 12, 18,
   27–8, 32, 36